Social Consequences of Testing for Language-minoritized Bilinguals in the United States

BILINGUAL EDUCATION & BILINGUALISM
Series Editors: **Nancy H. Hornberger** *(University of Pennsylvania, USA)* and **Wayne E. Wright** *(Purdue University, USA)*

Bilingual Education and Bilingualism is an international, multidisciplinary series publishing research on the philosophy, politics, policy, provision and practice of language planning, Indigenous and minority language education, multilingualism, multiculturalism, biliteracy, bilingualism and bilingual education. The series aims to mirror current debates and discussions. New proposals for single-authored, multiple-authored, or edited books in the series are warmly welcomed, in any of the following categories or others authors may propose: overview or introductory texts; course readers or general reference texts; focus books on particular multilingual education program types; school-based case studies; national case studies; collected cases with a clear programmatic or conceptual theme; and professional education manuals.

All books in this series are externally peer-reviewed.

Full details of all the books in this series and of all our other publications can be found on http://www.multilingual-matters.com, or by writing to Multilingual Matters, St Nicholas House, 31–34 High Street, Bristol BS1 2AW, UK.

BILINGUAL EDUCATION & BILINGUALISM: 117

Social Consequences of Testing for Language-minoritized Bilinguals in the United States

Jamie L. Schissel

MULTILINGUAL MATTERS
Bristol • Blue Ridge Summit

DOI https://doi.org/10.21832/SCHISS2708
Library of Congress Cataloging in Publication Data
A catalog record for this book is available from the Library of Congress.
Names: Schissel, Jamie L., 1980– author.
Title: Social Consequences of Testing for Language-minoritized Bilinguals in the United States/Jamie L. Schissel.
Description: Blue Ridge Summit: Multilingual Matters, [2019] | Series: Bilingual Education & Bilingualism: 117 | Includes bibliographical references and index. | Identifiers: LCCN 2018046318 (print) | LCCN 2019001357 (ebook) |
ISBN 9781788922715 (pdf) | ISBN 9781788922722 (epub) |
ISBN 9781788922739 (Kindle) | ISBN 9781788922708 (hbk : alk. paper) |
ISBN 9781788922692 (pbk: alk. paper)
Subjects: LCSH: Bilingualism–Social aspects–United States. | Linguistic minorities–Social aspects–United States. | Children of minorities–Education–United States. | Multicultural education–United States–Evaluation. | Education, Bilingual–Social aspects–United States. | English language–Study and teaching–Foreign speakers.
Classification: LCC LC3731 (ebook) | LCC LC3731 .S345 2019 (print) | DDC 306.44/60973–dc23
LC record available at https://lccn.loc.gov/2018046318

British Library Cataloguing in Publication Data
A catalogue entry for this book is available from the British Library.

ISBN-13: 978-1-78892-270-8 (hbk)
ISBN-13: 978-1-78892-269-2 (pbk)

Multilingual Matters
UK: St Nicholas House, 31–34 High Street, Bristol BS1 2AW, UK.
USA: NBN, Blue Ridge Summit, PA, USA.
Website: www.multilingual-matters.com
Twitter: Multi_Ling_Mat
Facebook: https://www.facebook.com/multilingualmatters
Blog: www.channelviewpublications.wordpress.com

Copyright © 2019 Jamie L. Schissel.

All rights reserved. No part of this work may be reproduced in any form or by any means without permission in writing from the publisher.

The policy of Multilingual Matters/Channel View Publications is to use papers that are natural, renewable and recyclable products, made from wood grown in sustainable forests. In the manufacturing process of our books, and to further support our policy, preference is given to printers that have FSC and PEFC Chain of Custody certification. The FSC and/or PEFC logos will appear on those books where full certification has been granted to the printer concerned.

Typeset in Sabon and Frutiger by R. J. Footring Ltd, Derby, UK.

Contents

Acknowledgments vii

Introduction 1
   Language-minoritized Bilingual Test-takers in the United States 1
   Tests and Assessments 4
   Brief Histories of Testing 6
   Overview of the Book 12

1 Conceptualizing a Historical Narrative of Social Consequences 14
   Conceptualizing Histories of Discrimination 15
   Validity and Language-minoritized Bilinguals 19
   The Task That Follows 34

Part 1: Immigration Policy in the United States 37
   Pre-Civil War Period 37
   Post-Civil War Period 38
   World War I era 38
   World War II and the Beginning of the Cold War 39
   Civil Rights Discussions 40
   Immigration During the Civil Rights Movement and Vietnam War 41
   Amnesty 43
   The 'War on Terror' 44
   Summary 44

2 Seeking Access to Civic Participation 45
   Literacy Testing 45
   Naturalization and Citizenship 52
   Testing in the Military 62
   Discussion 74

3 Seeking to Enter the United States: A Focus on the Ellis Island and Angel Island Ports of Entry 77
   Ellis Island 78

Angel Island	91
Discussion	96

Part 2: Educational Trends — 99
    Early Court Cases About Language Education — 99
    Legislation on Bilingual Education — 100
    Bilingual Education and Segregation — 104
    Federal Policy Shifts with NCLB and ESSA — 105
    Summary — 107

4 Seeking Education in K-12 Schools — 108
    Intelligence Testing — 109
    Standardized Testing of Content and English Proficiency — 119
    Discussion — 127

5 Seeking Higher Education — 129
    College Admissions Testing — 130
    English Proficiency Testing — 136
    Discussion — 142

Concluding Thoughts — 143
    Language-minoritized Bilinguals as Intersectional Individuals — 144
    Language-minoritized Bilinguals and Histories of
        Discrimination — 145
    Thoughts Moving Forward — 146

References — 148

Index — 165

Acknowledgments

While meandering and muddling through this writing process, I have much appreciated the support of so many who are connected to me and with this moment. Summer and Travis, my sister and brother, and Erin and Adam, who are like a sister and brother too, have been great people to travel together through life with, as have been my great-grandparents, grandparents, parents, aunts, uncles and cousins, who really are too numerous to begin to name. I want to offer so much love and gratitude to Alma, Amy, Ana, Andres, Ann, Belem, Beni, Beverly, Bridget, Chris, Colleen, Crissa, Daniel, Daniela, Donna, Edwin, Fabiola, Fany, Fatima, Haley, Hannah, Inky, Jacqi, Jeannette, Jen, Jenice, Jiyoon, Johan, John, Joy, Juan Manuel, Julio, Karam, Kate, Katie, Kiara, Lan, Laura, Lizzy, Lore, Luisa, Margaret, Marypaz, Meg, Melody, Micheline, Mody, Monica, Nick, Nina, Pam, Randy, Sara, Sara, Sarah, Saskia, Sofia, Talo, Tatyana, Traci, Vero, Vilma, Yareni, Ye, Yesenia, Yubi and Zhaleh for everything.

For feedback early on in the process, I want to thank Tim McNamara. To Nelson Flores, Kamran Khan, David Low and Miranda Weinberg, your comments were meticulous and I hope I did them justice. Thank you to Asya Taylor, who helped with reference logistics, to Martha Reyes, who helped keep other projects going while I finished up this book, and to Alex Reyes, who made sure names and dates were on point. Thanks also to the team at Multilingual Matters for all your support. I want to express endless appreciation to Constant Leung, Mario López-Gopar and Elana Shohamy for guiding me and my work, and in particular for our shared enthusiasms in life and being. And I have so much gratitude to give to Tommi Grover, Nancy Hornberger and Wayne Wright for their compassion, empathy and conversations.

You all and so many others have done more for me than I can express here. Thank you for being simply amazing.

Dedicated to the memory of my mom, June, whose feisty spirit I honor on a daily basis, to my sister, Summer, who still finds a way to look after me, and to brother, Travis, with whom I share so many wonderful traditions.

Introduction

Tests and assessments have had a long history across the world. Before delving into the intricacies of constructing a historical narrative of the social consequences faced by language-minoritized bilinguals in the United States, in this introductory chapter I begin by exploring who language-minoritized bilinguals are and who they are positioned with respect to testing terminology. Starting by exploring who the test-takers are is purposeful, as this book centers their experiences through a use-oriented testing approach (Shohamy, 2001, 2006). This is followed by background on how tests, assessments, exams and evaluations are understood in this book. Finally, the introduction presents an overview of the development of tests as practices that are commonplace in most institutions in the United States. The discussions of tests and the processes leading to their development are largely descriptive.

Language-minoritized Bilingual Test-takers in the United States

In identifying who is a language-minoritized bilingual, I turn first to *The Standards for Educational and Psychological Testing* (AERA, APA & NCME, 2014). *The Standards* have been developed by three leading research organizations in education (American Educational Research Association, AERA), psychology (American Psychological Association, APA) and psychometrics/testing (National Council on Measurement in Education, NCME). *The Standards* was first published in 1966 and is consulted by test developers throughout the process of creating a test. The rationale for starting with the definition of a 'language-minoritized bilingual' in relation to *The Standards* is to connect the historical narrative that follows and the experiences of language-minoritized bilinguals to the guidelines that are in place to inform test design, development and interpretation. That is to say, to ensure that the historical narrative presented in this book is applicable to an audience that has the power to make meaningful changes in testing practices related to language-minoritized bilinguals, I first present how the individuals whom I refer to as language-minoritized bilinguals co-inhabit the category of 'English language learner' articulated in *The Standards*.

The conceptualization of individuals as English language learners informs whose experiences are included in this history. The term 'English language learner' will be particularly familiar to those who have worked in K-12 educational settings in the United States. Local, state and federal policies have used this or similar terms (e.g. 'English learner', 'limited English proficient student') that connect closely with *The Standards*' definition:

> English language learner (ELL): An individual who is not yet proficient in English. An ELL may be an individual whose first language is not English, a language minority individual just beginning to learn English, or an individual who has to develop considerable proficiency in English. Related terms include English learner (EL), limited English proficient (LEP), English as a second language (ESL), and culturally and linguistically diverse. (AERA, APA & NCME, 2014: 218)

Arguably, this definition presents the most current and widely accepted conceptualization of individuals who could also be conceived of as language-minoritized bilingual test-takers in the United States (and other regions of the world as well). The underlying characteristic used to identify who is an English language learner, according to *The Standards*, is being not yet proficient in English.

Not yet proficient in English

For this history, I posit that the individuals whose experiences are used to construct the historical narrative of this book co-inhabit a categorization that terms them as English language learners or language-minoritized bilinguals. And further, the choice of a particular term serves not to draw distinctions between those individuals who are being tested, but instead the choice of terminology reflects different purviews of those involved in testing. That is to say, the term 'English language learner' indexes how these individuals are perceived by other individuals, tests, institutions or policies as not possessing 'English language proficiency' according to monolingual constructs and ideologies of proficiency. 'English language learner' also is an institutional category in K-12 contexts in the United States that relies on assessment data to divide students into different categories. In contrast, 'language-minoritized' can be a term that points to the disenfranchisement of communities and is related to the 'near-universal agreement among language education scholars about the legitimacy of minoritized linguistic practices' (Flores & Rosa, 2015: 149). The contrast in the terms 'English language learners' and 'language-minoritized bilinguals' reflects a different positioning of the individuals, with those using the latter term critically engaging in perceptions of and ideologies around language proficiency.

The above definition of 'English language learner' in *The Standards* centers on the lack of a trait: English proficiency. The definition thereby erases the bilingualism of these individuals. In the United States, there has been a history of presenting the country as *de facto* English monolingual, marked recently by the removal of the very word 'bilingual' from educational policies (Hornberger, 2006). Yet the trait of not being proficient in English can be viewed with respect to bilingualism, which adds nuance to understanding the different ways in which people can be perceived of as bilinguals. Distinctions between types of bilingualism are contextually embedded, and often denote the processes by which a person develops bilingualism. Language-minoritized bilingualism may be seen as similar to what has been referred to as *folk* bilingualism, or when individuals 'have usually been forced to learn the other language in practical contact with people who speak it' (Skutnabb-Kangas, 1981: 97). This portrait of bilingualism contrasts with *elite* bilingualism, which describes individuals who are 'usually highly educated, and some part of their education has been in foreign languages' (Skutnabb-Kangas, 1981: 97). Which languages have national or international prominence also factor into this understanding of bilingualism. For folk bilinguals, the 'other language' is typically the dominant language of the area, which may hold official or *de facto* official status. In contrast, elite bilinguals are learning a non-dominant language, and generally already possess the dominant language of the region, usually as a 'native speaker'. Though there are exceptions, those who are best described as elite bilinguals are not thought to be included in the category 'English language learners' or 'language-minoritized bilinguals'.

In looking at how language proficiency functions in testing, what is missing from *The Standards*' definition is the agent (or agents, or institutions) that make the choice about what English proficiency is. English proficiency is presented as a binary category, where an individual is either English proficient or is not (Abedi & Linquanti, 2012). This is an oversimplification of language proficiency (Leung & Scarino, 2016). Looking to categorizations other than 'English language learner' allows me to take a more inclusive view of bilingualism. García also argues that this position has great potential for meeting the needs of all individuals, in particular in terms of testing.

> Without an ELL [English language learner] or LEP [limited English proficiency] category, it would also be easier for educational policymakers to demand that assessment be valid for all bilinguals. A more flexible norm could then be adopted that would include all children along a bilingual continuum, instead of insisting on a rigid monolingual standard. (García, 2009: 324)

Moving away from monolingual standards is a crucial perspective that is often missing from the creation or interpretation of tests.

In terms of who decides, membership of the 'English language learner' category is not largely a choice made by the individual. And yet, it is not always clear who is ascribing this categorization. In educational contexts, for example, a combination of interpretations of test results, home language surveys and/or perceptions of teachers and parents or guardians can be used to make this determination. Outside educational contexts, being seen as a language-minoritized bilingual can be based on appearance, name, the perception of non-American English pronunciation, or speaking a language other than English. Thus, a limitation in *The Standards*' definition of 'English language learner' is that it is not clear who decides that an individual meets this description.

For this book, I have chosen the term *language-minoritized bilingual*, as it foregrounds the role of language and bilingualism in uniting this group, one that is situated and resituated within social, political and historical processes. The reason for this choice in terminology is also practical, as 'English language learner' is most commonly associated with students in K-12 schools in the United States, yet this history includes the experiences of individuals of different ages inside and outside of educational contexts. There are, though, limitations to this term, as those whom I am including in this group may not have chosen to identify themselves by their minoritized or bilingual statuses. Also, I am not directly including some individuals whose experiences are connected with the history of the United States as a white settler colonial society, specifically, individuals who were colonized, such as Native Americans, or Indigenous or First Nations persons, and African Americans brought to the United States as slaves. In both cases, the languages of their ancestors have systematically been targeted and erased. And though there remain efforts for the continued use of the languages of Native Americans and of African Americans, their histories in relation to testing merit specific attention that is beyond the scope of this book. Yet arbitrarily excluding their experiences, in particular with respect to histories of the United States as a white settler colonial society, would be misaligned with the underlying motivations for this book. Thus, although a thorough inclusion or analysis of the experiences of Native Americans and African Americans is not within the purview of this text, this historical narrative will highlight some of the key intersections of the experiences of these different communities.

In moving from people to objects and actions, the next section reviews the terminology of testing. Much like the examination of English language learners and language-minoritized bilinguals, the section first looks at how *The Standards* defines tests and assessments. It then transitions into a discussion of the ways in which terminology is used throughout this book from a use-oriented testing approach that foregrounds the perspective of language-minoritized bilinguals.

Tests and Assessments

There is a long-standing tradition of delineating the differences between 'tests' and 'assessments', and their corresponding verb forms, 'testing' and 'assessing'. Assessments are conceived of more expansively in terms of what might be considered to be included. *The Standards* defines 'assessment' as follows:

> Any systematic method of obtaining information, used to draw inferences about characteristics of people, objects, or programs; a systematic process to measure or evaluate the characteristics or performance of individuals, programs or other entities, for purposes of drawing inferences; sometimes used synonymously with *test*. (AERA, APA & NCME, 2014: 216, original emphasis)

The term 'testing' is more specific, relating to a particular instrument or practice. According to *The Standards*, a 'test' is 'an evaluation device or procedure in which a systematic sample of a test-taker's behavior in a specified domain is obtained and scored using a standardized process' (AERA, APA & NCME, 2014: 224). Such definitions and the differences they express are essential in understanding the perspective of the professions or professionals that are invested in the design and development of assessments and tests.

The task in this book, however, is to move away from emphasizing specific assessment or testing practices with respect to the psychometric or measurement concerns that arise, and to center instead on the perspectives of test-takers. Like Shohamy's book *The Power of Tests*, 'this book is not about tests, but rather about their uses, effects, and consequences' (Shohamy, 2001: xvi). As such, I have adopted a more flexible conceptualization of assessment and testing that nevertheless remains inclusive of *The Standards*' definitions of assessments and testing. The flexibility comes in trying to understand the situatedness of definitions and how inferences are made, or, more precisely, who is making the inferences and who is impacted by these inferences. Such a conceptualization is rooted in critical perspectives on testing and assessment from the field of language testing (Lynch, 2001; McNamara, 1998; Safari, 2016; Shohamy, 1998, 2001, 2006, 2011, 2016) which argue for understanding the power relationships in assessment and testing.

These perspectives move away from concerns with fidelity of test administration or implementation to sustain objectivity or test security. Instead, critical perspectives on testing, also referred to as use-oriented testing (Shohamy, 2001, 2006), look at the experiences of individuals who not only take the test and need to adapt to the decisions attached to their scores, but also their broader experiences that come into play around how and what kinds of interpretations and decisions are made. In this view, tests and assessments function as part of a larger tapestry of life, and cannot be discussed solely in terms of their purported systematicity or objectivity of their design and implementation.

The term 'evaluation', though typically used with respect to program evaluation, offers an additional perspective that is key to identifying trends of experiences of language-minoritized bilinguals as a group as well as individuals. This viewpoint also allows the scope of understanding these trends to encompass how patterns of experiences are constructed across scales of space and time. In short, in centering the perspective of the test-taker, the distinctions between what constitutes an assessment or and what constitutes a test as defined by *The Standards* lack relevance because the main concern for most test-takers is how taking the assessment, test or broader form of evaluation will impact their lives.

In taking this approach, this book is positioned to present a nuanced understanding of how assessments, tests and other forms of evaluation relate to the socio-political historical context in which they exist, and in particular with respect to the range of immediate to long-term consequences that this poses for language-minoritized bilinguals in the United States. Thus, rather than engaging in discourses that are invested in the distinctions between 'assessments' and 'tests', this book uses the term 'test' or 'testing' to refer to a broad range of instruments and practices, though the terms 'assessment' and 'evaluation' also arise in situations when they are contextually relevant for understanding the test-takers' perspective. In this book, 'tests' are mediating mechanisms that language-minoritized bilinguals encounter when they seek any of four things: (1) access to civic participation, (2) entry into the United States, (3) education in K-12 schools or (4) higher education opportunities.

Although the historical narrative in this book centers on the late 1800s to the present day and is focused on the United States, in this introduction I would like to dedicate space to presenting how the history of tests (and the consequences of testing) dates back thousands of years and can be traced to multiple regions of the world. In the following section, I provide an overview of the major developments of testing as a backdrop for the specific events that are detailed throughout the book with respect to language-minoritized bilinguals.

Brief Histories of Testing

Many histories, this one included, trace practices that resemble testing to the Han Dynasty in 201 BCE to 8 CE in China, where the civil service exam tested individuals on a variety of topics, including Confucian doctrines. The Han Dynasty – and subsequent dynasties – claimed that the exam allowed any test-taker access to elite government and military positions, regardless of their background. This notion that the test was objective and promoted equal access to opportunities, however, was largely rhetorical. First, the content of the test, such as law, agriculture and poetry composition, placed demands on the test-taker that required hours of study. The amount of time needed to prepare adequately for the exam was too much for persons without sufficient economic means. Second, China was and is a linguistically diverse region and the literacy and oral language requirements effectively excluded speakers of other languages or other varieties of Chinese from meaningful participation. The exam was used to create and maintain social hierarchies, until the Qing Dynasty in 1905. It fell out of favor during the Boxer Revolution and was replaced with other types of credentialing, such as degrees in higher education (Higgins & Sun, 2002; Zhang, 1988).

The consequences of the world's first recorded language test were more severe than the those of the Chinese civil service exam and modern testing practices. During approximately 1370–1070 BCE, near the Jordan River, the shibboleth test was used, as described in the Book of Judges in the Bible, to indicate where a person was from, based on their regional dialect. The test administrators, so to speak, tried to determine if an individual was from the region they recently conquered. If test-takers could not produce the palatal alveolar fricative /ʃ/, as in shibboleth, and instead produced the alveolar fricative /s/, as in sibboleth, they were killed on the spot (Spolsky, 1995). The shibboleth test presents some of the most extreme consequences.

Educational institutions have played some of the largest roles developing or sustaining testing practices. Universities in the United States, for example, have required entrance exams since 1620. Barker (1967) documented the history of entrance exams for US universities. Initially, most universities during colonial times required oral exams of Latin and Greek. Harvard University additionally required a written essay in Latin. With changes over time, these entrance exams came to reflect new areas of study in secondary education, which shifted from a focus on the classics to include subjects such as mathematics, geography, science, history and English. These changes occurred around the time of the Civil War. Before the war, the classics dominated tests. After the Civil War, through to the end of the 1800s, tests in the classics were replaced by the above subject matters and modern languages. In 1900, the College Entrance Examination Board, now known as the College Board, formed and began to centralize written entrance exams. Applicants could visit locations outside the university to take these tests, and this led to the creation of some of the first testing centers. University entrance exams changed again and dramatically with the advent of the multiple-choice testing format. Once these tests were introduced in the 1910s, universities became part of a larger national trend that looked towards technology, quantification and a culture of objectivity, including in testing methods (Clarke *et al.*, 2000).

Standardizing testing

The use of various types of multiple-choice or 'new-style' tests became widespread. Frederick J. Kelly (1916) developed what are widely accepted as the first multiple-choice tests in 1914: the Kansas Silent Reading Tests. These were designed using four overarching criteria for test development: (1) test a skill that has value in being measured, (2) provide simple administration and scoring methods for teachers unfamiliar with standardized tests, (3) measure learning progress and present standing, and (4) not demand too much time for the test. Kelly's design moved away from individually administered tests – which were the norm – allowing larger numbers of individuals to take a test simultaneously, administered by one person, and scored relatively quickly and objectively. Kelly's four criteria, but in particular the second and the fourth, served as motivation for developing large-scale standardized tests nationwide.

Following Kelly's work, the US military also developed multiple-choice tests. These tests were part of larger movements around the development and use of intelligence tests. Early work in test development centered on creating measurements for the newly defined concept of intelligence, which was used to justify claims undergirded by white supremacist, ableist, sexist and other far-reaching discriminatory positions. In the 1880s, Sir Francis Galton in the United Kingdom argued that test scores of intelligence represented a fixed, genetically inherited trait that was directly linked to race. He coined the term 'eugenics' to describe how his theories of intelligence could be used to recommend severe consequences, from institutionalization to forced sterilization and social isolation (Buchanan & Finch, 2005). He argued that 'Eugenics is the science which deals with all influences that improve the inborn qualities of a race' (1909: 35). His invoking of presumed objectivity attached to scientific measures obscured how interpretations of the results reflected connections between highly discriminatory ideological agendas and the role of testing in promoting or sustaining these perspectives.

The expansion of multiple-choice tests soon thereafter was enormous. Soon after the first use of multiple-choice tests by Kelly, the military in the United States reported to have administered its multiple-choice intelligence tests, the Army Alpha and Beta, to around 1,588,904 to 1,726,966 individuals. It is important to note that these tests, and interpretations of these tests, were linked with ideological agendas to substantiate discrimination based on race, country of origin and disability. Brigham (1923) used the data from these tests to argue for the intellectual superiority of a small group of people – whom he referred to as 'Nordic' and who the narrow criteria for 'whiteness' (see also the racial prerequisite trials in Chapter 2). The people who created these military tests were also responsible for the expansion of multiple-choice and standardization of tests for other institutions. Yerkes and Terman sold over a half million copies of the National Intelligence Test – based on the Army Alpha and Beta – in 1919 to businesses, hospitals and primary and secondary schools (Kevles, 1985). By 1922, most commercially available tests were the multiple-choice format (Pressey & Pressey, 1922). Brigham developed the Scholastic Aptitude Test (SAT) for college admissions in 1926, also based on the Army Alpha and Army Beta tests (Spolsky, 1995). After multiple-choice tests became commonplace in the 1930s, many researchers involved in testing had rescinded their previous comments that explicitly discriminated on the basis of race, national origin and disability.

Soon after the development of these tests, and their proliferation in education in particular, criticisms emerged about tests influencing teaching. In the mid-1930s, Lindquist detailed the common critiques of testing:

> criticisms have included the contentions that, in their desire to secure higher test results, the teachers in the participating schools will 'point' their instructions toward the examinations used; that they will become 'drill masters,' primarily concerned with the rote learning of facts culled from previous examinations; that they will seriously neglect the less tangible but more important outcomes of instruction which are not measured by the examinations; and that they will secure spuriously high standing on the tests through intensive last-minute cramming procedures. It has been claimed consequently that the tests used will 'dominate' the high school curriculum and that the cooperative testing program is but another device for taking from the high schools the right to determine their own curriculum policies. (Lindquist, 1935: 515)

In reading Lindquist's descriptions of these criticisms, it is difficult to ignore how these same issues remain unresolved in the present day. Research on quantitative methods for detecting cheating on tests (Cizek & Wollack, 2017), continued questions about teaching to the test (Popham, 2001), issues around curriculum narrowing (Berliner, 2011) and the thriving test-preparation industry (Buchmann et al., 2010) are some of the examples of how the concerns about testing from its early inception in the 1930s remain relevant today.

Technology and testing

Technological innovations increased the efficiency of scoring, and aided the continued growth and development of testing. In 1937 IBM made the 805 Test Scoring Machine commercially available. It had been designed by a teacher hired by IBM in 1934 to develop an automated scorer. It was not of course wholly automatic, in that a person needed to insert sheets and manually record the scores. IBM advertised that 800–1000 tests could be scored per hour (IBM, n.d.).

Major innovations were made within the testing industry during the 1950s and through to the 1980s to increase speed and efficiency while reducing the cost of test production and scoring. In 1955, high-speed scanners that did not need humans to feed sheets or record the scores were developed. Businesses began to enter the testing industry not as test developers but primarily as test scorers. The National Computer Systems company, founded in 1962, scored tests and some surveys. In the mid-1970s

Scantron was founded and has now become a metonym for multiple-choice answer sheets. Scantron's unique business model may explain how it became synonymous with standardized-test answer sheets. The company developed a desktop scanner that would score using a microcomputer and this scanner was given for free to schools. Schools needed to pay only for the Scantron sheets that fit specifically in this scanner (Clarke et al., 2000; Kopriva, 2008).

These technological investments aided the growth of testing as a profitable business. In the United States, annual revenues from testing reached $40 million in 1960, solidly establishing testing as an industry, had increased to $100 million by 1989 (Rigney et al., 2008) and were estimated to be $700 million in the late 2000s (Supovitz, 2009).

Accountability testing and pushback

As testing become linked to larger accountability frameworks, states began to require educational testing. California mandated testing statewide in 1962; in 1977 Florida was the first state to mandate a high school graduation test. From 1962 to 1985, state-mandated testing programs jumped from one to 35 states (Clarke et al., 2000; Kopriva, 2008). With the No Child Left Behind Act of 2001 (NCLB), all states were required to have state accountabilities systems in place that reported to the federal government. Wiliam (2010) explained the presuppositions underlying NCLB that these annual, standardized tests for mathematics and language arts would uncover 'differences between students in terms of their educational outcomes', and that the outcomes, 'as measured by the tests, should be largely, if not wholly, attributable to differences in the quality of education provided by schools' (Wiliam, 2010: 110).

At the national level, a low-stakes standardized testing accountability system was put in place in 1969 with the National Assessment for Educational Progress (NAEP) for language arts and mathematics. The scores from the NAEP tests are still used to compare student performance by state. In these, and across similar accountability systems defined by testing, 'policymakers have used tests in an attempt to discover which schools and districts are fulfilling their responsibilities and which are falling short' (Haertel & Herman, 2005: 28). Tests continue to occupy this role in the United States, though recent movements at universities away from the use of standardized entrance exams and the opt-out movement in K-12 education have pushed back against these entrenched testing practices.

As of the fall 2018, over 1000 accredited colleges and universities in the United States did not require students take the standardized entrance exams in the form of the SAT (Scholastic Achievement Test) or ACT (American College Test) (FairTest, 2018) and as of August 2016 a total of 225 universities had flexible SAT/ACT requirements for international students (Test Optional Survey, 2016). The GRE (Graduate Records Exam) has been eliminated at the program or department level as a requirement for applications to masters and PhD programs (McCammon, 2016). Universities can choose to waive English proficiency testing requirements (e.g. the TOEFL – Test of English as a Foreign Language) by having international students enroll in university-run intensive English programs (American Educational Group, 2010). Information about the bachelor's degrees is readily available and highly publicized. Universities or programs that do not require the GRE or a standardized English proficiency test have been compiled more informally, and have not received similar widespread publicity.

Beginning in the autumn of 2011, the United Opt Out National formed as a non-profit organization, providing support to parents, teachers and students who do not want to participate in standardized testing in K-12 schools (http://www.unitedoptoutnational.org). During the 2014–2015 school year, it is estimated that 670,000 students opted out of standardized tests nationwide (FairTest, 2016). The case for opting out of annual, standardized testing is put by FairTest (the 'National Center for Fair and Open Testing'):

> *Testing overuse and misuse is damaging public education.* It eats up classroom time, narrows curriculum and drives many students out of school. It perpetuates a false narrative of failure and puts schools in low-income communities at risk of closure or privatization. (FairTest, 2017: para. 1, original emphasis)

In their national survey investigating the opt-out movement, Pizmony-Levy and Green Saraisky received 1,641 responses from 47 states. 'The typical opt out activist is a highly educated, white, married, politically liberal parent whose children attend public school and whose household median income is well above the national average' (Pizmony-Levy & Green Saraisky, 2016: 6). Key findings included that 74.5% of respondents who were parents or guardians of school-aged children had opted out of testing, and 92.1% stated they were likely to opt out in the future. Most had been involved in the opt-out movement for three or four years. In addition to protesting against testing, many were vocal about the narrowing of the curriculum based on testing, privatization of education and the Common Core State Standards. New York State has had the largest number of students opting out. The organization New York State Allies for Public Education (2016) reported that 265,000 students refused to take tests in 2016, a 16.8% refusal rate for the English language arts test and a 12.7% refusal rate for mathematics. The movement has continued to expand each year, and the growing infrastructure at state and national level may serve to support this resistance.

Conclusion

In reviewing these testing practices, it is evident that some issues were (and remain) largely unaddressed throughout the expansion of testing. Throughout this time, there have been vocal criticisms of and contentions with testing practices, yet the growth of testing appears to have been unaffected. Further, despite the ubiquity of testing with language-minoritized bilinguals since the beginning of testing in China, their histories and experiences remain largely unexplored. This book aims to fill this gap by constructing a historical narrative of the consequences language-minoritized bilinguals have faced, as a means to interrogate approaches that have negatively impacted these individuals, focusing on testing in the United States.

Overview of the Book

The book consists of five main chapters. The first chapter introduces the conceptual framework that underpins the analysis in the subsequent chapters. Part 1 comprises two chapters that trace histories centered around major issues of immigration. Part 2 focuses more on educational issues and is divided into K-12 and higher education contexts. Chapters 2–5 provide rich descriptions of historical and modern events, with commentary on concepts introduced in Chapter 1. Finally, the 'Concluding Thoughts' chapter serves as a critical synthesis of the content of the earlier chapters, reflecting on the implications of the analyses for those in the field of testing, with particular attention to the contribution to perspectives on validity, as well as for audiences more generally invested in working against legacies of colonialism, slavery, imperialism and other systematic oppressive practices.

In Chapter 1 I describe the process of constructing a historical narrative. The conceptual framework foregrounds histories of discrimination through the use of scholarship on intersectionality and white supremacy. This analytical lens situates how consequential validity has been conceptualized with respect to language-minoritized bilinguals. In doing so, this chapter introduces key issues that are then taken up in part in Chapters 2–5 and revisited more in depth in the 'Concluding Thoughts'.

Chapters 2–5 illustrate different ways in which language-minoritized bilinguals have encountered tests, each centered around what these bilinguals are seeking. Chapter 2 examines civic participation, including gaining access to the United States, to voting, naturalization or citizenship, and military service, discussing how racial background, country of origin and citizenship impact the consequences of testing. Chapter 3 explores the ports of Ellis Island and Angel Island and the different treatment of children and adults at each port of entry, while also highlighting discriminatory treatment based on country of origin and race.

Shifting to seeking education, Chapters 4 and 5 look at K-12 schools and higher education, respectively. Chapter 4 provides information about K-12 testing in US public schools, including intelligence testing, content area and English proficiency testing. This chapter more than others discusses some of the long-term consequences of testing, and how multiple factors, notably race, sexuality and disability, contribute to the severity of the consequences. In Chapter 5, I present information about the major tests for college admissions – achievement tests and English proficiency tests – as well as post-admissions testing of international teaching assistants. This chapter explores how the treatment of language-minoritized bilinguals who live in the United States contrasts with the treatment of those coming from non-US contexts.

To conclude, I revisit the argument for including a historical narrative as an aspect of consequential validity. The conclusion is a synthesis of the previous chapters and weaves together the myriad experiences of language-minoritized bilinguals to critically engage with the histories and legacies of white settler colonialism in the United States, with implications for testing in other regions of the world as well. The conclusion ends by posing questions to the different parties involved, putting this history to use in future decision making.

1 Conceptualizing a Historical Narrative of Social Consequences

This history centers language-minoritized bilingual test-takers' experiences with tests and the consequences of that testing for those bilinguals. In this chapter, I outline key conceptual issues that arise in constructing a historical narrative of the social consequences of tests for language-minoritized bilinguals. One of the motivations for this book is the lack of a current narrative on the social consequences of testing for language-minoritized bilinguals.[1] Another is to support change in testing practices (this is taken up in depth in the 'Concluding Thoughts' chapter). According to Shohamy, testing approaches for language-minoritized bilinguals have remained largely unchanged despite innovations in the field of education:

> Although dynamic, diverse, and constructive discussions of multilingual teaching and learning are currently taking place within the language education field, the phenomenon is completely overlooked in the assessment field that continues to view language as a monolingual, homogenous, and often still native-like construct. (Shohamy, 2011: 419)

A history is presented here that highlights persistent and often repeated consequences, and specifically negative consequences of testing for language-minoritized bilingual populations. That testing has largely operated using monolingual standards, and the narrative provided here should serve as a motivation for innovations in testing to work actively against these negative social consequences. Such work is needed because, as Otheguy, García and Reid have stated, '[m]any language assessments [...] work to the detriment of bilingual children [and adults] worldwide' (Otheguy *et al.*, 2015: 283).

This historical narrative examines the social consequences of testing faced by language-minoritized bilinguals, and elucidates how negative consequences persist. This book, then, is a direct engagement with a question that has been asked in various forms by many people: do the results of these tests – and the consequences of testing – merely reflect social inequities, or do they reproduce them? This narrative seeks to illustrate through historical evidence that language-minoritized bilinguals have faced repeated, often severe, consequences which have both exacerbated existing inequities and introduced new ones.

To begin this task, I describe scholarship on intersectionality and historical perspectives of white supremacy, primarily in the United States but also as a global phenomenon. These views inform my approach to describing social consequences and validity, with an emphasis on how previous approaches to validity have treated language-minoritized bilingual test-takers; the discussion ends with the proposal that a use-oriented testing perspective be adopted in constructing a historical narrative of the consequences of testing. These different lenses highlight myriad separate factors at play in relation to the social consequences of testing, and importantly when looking at these experiences collectively. Thus, in this chapter I put forth a framework that is used throughout the book to provide evidence that can be used to inform new, shifting approaches to testing, with the explicit purpose of confronting and mitigating the reproduction of negative social consequences of testing for language-minoritized bilinguals through the construction of a cohesive, though not exhaustive, historical narrative.

Conceptualizing Histories of Discrimination

For an investigation of histories of discrimination, the scholarship on intersectionality and white supremacy provides an overarching framework to locate cohesion across the array of experiences related to themes of oppression and privilege. Intersectionality is particularly well situated because it would be challenging to conceive of a historical narrative of language-minoritized bilinguals in the United States that ignored the role of racism, ableism, sexism, anti-LGBTQ+, xenophobia, classism and ageism. Combined with the literature on white supremacy, these views of history also serve as a lens for critiquing validity and how validity has been produced within a history of white supremacy.

Intersectionality

Including identities based on race, age, gender, sexual orientation, nationality, class and religion is essential to understanding the social consequences of testing because many language-minoritized bilinguals have faced negative social consequences not only because of their language background, but also because they inhabit one or more of these other identities as well. Intersectionality frameworks help to make sense of the interactions of these multiple minoritized identities, and the various forms of oppression entailed. In her seminal work on intersectionality, Crenshaw (1989, 1991) examined how Black women were uniquely impacted by violence with respect to structural, political and representational intersectionality around race, class and gender. Crenshaw's work has been expanded to understand the experiences unique to individuals who inhabit two (or more) historically marginalized identities. Intersectionality frameworks facilitate the documentation of historical accounts of the forces that perpetuate oppression with respect to language-minoritized bilinguals.

Looking at these different perspectives of structural, political and representational intersectionality provides interpretive lenses that aid in framing how language-minoritized bilinguals have experienced the consequences of testing in relation to other social, political and historical phenomena. Structural intersectionality presents how different aspects of societies are linked to, make possible or sustain oppressive acts (Crenshaw, 1991, 2014). Political intersectionality emphasizes the laws or policies that are put in place to address one aspect of inequities, but that introduce a bevy of other complications when they do not take the impact of other intersectional identities into consideration. Representational intersectionality is understood as 'when one discourse fails to acknowledge the significance of the other' and 'the power relations that each attempts to challenge are strengthened' (Crenshaw, 1991: 1282).

For language-minoritized bilinguals, intersectionality has been applied in research on *raciolinguistic ideologies* and on language-minoritized bilinguals in K-12 schools who have also been diagnosed with disabilities. Rosa and Flores integrate intersectionality as one of five components of a raciolinguistic perspective. They argue that this bringing together of language and race 'is not intended to displace, avoid, or distract from important analyses of categories such as gender, socioeconomic class, sexuality, ethnicity, and religion' and that they instead align their argument with scholarship in intersectionality that 'refuse[s] dichotomies between categories such as race, class, gender, and sexuality' (Rosa & Flores, 2017: 15). They review research that has looked at how these intersections of language, race and additional identities have coalesced to impact individuals. Kangas (2017, 2018) and Schissel and Kangas (2018) have applied intersectionality to understand the unique concerns that arise for language-minoritized bilinguals who are also diagnosed with disabilities in US public schools. These works illuminate a lack of examination of what separate practices and policies – on the part of teachers, schools and tests – for language-minoritized bilinguals or students with disabilities mean for students who are both.

Intersectionality is itself not beyond critique, however. In general these critiques are essential to move intersectionality forward as a reflective, contextually attuned theory or framework. Cho (2013), for example, has called into question how dominance and oppression are often prescriptively ascribed to particular racial groups or sexes. She points to somewhat reductive portrayals of race as Blackness and sex as women, to the exclusion of more fluid frames for identifying race, sex and other identities. Others have questioned the application of intersectionality in research centered on identity (Anthias, 2012; Cho *et al.*, 2013; Guidroz & Berger, 2009; Núñez, 2014). Yet the prevalence of particular emphases in critiques has been problematized as well. May (2015) has claimed that many critiques are more indicative of how intersectional research has been misunderstood or poorly executed. She calls for researchers engaging in work with intersectionality to reflect on how power operates in scholarship as well. Moreover:

> [what researchers] may not have accounted for adequately is how [they] are regularly invited to adhere to and think within the confines of existing and established frameworks. [… These frameworks] consistently seem more logical or plausible and those who use them, or adhere to their norms, are more likely to be perceived as rational or as making reasoned claims. This is what intersectionality, in great part, has to teach us: and this is also, in great part, how it gets dropped or distorted. (May, 2015: 67–68)

The point that May has made is that intersectionality is not a straightforward interpretive frame. Rather, it is 'about "both/and" thinking, relational power and privilege, ontological multiplicity, and intermeshed oppressions' (May, 2015: 98). Thus, many of the critiques of intersectionality are reflective of degrees of incompatibility between intersectionality and some paradigms within research and how central tenets are 'dropped or distorted'.

For this historical narrative, intersectionality highlights how the multiple minoritized categories that language-minoritized bilinguals occupy can impact the social consequences of testing. More specifically, it looks how these bilinguals are more susceptible to different testing consequences because they inhabit multiple minoritized identities. These identities are often foregrounded and even isolated in ways that make a test or testing consequence more readily applied.

Focus on race and white supremacy

In constructing a historical narrative of testing and its consequences, it is important to understand that colonialism, slavery and imperialism are global phenomena with clear histories in testing and in the United States. Viewing testing and its consequences with respect to white supremacy makes visible the systemic oppressive forces (Allen, 2001; Ansley, 1989; Doane & Bonilla-Silva, 2003; Flores & Rosa, 2015; Gillborn, 2006; Omi & Winant, 1993; Sledd, 1969; Smith, 2012, 2016) that circulate around, through and with testing. In reviewing the literature on white supremacy, conceptualizations comprehensively encompass historical, political, social and economic influences and events. The linguistic elements generally link whiteness with monolingual or native speaker ideologies about English proficiency that align with standard language varieties (Sledd, 1969). That is not to say that whiteness could not include speaking other languages, but the assumption is steeped in perceived fluency in English. One example is the practice of hiring 'native English speakers' in different regions of the world, which has favored white individuals. In looking to definitions of white supremacy, there is an emphasis on these factors, and the ways in which supremacist acts represent power relationships that marginalize. Ansley explained how white supremacy represents

> a political, economic, and cultural system in which whites overwhelmingly control power and material resources, conscious and unconscious ideas of white superiority and entitlement are widespread, and relations of white dominance and non-white subordination are daily reenacted across a broad array of institution and social settings. (Ansley, 1989: 1024n)

The inclusion of unconscious ideas is particularly relevant for the understanding of white supremacy in relation to testing. The United States has a history of policies and laws explicitly formed on the basis of white supremacy, around, for example, immigration and naturalization. Such practices and their impact have not disappeared; rather, white supremacy has shifted from *de jure* to *de facto* practices (Mills, 2003).

Smith (2016) has explored how white supremacy is sustained through three primary logics which are anchored in systems which often do little to question their practice: slavery anchored in capitalism; genocide anchored in colonialism; and orientalism anchored in war. These logics are literal in their description of historical events, yet bear relevance to modern, *de facto* versions of white supremacy. From slavery to the current for-profit prison and immigration detainment systems, economic growth through capitalism has been achieved. Genocide speaks to the disappearance of Indigenous peoples, and in particular to their removal in order to gain their lands. The forcible removal of Native Americans throughout the history of the United States is not far removed from the government actions at Standing Rock Reservation, where from April 2016 there were protests against the Dakota Access Pipeline (which had raised serious concerns about endangering water supplies and destroying ancient burial grounds). The third logic of white supremacy argued by Smith is orientalism anchored in war. Based on the work of Edward Said, orientalism describes the process whereby Western countries (inclusive of the United States) are deemed to have a superior or exceptional civilization, while other regions of the world are less advanced or exotic. The exoticism or 'foreignness' is often seen as a threat, which is then used to justify war or other forms of military action. The 'war on terror' and the differential treatment of domestic terrorist events based on the race or ethnicity of the person committing the act exemplify this logic of white supremacy.

In seeking a way to understand how language-minoritized bilinguals have been treated historically, this book looks to Omi and Winant's (1993) concept of *racial projects*. 'Racial projects connect an interpretation of race in a given historical moment or context to the organization of social structures and everyday practices' (Carbado & Harris, 2012: 183). Understanding the interpretation of language-minoritized bilinguals in a given historical context in connection with the organization of social structures and everyday practices foregrounds the relevance of the social consequences of testing. While racial projects seek in a similar way to understand the interpretation, representation or organization of racial dynamics, this historical narrative seeks to understand the dynamics of being perceived as 'not yet proficient in English' in relation to a multitude of other characteristics that serve to perpetuate the use of tests to delegitimize the participation of language-minoritized bilinguals in various facets of US society.

Exploring the contexts of white supremacy outside the United States also factors into this understanding of white supremacy. Allen (2001) examines how conceptualizations of globalization and the influence of capitalism in driving global connections are indicative of global applications of white supremacy. Twine (1998) has explored the dynamics of white supremacy in Brazil in the views of Afro-Brazilians. Hage (2012) has detailed racialization and discourses of superiority in Australia. In connecting white supremacy to testing, Gillborn (2006) showed how white norms are applied in the national assessment system in schools in the United Kingdom, questioning – like this book – whether tests record or produce inequalities. He outlined the shifts in tests and accountability frameworks, most of which obscure the heterogeneity of achievement of students from different racial backgrounds, and the enactment of policies with almost no regard to how they could affect non-white students. To draw attention to the ubiquity of subjugation of language-minoritized bilinguals in testing, Gillborn remarked, 'It is difficult to imagine a contrary situation where no action would be taken were a new assessment system to result in white children being out-performed by their peers in every minority group' (Gillborn, 2006: 334). This then leads into a discussion of the purpose of testing, which connects with test validity. These understandings of white supremacy serve as a backdrop for constructing a historical narrative of the consequences of testing faced by language-minoritized bilinguals.

Validity and Language-minoritized Bilinguals

Modern definitions of validity stem from a view that the interpretations of or actions based on a test score are used for intended purposes. *The Standards* define validity as:

> The degree to which accumulated evidence and theory support a specific interpretation of test scores for a given use of a test. If multiple interpretations of a test score for different uses are intended, validity evidence for each interpretation is needed. (AERA, APA & NCME, 2014: 225)

Within this current definition of validity, there is a clear distinction between the testing instrument itself and the inferences and decisions, or uses, associated with the scores achieved by test-takers.

The development of the concept of validity with regard to language-minoritized bilinguals in the United States is discussed in this section. It begins with the first assessments to be used on a large scale – intelligence tests – and how these first tests were created and interpreted in relation to racist and anti-immigrant discourses and policies – in related to white settler colonialism, slavery and imperialism. Indeed, the very idea of validity can be viewed as coming from a particular epistemological framework that suggests that intelligence can be objectively assessed. The rise of intelligence testing was part of the sorting of populations into different levels of intelligence, itself a continuation of colonial discourses. On one side were biological racists – often in the eugenics movement – who thought that these differences were genetic. On the other side were cultural (or perhaps epistemological) racists, who attributed this to environmental factors. As the biological argument waned with the decline of eugenics, the cultural argument rose to prominence and is still a primary discourse within educational circles.

It is important to note that although the initial development of tests in the United States engaged directly with language-minoritized bilinguals, including the creation of tests in part for individuals who did not speak English (i.e. Army Beta), the period when the majority of work on approaches to validity was *after* the number of language-minoritized bilinguals in the United States had dramatically decreased, from the 1930s on. That is, many of these early tests were developed during the 1910s and 1920s, when restrictive immigration policies and pro-English legislation in states and schools drastically reduced the number of language-minoritized bilinguals. What is relevant here is that perhaps because of the smaller population of language-minoritized bilinguals taking tests, the development of validity theories for these bilinguals received less attention. In turn, this also points to issues around how – aside from denouncing affiliation with eugenics – those working with the concepts of validity did not systematically address the historical links with eugenic, anti-immigrant, racist ideologies and any potential implications of such origins.

With respect to work on validity, attention was paid to language-minoritized bilinguals more specifically around the 1980s and 1990s. Social consequences of testing under a unitary definition of validity (Messick, 1989), and specifically construct-irrelevant variance, was applied to these individuals in the 1990s. This marked a time when theories and conceptualizations of validity more directly addressed the testing of language-minoritized bilinguals. These conceptualizations have worked to identify how test developers contribute to the consequences of testing by distinguishing between positive and negative, intended and unintended consequences. Since then, innovations such as the concept of cultural validity (Solano-Flores, 2011; Solano-Flores & Nelson-Barber, 2001) have presented some of the most promising new directions in validity that specifically address language-minoritized bilinguals.

Early approaches to validity addressing language-minoritized bilinguals

Early research on what would develop into modern testing began by engaging in how to define validity, emphasizing what came to be called criterion-reference validity (Kane, 2013; Sireci, 2009). The criterion referred to the specific attribute being measured, for example intelligence or language proficiency. Analyses of the first large-scale, standardized intelligence tests – the Army Alpha and Beta, and the Army Performance Examination – present validity on a continuum from a focused to a vague engagement with the theoretical or practical definitions of validity. Yerkes (1921) and Brigham (1923) published extensive volumes analyzing the data from estimates of 1,588,904 to 1,726,966 recruits who took the tests, many of whom were language-minoritized bilinguals.

These army tests were administered to draftees during World War I, when the US military was racially segregated. Groups of individuals who were not born in the United States were called 'foreign born white' and were listed as from the following countries of origin: Austria, Belgium, Canada, Denmark, England, Germany, Greece, Holland, Ireland, Italy, Norway, Poland, Russia, Scotland, Sweden and Turkey. Individuals who would then have been classified as 'foreign born non-white' generally came from Mexico or Central and South America, as well as from Asian and African countries; information on them is largely absent from the analyses presented by both Yerkes and Brigham.

Validity it was more clearly defined and explored by Yerkes (1921) than Brigham (1923). Yerkes (1921) claimed 'Validity as a measure of intelligence – A majority of the tests [Army Alpha, Beta and Performance] were known to correlate highly with good measures of intelligence [Stanford–Binet]' (Yerkes, 1921: 303). Describing the role of correlation with other tests, Yerkes explained:

> A test which will not correlate fairly well with the total score of a good battery of tests is ipso facto under grave suspicion; there is little likelihood that it will consistently correlate well with any other proved measure of intelligence. (Yerkes, 1921: 338)

Thus Yerkes placed a great deal of importance on this method of defining validity. In conjunction with these definitions of validity, Yerkes compared scores with the opinions of or informal evaluations by officers who had been well acquainted with the test-takers. Though not included in his official definition of validity, these descriptions feature prominently throughout the volume. In summarizing the links between test results and officers' opinions, Yerkes wrote of the specific case of one officer:

> Maj. Schitter, commanding the base hospital, is firmly convinced of the value of the test as an aid in sizing up the capabilities of his men. He told me of a number of instances where the psychological scores have an accurate index as to practical worth. (Yerkes, 1921: 20)

Yerkes generalized the implications of this support in relation to validity:

> It may be well emphasized that the psychological examination furnishes for immediate use a rating of the men which in validity compares not unfavorably with ratings furnished by officers after months of acquaintance. (Yerkes, 1921: 155–156)

These early definitions of validity were used to justify the consequences of test use, in this case placement in different military ranks, or dismissal.

Both Yerkes and Brigham explained the consequences faced by test-takers as a direct result of the test (i.e. regular service, assignment to a 'development battalion', domestic service, discharge, or referral to a psychiatrist – see Chapter 2 for more specific information about the consequences of military testing). In connecting the validity of score inferences to the criterion of intelligence, both researchers explained how the results aligned with their belief that intelligence was both innate and inherited. As presented in the Introduction, these views were linked with eugenics, and movements that purported that links between intelligence and race were biological, but also that policies and actions such as sterilization or deportation should be implemented as negative consequences for people who performed poorly on intelligence tests. Yerkes and Brigham also made generalizations about entire races or nationalities from these data, with Brigham expanding on Yerkes's more hedged assertions. Yerkes put forth the claim that the average intelligence score on these exams was 'lower than that of the country at large' (Yerkes, 1921: 785), and so concluded that the individuals who were tested were not representative of the overall population, due in part to the large number of foreign-born recruits. Brigham was more specific about which particular language-minoritized bilinguals were impacting the scores in stating the 'intellectual superiority of the Nordic race group' (Brigham, 1923: 207). Brigham focused on the implications of the scores and drew broad conclusions about groups of individuals based on racial and national backgrounds, with strong claims about superiority.

And yet, Brigham's (1923) analysis of the Army Alpha, Beta and Performance exams did not include a definition of validity; in fact, he discussed validity only twice throughout his volume. This included discussing how the validity of the test scores impacted language-minoritized bilinguals. In making claims about foreign-born test-takers, Brigham expanded upon claims made by Yerkes (1921) about what types of inferences could be drawn from data that showed that scores increased with the test-takers' length of residence in the United States. Yerkes posited that 'the more intelligent immigrants succeed and therefore remain in this country, but this suggestion is weakened by the fact that so many successful immigrants do return to Europe' (Yerkes, 1921: 704). Brigham questioned the validity of the measurements, presupposing that a factor other than intelligence was being measured with these tests. In the hypothetical, he posited:

> If our results reflect another factor independent of intelligence, which might be designated 'the better adaptation of the more thoroughly Americanized group to the situation of the examination,' we have no means of controlling this factor. Ultimately, the validity of our conclusion from this study rests on the validity of the alpha, beta, and the individual examinations. [...] If the tests used some mysterious type of situation that was 'typically American,' we are indeed fortunate, for this is America, and the purpose of our inquiry is that of obtaining a measure of the character of our immigration. (Brigham, 1923: 95–96)

Brigham ultimately accepted that the scores from the test could be trusted, and returned to theories of innate or inherited intelligence to make claims about immigrants from particular backgrounds. He specifically rejected the claim that there could be some issues with the test itself. He asked:

> does it [the test result] represent an error in the method of measuring intelligence, or, looked at from another angle, does it show gradually decreasing intelligence of the more recent immigrants examined in the army? (Brigham, 1923: 100)

Starting with the assumption that they were measuring 'native or inborn intelligence', he argued that these scores reflected static qualities, rejecting the possibility of an individual's scores changing over time. For foreign-born test-takers, he concluded that the scores reflected 'a change in the character of the immigrants examined' (Brigham, 1923: 100). In defending the precision of the measurements, he made strong negative claims about immigrants:

> We must therefore accept the conclusion that under the conditions of this experiment the differences shown in the average scores of the five years of resident groups [of immigrants] indicate real differences in intelligence and not a defect in the measuring scale [...] we accept the hypothesis that

the curve indicates a gradual deterioration in the class of immigrants examined in the army, who came to this country in each succeeding five year period since 1902. (Brigham, 1923: 110–111)

Brigham's analyses lacked a strong validity argument and, rather, reflected national, anti-immigrant sentiments. The Emergency Quota Act (also known as the Emergency Immigration Act) of 1921 restricting immigrants from southern and eastern Europe was already in effect by the time Brigham published his volume. Brigham's purported scientific evidence from these testing data aligned with the common knowledge circulated against these immigrants. The Immigration Act of 1924 then increased the restrictions on southern and eastern Europeans (Hing, 2004).

As validity continued to develop as a concept in the field of testing, researchers often emphasized how test scores either related to the underlying factors being measure or how it correlated with other measurements of the same factors. They moved away from making sweeping conclusions about the test-taker based on the results, especially for intelligence tests. Brigham (1930), in a paper which largely retracted many of his earlier statements, explained this shift as follows:

> Psychologists have been attacked because of their use of the term 'intelligence,' and have been forced to retreat to the more restricted notion of test score. Their definition of intelligence must now be score in a test which we consider to measure 'intelligence.' (Brigham, 1930:158)

In making this shift to begin to focus on the implications of test scores – more in alignment with modern definitions – Brigham also explicitly addressed the fallacies underlying his previous work. He thus argued against using test scores to draw conclusions about innate intelligence based on race or nationality:

> comparative studies of various national and racial groups may not be made with existing tests, and show, in particular, that one of the most pretentious of these comparative racial studies – the writer's own – was without foundation. (Brigham, 1930: 165)

Yet testing of language-minoritized bilinguals continued, with sometimes far-reaching implications. Intelligence testing in particular became commonplace for children. While Yerkes and Brigham examined data from the army tests, Pintner and Keller (1922) published the first use of an intelligence test with language-minoritized children, aged 5–16, comparing the Binet and (revised) Stanford–Binet tests with the Pintner non-language test and performance tests (e.g. the Pintner Cube test, the Foam Board). Although validity was not addressed explicitly, this was the first article to critique the use of intelligence tests with language-minoritized bilinguals. The authors concluded that 'when classified according to mental age, those children who hear a foreign language in their homes may suffer a serious handicap when tested only by the revisions of the Binet Test' (Pintner & Keller, 1922: 222). This 'handicap' is not clarified in the article. The authors, however, discuss how language-minoritized bilinguals' scores on different intelligence tests varied more than those of their English-speaking counterparts, pointing to potential bias in these exams.

For language-minoritized students, research about the validity of intelligence test methods, performance and inferences continued to be richly debated. In particular, researchers continued to investigate whether heredity, environment or language could be identified as the cause for differences in performance when comparing language-minoritized students' scores with those of white, English-speaking students (Sánchez, 1932). Testing techniques were sought that were more developed specifically for the language-minoritized population. To determine whether heredity was the distinguishing factor, non-verbal tests were touted as free of linguistic influences and able to measure innate intelligence (Goodenough, 1926). To determine whether environment, instead, was the responsible factor, scores from siblings who were separated were compared, and descriptions of their vastly different socio-economic realities were presented (Gonzales, 1928, as cited in Sánchez, 1932). To determine whether language was the responsible factor, studies tested whether bilingualism could result in a confusion that hindered a child's intellectual development (Colvin & Allen, 1923; Wang, 1926; Yoshioka, 1929).

Critiques of the validity of applying these testing approaches to language-minoritized bilinguals were vocalized by one of the few Mexican America bilingual scholars involved in these debates: George Sánchez. Best known for his book *Forgotten People* (1940) and his work furthering equity movements for the education of Mexican Americans, his writing about standardized testing highlighted the consequences that language-minoritized bilinguals faced, and these are issues that remain at the forefront of many debates on testing of bilinguals:

> a test is valid only to the extent that the items of the test are as common to each child tested as they were to the children upon whom the norms were based. Only when community of experience actually exists can checks based on that assumption be valid, even if we grant that such checks do symbolize intellectual capacity – an 'if' that has serious questions in itself. (Sánchez, 1940: 766)

He further stated:

> As long as the tests do not at least sample in equal degree a state of saturation that is equal for the 'norm children' and the particular bilingual child it cannot be assumed that the test is a valid one for that child. (Sánchez, 1940: 771)

Ultimately, he concluded that many test scores were a reflection of institutional problems around access to equitable educational opportunities for Spanish-speaking children. He did not argue against the use of tests, but instead called for educators and testers to take into account the broader economic, socio-political and cultural circumstances of these children, and the interactions of these factors with interpretations of test scores.

The burgeoning explorations of validity within these analyses of the early forms of intelligence tests offer a glimpse into the early positioning of language-minoritized bilinguals. The explorations in particular of the inferences being draw from the test scores and some of the proposed consequences are interconnected with socio-political views that devalued language-minoritized bilingual experiences. Sánchez's work illustrates how the use of test scores to substantiate views that marginalized bilinguals were challenged. Language-minoritized bilinguals were more actively included in validity conversations in testing in the late 1970s and 1980s (Duran, 1989), in particular with the introduction of consequential validity.

Social consequences

From the 1930s onwards, definitions of validity became more fleshed out within the field of testing as a whole. Yet language-minoritized bilinguals remained peripheral, in part due to restrictions on immigration imposed by the United States, economic factors such as the Great Depression and global conflicts such as World War II. Centralized clarifications in definitions of validity were taken up again in drafting early editions of *The Standards* in the 1950s and 1960s. During this period, more attention was paid to language-minoritized bilinguals in the field of language assessment (in contrast to the other types of testing, such as intelligence) as tests of English language proficiency were being developed (e.g. Lado, 1961), such as the Test of English as a Foreign Language (TOEFL) introduced in 1965. Duran (1989) summarized the testing of linguistic minorities and noted the following: (1) there were significant problems with language proficiency testing; (2) intelligence tests needed to account for test-takers' English proficiency and cultural background; (3) there were limited data on testing school achievement; (4) there were complications with evaluations for language-minoritized bilinguals in special education; and (5) there were problems with relying on college admissions exams (e.g. the SAT). Although these issues are far from resolved, Messick's work on a unitary view of validity inclusive of social consequences of test use and construct-irrelevant variance was a necessary step towards providing validity frameworks more specifically for language-minoritized bilinguals in the United States.

Messick's discussion of the social consequences of testing gained traction in test development and testing research. His views on validity are encapsulated in the overarching unitary validity theory: 'the appropriateness, meaningfulness, and usefulness of score-based inferences are inseparable and [...] the integrating power derives from empirically grounded score interpretation' (Messick, 1993: 12). Before the unitary theory of validity, there were generally several disparate aspects of validity. I previously mentioned criterion-reference validity in the early development of intelligence tests, which is the comparison of a test score to other external variables that have already been used to measure the behavior or skill in question. Predictive validity can indicate a test-takers' future performance on a related measure. Concurrent validity indicates the test-takers' presumed performance on other measures at the present moment. Content validity describes the breadth and depth of skills or topics used to get a score on a particular test. Construct validity is investigated by evaluating the qualities or characteristics that the test is measuring (Messick, 1990).

Consequences have traditionally been defined in terms of areas that a person creating tests can take into account in test design and development: construct under-representation and construct-irrelevant variance. Construct under-representation refers to when a test is too narrow in scope. Construct-irrelevant variance is caused by extraneous, uncontrolled attributes that affect test performance (Messick, 1980, 1989, 1994). Construct-irrelevant variance has become particularly relevant in creating different approaches to the testing of language-minoritized bilinguals, in particular for content tests of academic performance (e.g. mathematics, science). Presently, the most prevalent and expanding way to adapt content tests for language-minoritized bilinguals in the United States is using test accommodations (Abedi, 2017; Rivera & Collum, 2006). Test accommodations or changes to the test administration (e.g. to small groups), test response (e.g. transcription) or the test itself (e.g. bilingual test forms) aim to reduce construct-irrelevant variance due to language proficiency or the cultural background of language-minoritized bilinguals while not changing the construct that is intended to be measured (see Chapter 4).

Kane (2013) has argued for the inclusion of consequences within his interpretative argument validity framework, renaming the framework 'interpretive use argument' to include test use and the consequences of test use within validity studies. Yet the work by Messick and Kane is limited. McNamara has argued that the social consequences of testing remain largely peripheral because of the 'lack of an appropriate model of the broader social context in which to consider the social and political functions of tests [...] in validity theory in general, even in progressive theories such as Messick and Kane' (McNamara, 2008: 423). Chalhoub-Deville has similarly pointed out that the efforts of Kane and others to include the social consequences of testing within validity research have fallen short:

> while consequences are acknowledged as relevant to testing practices, disagreement prevails on whether they should be part of validity. The dominant perspective has been to restrict the scope of validity to semantic, construct-related research and explorations of fairness and bias. This view of validity has tended to exclude arguments and investigations that pertain to sociopolitical consequences. (Chalhoub-Deville, 2016: 461)

In moving beyond these criticisms, she has posited how to include consequential validity with respect to a theory of action and global educational reform movements. In her framework, she has made 'policy formulation, assessment design/development, and the ongoing administration of a testing program [...] part of a coherent validation program' (Chalhoub-Deville, 2016: 464). Additionally, she has included time as part of her scale for role and responsibility allocation for consequences in validity. Her conception of time, however, differs from how this historical narrative is constructed. Her inclusion of the time dimension is more from the beginning of the development of the test onwards. She writes that 'the time element and related stages are also important in defining roles and allocating responsibility. Responsibilities alter with the passage of time' (Chalhoub-Deville, 2016: 468). In doing so, she is allowing for shifting, changing views of social consequences related to testing, but does not explicitly connect these current consequences or practices with historical contexts. Within this framework there could be space for a consideration of how socio-political contexts have been developed over time and remain connected with various historical origins and influences. Yet histories or historical perspectives have not been explicitly integrated.

Controversies about including consequences as an aspect of validity

Controversies about the inclusion of consequences and uses of testing remain part of a long-standing debate. Central to that debate over the value of studying consequential validity is whether or not test *misuse* is part of consequential validity. Misuse from this perspective means using a test for purposes other than those that were intended. Misuse is problematic, as it can often take a great deal of time before misuses are uncovered, and it assumes that the intentions behind creating tests are benevolent. Messick (1998) clearly states that he does not intend for the misuse of a test to be included in his concept of the consequential validity of an instrument: he and others agree that responsibility lies with the test misuser, and therefore is beyond the scope of the consequential validity (Cronbach, 1971; Messick, 1989; Shepard, 1997). However, when discussing consequential validity, he does include the potential consequences of inferences made from test scores in addition to test use. In making the case for consequential validity, Messick states:

> All educational and psychological tests underrepresent their intended construct to some degree and all contain sources of irrelevant variance.

> The details of this underrepresentation and irrelevancy are typically unknown to the test maker or are minimized in test interpretation and use because they are deemed to be inconsequential. If noteworthy adverse consequences occur that are traceable to these two major sources of invalidity, however, then both score meaning and intended uses need to be modified to accommodate these findings. If these sources of underrepresentation and irrelevancy were known in advance, they would be taken into account in test development. There is *no way* that such unanticipated consequences of legitimate test interpretation and use can be considered to be irrelevant to the validation process. (Messick, 1998: 42, emphasis added)

In explaining ways that consequential validity is being ignored in testing, Shohamy (2006: 95) provides three examples of aspects of the consequential validity of tests that have been overlooked in test development:

(1) determining the prestige and status of languages;
(2) standardizing and perpetuating language correctness; and
(3) suppressing language diversity.

These test consequences relate to ideological orientations inherent in the test construction. These 'social consequences of score interpretation' (Messick, 1998: 41) connect testing to assumed broader societal influences that may go unnoticed.

Shohamy's (2001) argument, which also seeks to account for how those in positions of authority use of tests to change the behavior of test-takers to further their own agendas, straddles the boundary of inclusion in considerations of consequential validity. On the one hand, the construction of the test itself, perhaps the use of one standard language variety over another, belongs in the category of consequential validity. On the other hand, the agenda of the person in authority comes into question and borders on misuse. But Shohamy's argument bears continued reflection because, if in developing a test an agenda such as suppressing linguistic diversity is quite clear, then the case could be made to include this within consequential validity.

In 2016 a special issue of *Assessment in Education: Principles, Policy and Practice* was published on the question of validity articles by Sireci (2016) and Cizek (2016) addressed the role of test use in understanding validity. Sireci's article 'On the validity of useless tests' is aptly titled and uses *The Standards*' definition of validity in addressing how interpretation of a score and use of a test are both necessary for a sufficient validity argument. Cizek challenges *The Standards*' definition and argues for a systematic integration of test use as evidence of defensible testing. He posits:

> Modern validity theory must continue to evolve. Failure to do so would perpetuate perhaps the greatest injustice in modern testing. [...] of greatest concern – validation in practice that is too often anaemic (Ebel, 1961) and

justification in practice that too often reflects a Machiavellian approach wherein simply the loudest, most persuasive, and most powerful or well-funded voices determine the legitimate uses of tests. Decisions about the appropriate use of a test should depend more on the evidence supporting the intended use than the rhetorical force of any entity with a pecuniary or political interest in its implementation. For the greater good of those who are the consumers of test data, and to make progress towards a more comprehensive approach to defensible testing practice, we must begin to pursue the potential for more systematic, rigorous, transparent and democratic justification efforts that rival those that have been developed for validation of score meaning. [...] Such efforts also have potential to enhance the quality and utility of test results and to enable those who develop and use tests to improve the outcomes for their clients, students, organisations and others that are the ultimate beneficiaries of high quality test information. (Cizek, 2016: 217)

In transitioning from these broader views of validity to those more narrowed and focused for language-minoritized bilinguals, there are several important points to emphasize. Throughout the history of validity, bilingualism has generally been treated as a measurement error, such that, at its worst, testing has systematically disadvantaged language-minoritized bilinguals. Cizek's call for a framework for defensible testing directly calls out some of the limitations of previous approaches to validity, but does little to unpack the challenges of creating validation frameworks for language-minoritized bilinguals.

The consequences of testing have been conceptualized as being beyond the immediate testing situation in work on test impact and washback. Impact includes the broader social and political implications of test use, and washback is the influence of testing on teaching (Shohamy, 2001; Wall, 1997). Within these approaches to understanding test consequences has been a focus on what constitutes positive and negative consequences, and whether these were intended or unintended. Messick connected these issues with consequential validity or the 'unanticipated side-effects of legitimate test use, especially if unanticipated adverse effects are traceable to sources of test invalidity' (Messick, 1989: 40).

When looked at as washback, the positive and negative testing consequences are framed as changes introduced by a test that could potentially improve learning or impede learning. Both can be intended or unintended consequences of the use of the test. In the ideal situation, tests are designed to contribute to positive, intended consequences. Positive unintended consequences are also generally welcomed. Positive consequences can include having instruction align with learning standards that are also used in the construction of the test, or more simply include having instruction and the test match each other to encourage learning. Intended negative consequences are also common with tests, such as high-stakes tests in which inadequate performance denies admission to a particular program.

This type of consequence is paired with an intended positive consequence, which is admission. This book focuses closes on negative consequences, intended and unintended, and questions the relevance of intention. Centralizing the consequences of test use connects this historical narrative to aspects of validity in test construction and use. Linking a history of negative social consequences in particular to approaches to validity in the testing of language-minoritized bilinguals serves to challenge current conceptualizations of intended and unintended consequences. These current approaches to the consequences of testing often neglect both the cumulative impact of testing that a historical lens emphasizes and *the irrelevance of intention in light of the long-standing histories of test use that show the marginalization of language-minoritized bilinguals regardless of the intent behind testing.*

All of these perspectives on the consequences of testing remain firmly aligned with a unitary view of validity, and thus my claim is that the historical narrative presented in this book can be connected to validity approaches. Within this historical analysis, I focus on test-takers' experiences and the negative social consequences that have occurred over a long period of time. Kane has stated that 'the validity of a proposed interpretation or use of test scores at any point in time can be defined in terms of the plausibility and appropriateness of the proposed interpretation/use at that time' (Kane, 2013: 2). This statement reflects a view that detaches the consequences of a test score from the full life of the test-taker, and points to how the definition of a point in time can be quite arbitrary. To be clear, it is not my intention with this text to create a 'new' validity. Rather, I aim to highlight one limitation: the lack of a historical lens. This has contributed to test-takers' experiences being ignored for over 100 years, during which time consequences have accumulated without critical acknowledgment or changes to testing that has often perpetuated these consequences. This historical narrative presents test-takers' cumulative experiences, rather than test score inferences in isolation, to contribute to validity approaches for this particular population of test-takers. To accomplish this, I introduce use-oriented testing and cultural validity to propose a shift towards a more equitable approach to validity specifically for language-minoritized bilinguals in the United States.

Use-oriented testing and cultural validity

Shohamy who views use-oriented testing as being 'embedded in educational, social, and political contexts'). This view of testing 'is concerned with what happens to the test-takers [...] the ethicality and fairness of the tests, the long- and short-term consequences that tests have on education and society' (Shohamy, 2001: 4). Importantly, use-oriented testing emphasizes the experiences of the test-takers. In addition to use-oriented testing, I foreground cultural validity, which no longer treats linguistic and cultural diversity as potential measurement error. Solano-Flores and Nelson-Barber (2001) introduced cultural validity to position cultural and linguistic diversity as integral to test design. Viewing linguistic and cultural diversity as 'the essence of validity' (Solano-Flores, 2011: 3) seems vital, in particular when the group of individuals taking tests are also defined by these characteristics. Thus Chapters 2–5 will explore how language-minoritized bilinguals are seeking different types of access or opportunities. In doing so, the history pushes back against the notion that viewing an individual as not yet proficient in English is neither a necessary nor a sufficient unifying characteristic in understanding this heterogeneous group.

Embedded within Messick's (1989) concept of unitary validity, this construction of a historical narrative of the consequences of testing also links to institutional and research-based definitions of fairness in testing. For *The Standards*, fairness is 'responsiveness to individual characteristics and testing contexts so that test scores will yield valid interpretations for intended uses' (AERA, APA & NCME, 2014: 50). For language tests, fairness in the International Language Testing Association's Code of Ethics states that test developers 'shall not discriminate against nor exploit their test-takers on the grounds of age, gender, race, ethnicity, sexual orientation, [or] language background, creed, political affiliations or religion' (ILTA, 2000: 2). McNamara and Ryan (2011) have introduced a fine-grained distinction between fairness and justice with respect to validity:

> Questions of test *fairness* involve not only a concern with equal treatment of groups and avoidance of psychometric bias but all aspects of the empirical validation of test score inferences in the interests of yielding reasonable and defensible judgments about individual test takers. Questions of the *justice* of tests include considerations of the consequential basis of test score interpretation and use but also, and particularly, the social and political values implicit in test constructs. (McNamara & Ryan, 2011: 167, original emphasis)

Fairness and justice for language-minoritized bilingual also connects to Solano-Flores's (2011) concept of cultural validity, which views sociocultural factors, including linguistic diversity, as intrinsic to test development and use, rather than as a threat to validity.

And yet, although the attempts within this work to delineate, define and address validity in a more nuanced way make sense with respect to applying an analytical lens to conceptualizing validity, these fine-grained distinctions – like the distinctions between definitions of assessments, tests and evaluations (see Introduction) – can obscure test-takers' experiences with testing consequences, in particular when looking at these consequences as historically embedded within legacies of racism, ableism,

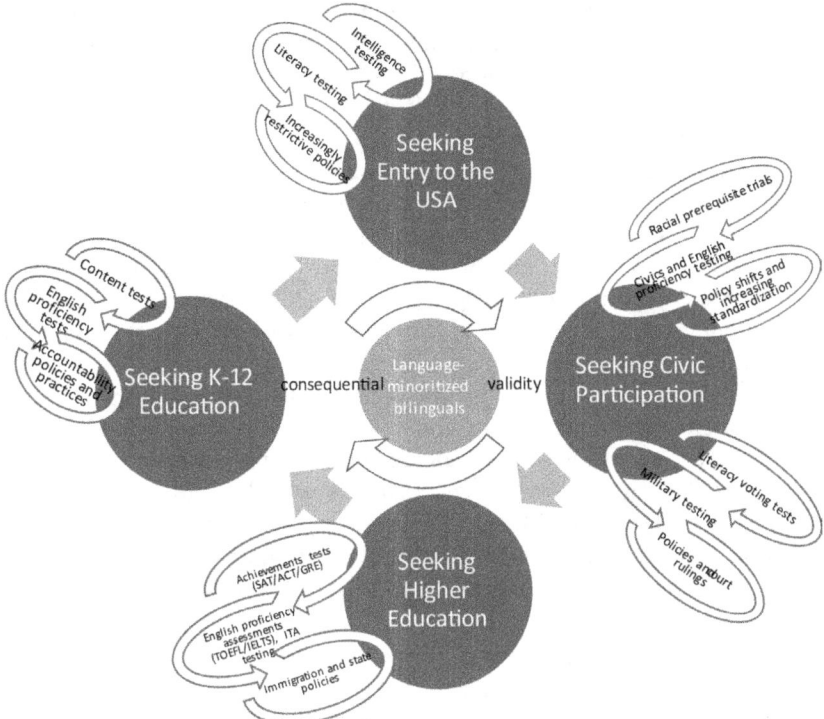

Figure 1.1 A use-oriented approach to the construction of a historical narrative of the social consequences of testing for language-minoritized bilinguals

sexism, anti-LGBTQ+, xenophobia, classism and ageism that continue to lack critical examination, and even to go unnamed. Focusing on how to differentiate between intended and unintended consequences and aspects of validity related to justice, fairness, values, roles and responsibilities and other, more specific delineations of consequential validity circumvents engaging directly with historic discrimination, disenfranchisement and other oppressive practices. That is to say, the instinct to try to organize or disentangle how these consequences are unique qualities of validity is a task that becomes counterproductive in constructing a historical narrative of the social consequences of testing faced by language-minoritized bilinguals, because it has the potential dilute the overall picture and the overarching impact of these consequences. In contrast, Figure 1.1 presents a visualization of a use-oriented test approach that begins with the test-taker.

In working to construct this historical narrative, a use-oriented perspective allows for an organizational framework that originates from test-takers. Beginning with language-minoritized bilinguals with this conceptualization centers their cumulative histories and experiences. The different goals of language-minoritized bilinguals are represented by the circles orbiting around the test-takers. Though presented with clearly delineated boundaries in terms of goals in Figure 1.1, in actuality they overlap and interact, which the arrows aim to represent. For example, many people seek entry into the United States by applying to study at a university. Tests in Figure 1.1 are seen as existing directly in relation to the goals of test-takers, and are linked with contextual influences such as policies and court rulings. Within Figure 1.1, consequential validity is presented as circulating between language-minoritized bilinguals and the goals they are pursuing. Placing consequential validity at this particular place in Figure 1.1 repositions some conceptions of this concept. Instead of investigating the intended or unintended consequences of test use, this perspective looks at the consequences as existing with respect to language-minoritized bilinguals pursuing particular goals. Thus, this history can be seen as contributing to Messick's unitary view of validity in connection with use-oriented testing, which allows for an approach that values the collective experiences of language-minoritized bilinguals.

The Task That Follows

This book seeks to construct a historical narrative to examine the social consequences of testing in relation to: test validity, the framing of consequences, as it shifts from foregrounding the perspective of test developers (e.g., intended and unintended consequences), to centering on the test-taker perspective; and how tests function to prohibit, exclude or discriminate. I am writing as a professional in testing who has been working to change the practice of testing language-minoritized bilinguals and I am writing this book for those concerned with and working with the testing of language-minoritized bilinguals to both scrutinize current practices and to propose new ways forward. Focusing on the perspective of language-minoritized bilinguals means that those in testing need to reflect on their position as they work in this field.

The conceptual framework laid out in this chapter frames the historical descriptions of social consequences faced by language-minoritized bilinguals in subsequent chapters of the book. Such work in testing can begin to address concerns that Cummins has noted: tests 'not only fail to sample the culturally-specific skills and knowledge of the minority child, they frequently penalize children for demonstrating this knowledge' (Cummins, 1986: 196). In this book I foreground the negative consequences, which serves two main purposes. First, negative consequences often have unjust repercussions for individuals, and understanding how and when these consequences occur can begin to counteract these practices. And further, by focusing on negative consequences, this book also is able to illustrate how profound negative experiences with testing have been for language-minoritized bilinguals. The cumulative nature of these consequences for this community serves to demonstrate how the mechanism of testing (often in conjunction with other forces) has contributed to the historic, systemic marginalization of language-minoritized bilinguals in the United States. Such an examination is done with a clear purpose: to disrupt and dismantle current practices, to make space for radical shifts in testing. Yet, there are limitations to testing, and this analysis also takes care not to overstate or minimize the role of testing.

Both short- and long-term consequences are considered here. Short-term consequences often have immediate impact, such as admission to or rejection from a program. Long-term consequences may be at the individual level, such as options made available for service in the military, while also extending beyond the individual to impact families, communities, policies, and social and political ideologies in US discourses. Though it is more difficult to pinpoint the exact role of testing in relation to the long-term consequences, this book serves to illustrate how testing has contributed across these different time scales.

In addressing the complexities of test consequences, I do not claim there is a one-to-one causal link between testing and the consequences faced by language-minoritized bilinguals. Instead, this historical perspective points to the multitude of factors that operate in a variety of ways with testing to create the institutions and structures of consequences. For example, how testing and policies have been laminated together for a shared purpose illustrates the strategic use of testing for particular purposes (with their own consequences). Yet, when testing results did not produce some intended negative consequences, rulings from judges and policies generally have been enacted to further these consequences, making testing more or less irrelevant. Immigration restrictions from the second and third decades of the 20th century are an example of this dynamic. And when testing was seen as over-reaching in terms of consequences, rulings from judges and policies were also enacted to mitigate these consequences, for example to push back against intelligence testing of language-minoritized bilinguals in US public schools in the 1970s. However, performing well on a test – which is often presented one way in which tests promote equity – is complicated by this history that illustrates ways in which test scores were dismissed and consequences were applied. That is to say, the way in which a history of testing is best understood is not in the broad patterns, but instead as the contextualized experiences language-minoritized bilinguals have with testing consequences based on what these individuals are seeking to do and how testing has often been put in place as a barrier or screen in reaching this goal. Working from these understandings, this book presents a historical narrative of testing consequences faced by language-minoritized bilinguals in the United States, from the late 1800s to the present day.

Note

(1) Although this history is focused on language-minoritized bilinguals, some of the events may connect to or in fact actually include speakers of non-standardized varieties of English.

Part 1: Immigration Policy in the United States

Part 1 provides an overview of events leading up to and informing the social consequences of testing for language-minoritized bilinguals seeking access to civic participation and entry to the United States through the ports of Ellis Island and Angel Island. The information is presented chronologically, and many of the coinciding geopolitical historical issues are laid out. This introduction to Part I, highlights the events that problematize the treatment of language-minoritized bilinguals with respect to their intersectional identities and the influences of white supremacy.

Pre-Civil War Period

The pre-Civil War spans from 1776, when the United States attained its independence, to 1861, which saw the start of the Civil War. Immigration policy was relatively unchanged over that period. The 1790 Naturalization Act created the first formalized immigration policy. It stated that only 'free white persons' living in the United States for a minimum of two years would be granted citizenship. All children of naturalized citizens could also become citizens. In 1798, the Alien and Sedition Acts changed the residency requirement to 14 years, and allowed for the executive branch of government to remove from US territory the citizens of countries with which the United States was at war. During this period, the United States was involved in a number of military conflicts to gain territory from other colonial countries and from Native Americans.

Ongoing battles between Mexico and the United States, and most notably the Mexican–American War 1846–1848, resulted in large territorial changes. The Treaty of Guadalupe Hidalgo in 1848 established the Rio Grande River as a border, in addition to present-day California, New Mexico and Arizona, amounting to 55% of Mexico's former territory. Mexicans in these territories had the choice of pursuing US citizenship or retaining Mexican citizenship. The majority chose US citizenship, but the process of gaining it was not immediate, and often not locally recognized. Rampant violence perpetrated by (mostly) white colonizing settlers against these individuals was fueled by dreams of 'striking it rich' during the California gold rush. In the end, the promises of the treaty were unfulfilled. The treatment of Mexican citizens who were also Native Americans was far worse. Their citizenship rights were overwhelmingly denied, their land rights were ignored, and violence against these individuals was common (Klein, 1996).

Post-Civil War Period

The Civil War ended in 1865, and in that year the 13th Amendment to the US Constitution abolished slavery. The ratification of the 14th Amendment in 1868 gave citizenship to individuals of 'African descent'. Immigration policies remained largely unchanged until the Immigration Act of 1882, which mandated a tax per passenger on ships bringing immigrants, to create an immigration fund for the Treasury Secretary to use (Migration Policy Institute, 2013). The same Act also initiated the screening of immigrants, which led to the establishment as immigration ports of Ellis Island in 1892 and Angel Island in 1910. The Naturalization Act of 1906 was the first to link knowledge of English with citizenship.

After the Civil War, immigrants from China were specifically targeted by immigration policies to prevent their entry into the United States. The wording of the 14th Amendment specifically excluded Chinese immigrants (Hing, 2004), Chinese women in part on the basis of an accusation of prostitution (Chan, 1991). The Chinese Exclusion Act of 1882 was followed by a number of reauthorizations and additional anti-Chinese Acts (e.g. the Scott Act of 1888 and the Geary Act of 1892). As the majority of those Chinese immigrants who had already arrived were young men who had come specifically to work on particular projects such as the railways, when an economic depression began in 1883, anti-Chinese sentiment intensified. State laws were also enacted during this time to bar immigrants from work or employment, and remained in place until 1942 (Hing, 2004).

World War I era

The beginning of World War I marked a period of heightened Americanization and anti-immigration sentiment. Some of the strictest immigration policies were enacted during and after this war. The 1917 Immigration Act created an 'Asiatic Barred Zone' that included India, Southeast Asia and most of the Middle East (Migration Policy Institute, 2013). The law expanded the reasons for deporting individuals. A provision for deporting 'anarchists' largely targeted Italian immigrants. Another provision, or particular relevance to the present context, allowed for the deportation of anyone aged over 16 who was illiterate (Hing, 2004). The literacy test, which was the basis for determining who was or was not illiterate, required immigrants to be able to read in their home language.

The 1921 Emergency Quota Act was the first time that numerical restrictions were instituted. It specified the numbers of immigrants allowed from any particular country in relation to a percentage of the population from that country already resident in the United States, according to the 1910 Census figures. But shortly thereafter, in 1924, the quota 'formula' was changed to reflect the 1890 figures, which amplified the restrictions against immigrants from southern and eastern Europe (Hing, 2004; Migration Policy Institute, 2013).

The Great Depression (1929–1939) decreased the number of immigrants, to around 7,000 individuals per year (US Department of Commerce, 1975). Also, individuals were forcibly removed from the United States. Between 1929 and 1936, between 400,000 to 1 million people of Mexican descent underwent repatriation, often forced, to Mexico (US Citizenship and Immigration Services, 2014).

World War II and the Beginning of the Cold War

During World War II, the ways in which the United States treated immigrants illustrated a critical lack of engagement with how different world events impacted the lives of individuals around the globe. It took years for the government to reconsider its entry policies for Jewish immigrants. Infamously, over 900 Jewish refugees were refused entry into the United States in 1939, and in 1941 the US State Department intensified immigration restrictions. At the end of World War II, the Truman Directive shifted these policies and allowed 16,000 Jewish refugees to enter the country, and between 1945 and 1952, the government allowed an additional 400,000 Jewish immigrants (US Holocaust Memorial Museum, n.d.).

From World War II and into the Cold War era, people from Mexico were both recruited to and removed from the United States with the Bracero Program and Operation Wetback Program, respectively. The Bracero Program brought millions of Mexicans to the United States to work as manual laborers, largely in ranching and farming. From 1942 to 1964, this bilateral agreement between the United States and Mexico resulted in 4.6 million work contracts. The Bracero History Archive houses descriptions of the experiences of the families of Bracero workers, documents, oral histories and images (see http://braceroarchive.org/items).

Throughout the duration of the program, the Mexican government lobbied for better working conditions and increased supervision, yet its requests were largely ignored by the US government. Moreover, at the same time, labor needs were also being met through smuggling and recruitment of non-contracted workers from Mexico. Federal policies were enacted that further supported the use of undocumented workers. An amendment to the Immigration and Naturalization Act of 1952 (also called the McCarran–Walter Act) that would have penalized the employers of undocumented workers was defeated and replaced with the explicit statements that hiring undocumented workers did not constitute the crime of 'harboring' (Hing, 2004).

A backlash against undocumented workers ensued almost immediately. In January 1954, Williard F. Kelly, Assistant Commissioner of the Border Patrol, Detention, and Deportation Division, wrote of ongoing and increasing concerns about people from Mexico in the south-west. He characterized Mexican workers as hungry, as suffering various diseases, and as criminals, who collectively presented a drain on the social welfare system. Undocumented workers in particular were portrayed negatively. As the numbers of document and undocumented workers increased with the Bracero Program, there were increasing calls for action to be taken against them. Rather than amend the policy, in the spring of 1954 the US Attorney General, Herbert Brownell, moved forward with plans to deport undocumented workers to Mexico – 'Operation Wetback'. In a highly publicized effort, Brownell worked with the US Border Patrol to deport over 1 million individuals. Thus, the access granted to Mexicans through explicit and implicit policies was revoked with Operation Wetback (Hernández, 2006).

Civil Rights Discussions

Policies on immigration had a legacy of being restrictive and overtly racist into the 1940s. Although legislation continued to discriminate, the use of explicit racial categories to bar access or to segregate or marginalize populations was slowly being removed. Desegregation was ended in the US military in 1948; racial categories were removed from citizenship or naturalization eligibility in 1952; and the Jim Crow Laws of segregation were repealed in 1964 (Hing, 2004). Racialized legislation and the repealing of these policies had implications for immigration policies. The McCarran–Walter Act stands out as a pivotal moment of discourse around racial discrimination in immigration policy. On 25 June 1952, President Harry S. Truman vetoed the Act because it maintained the quota system introduced with the Immigration and Naturalization Act of 1924 and perpetuated divisions among individuals and communities. In his veto statement, Truman detailed the implications of the explicit racial quotas in the 1924 Act, which limited immigration from non-Western European countries. He wrote:

> In one respect, this bill recognizes the great international significance of our immigration and naturalization policy, and takes a step to improve existing laws. All racial bars to naturalization would be removed, and at least some minimum immigration quota would be afforded to each of the free nations of Asia [...].
>
> But now this most desirable provision comes before me embedded in a mass of legislation which would perpetuate injustices of long standing against many other nations of the world, hamper the efforts we are

making to rally the men of East and West alike to the cause of freedom, and intensify the repressive and inhumane aspects of our immigration procedures [...].

The basis of this quota system was false and unworthy in 1924. It is even worse now. At the present time, this quota system keeps out the very people we want to bring in. It is incredible to me that, in this year of 1952, we should again be enacting into law such a slur on the patriotism, the capacity, and the decency of a large part of our citizenry. (Truman, 1952)

Truman's statement called for more policy changes. He acknowledged that the Act removed the 1790 designation that to become a naturalized citizen a person needed to be a 'free white person', which had been used to deny citizenship to many groups of immigrants. And although the Act included Asian countries in the system, the allotted quota number was extremely small and further complicated by how Asian immigrants would be defined, based on ethnicity and country of origin (Hing, 2004). Despite the call by Truman for revisions that would move the Act forward by removing some barriers to immigration, the Congress was able to override his veto and passed the McCarran–Walter Act without changes. It remained in place until 1965.

During the 1950s and 1960s, Presidents Eisenhower and Kennedy continued to press for changes in the discriminatory immigration policies. President Lyndon B. Johnson also pushed for the revision of immigration policy, despite opposition from southern senators Sam Ervin, Strom Thurmond and James Eastland, who claimed that the proposed reforms to the quota system would discriminate against English-speaking immigrants (Hing, 2004). During Johnson's presidency, the political climate shifted, however, and his administration moved forward with reforms. Johnson named 1965 as International Cooperation Year and called for people to come together to confront 'ignorance, poverty, and disease'. Leonard W. Gilman, Associate Deputy Regional Commissioner, Operations Regional Office Southwest, wrote a piece titled 'Bienvenidos Amigos' for the Department of Justice and Immigration and Naturalization Service's periodical *I&N Reporter* that characterized the relationship between individuals on the US–Mexican border as that of a 'Buena Vecindad' (good neighbor) – sharing holiday celebrations, and collaborative on medical care and city beatification projects (Gilman, 1965). In contrast to the tone of the contribution by Kelly to the same publication some 10 years earlier (Kelly, 1954), this article illustrated a growing positive portrayal of language-minoritized bilinguals in official discourses.

Immigration During the Civil Rights Movement and Vietnam War

It was on the heels of these shifts that the Immigration and Naturalization Act of 1965 (also called the Hart–Celler Act) was passed and signed into law. This legislation ended the quota system based on national origins. Yet there remained country-specific stipulations for immigration: 20,000 visas were granted to all countries outside of the Western hemisphere, regardless of the population of the country. Of the total of 170,000 visas, 75% were given to family members of people who were in the United States. The Western hemisphere was allotted 120,000 visas on a first-come, first-serve basis, if the applicant did not represent competition for US workers (Hing, 2004). The methods used to issue visas in the Western hemisphere following these changes in policy reflected the long-standing discrimination against individuals from Mexico. In the mid-1970s, immigration policies steadily disfavored Mexican immigrants and prioritized refugee populations from South East Asia following the US involvement in the Vietnam War. In 1976, Congress created a visa limit for Mexico of 20,000, which was half the previous average of 40,000. This change exacerbated the waiting list, which reached about 300,000 names in 1976 (Hing, 2004).

During this period, the United States gave increased access to migrants and refugees from communist countries. The Indochina Migration and Refugee Assistance Act passed in 1975 granted access to approximately 130,000 refugees from Vietnam, Laos and Cambodia. In the initial hearings to move the Act forward, Ambassador L. Dean Brown, the Director of the Interagency Task Force for the Department of State, presented information about current efforts to care for approximately 44,000 refugees in the US territory of Guam and urged for support of the individuals displaced on ships that other countries might turn away (Hing, 2004). The 1982 Amerasian Act and the Amerasian Homecoming Act of 1987 allowed individuals from Vietnam to seek refugee status if they had American fathers. Preference was also given to refugees from Cuba. From 1962 to 1979, several hundred thousand Cubans were granted entry under the Migration and Refugee Assistant Act of 1962, the Attorney General's parole authority and the Cuban Adjustment Act of 1966 (Wasem, 2016). The visas granted to Cubans during this time were miscounted as part of the total number of Western hemisphere visas – they were meant to be exempt from the total – further limiting access to visas by immigrants from Mexico (Hing, 2004).

With these additional admissions of refugees in the 1970s, Congress made revisions to policies to clarify and update the government's treatment of refugees. The Refugee Act of 1980 created an approach for addressing the immigration of refugees that was not present in previous immigration policies. The Act attempted to clarify, as far as possible, definitions of equitable treatment of refugees following six objectives: (1) redefine refugee designation in alignment with the United Nations Convention and Protocol on the Status of Refugees; (2) raise annual admissions from 17,400 to 50,000 individuals; (3) create flexibility in procedures in dealing with 'special humanitarian concerns'; (4) replace parole authority with Congressional control; (5) creation of an explicit asylum system; and (6) formalize provisions of federal programs to aid in resettlement (Kennedy, 1981).

Amnesty

In the 1980s, changes were made to immigration policies that again were targeted specifically at Mexican and other Latino immigrants. In 1986, the Immigration Reform and Control Act presented an amnesty provision to legalize approximately 3 million undocumented immigrants living in the United States, the majority of whom were from Mexico. But the Act also put in place new restrictions, including: (1) penalties for employers who hire undocumented workers; (2) a diversification visa program to limit the number of Latino immigrants; and (3) increased enforcement at the US–Mexico border.

Two groups of individuals were eligible to apply for residency: those who had lived in the United States before 1 January 1982 and those designated as 'specialized agriculture workers' (SAW), who had worked for a minimum of 90 days between 1 May 1985 and 1 May 1986. The application forms ran to three or four pages and required documentation of paying taxes, not being convicted of a crime, a list of all residences, dates and places of employment, fingerprints, and two color photographs, among other information. The fee for the application depended on how many people were in the family and ranged from $185 to $420 (the equivalent in 2018 would be $425 to $965, based on the Consumer Price Index inflation calculator from the US Department of Labor Bureau of Labor Statistics, at https://www.bls.gov/data/inflation_calculator.htm). In the end, approximately 1.75 million people who had arrived before 1982 applied, and 94% were approved for temporary residency; approximately 1.3 million individuals designated as SAW applied (Cooper & O'Neill, 2005; Hing, 2004).

An additional visa system was introduced under the 1986 Act that set to diversify the immigrant pool. The visa diversification program (NP-5 visa lottery) made 50,000 visas available via a lottery and defined diversity as individuals from countries that had had fewer than 50,000 visas in total awarded in the preceding five years. In the first year these visas were available, that is, 1987, immigrants from Ireland disproportionately were awarded visas via this lottery. The program was extended in 1988 and 1989, and then formally added to the Immigration and Naturalization Act of 1990 (see Wasem, 2011). Refugee Acts supporting immigrants from Nicaragua and Haiti in 1997 and 1998 respectively were two of the final immigration laws put in place before the shift in immigration policy after 11 September 2001 (Migration Policy Institute, 2013).

The 'War on Terror'

In response to the attacks on the United States on 11 September 2001, two key pieces of immigration legislation were passed in 2002: the Enhanced Border Security and Visa Entry Reform Act and the Homeland Security Act. The former implemented more regulated screening and security, and the development of a data system to share information about travelers, including the 'do not fly' list. The latter created a new federal department: the Department of Homeland Security. It then led all functions for immigration, including border protection and control, immigration enforcement and deportation. In 2001 the Real ID Act expanded grounds for exclusion or removal of immigrants on terrorism-related grounds (Migration Policy Institute, 2013).

Since Donald Trump became President in 2016, ongoing changes to restrict all forms of immigration have been commonplace. It is difficult to capture the specifics, as new policies are rescinded or enacted to limit immigration often, and many are also being debated in various court systems. For example, his executive order to ban immigrants from mostly Muslim-majority countries was upheld by the Supreme Court in June 2018 and the status of the Deferred Action for Childhood Arrivals (DACA) program remains in limbo at the time of writing. His reduction of the number of refugees allowed in the United States and the removal of temporary protected immigration status from individuals from El Salvador, Haiti and other countries illustrate additional policy shifts. Further, there are reports of increased numbers of raids by Immigration and Customs Enforcement (ICE) (Kulish *et al.*, 2017) and violence against perceived immigrants are on the rise (Okeowo, 2016). At the time of writing, it is clear that the administration is keen on limiting immigration using multiple approaches.

Summary

The wide range of policies and events impacting language-minoritized bilinguals are relevant to understanding the historical narrative of the consequences of testing. The direct and indirect impacts of these events gain importance when looking at the specific purposes behind and results of testing language-minoritized bilinguals.

2 Seeking Access to Civic Participation

Language-minoritized bilinguals have faced numerous forms of examination to gain US citizenship and the rights of citizens. The literacy test from the Immigration Act of 1917 served at first to deny initial entry and then transitioned into a tool to deport those already in the country. Additionally, literacy tests were also used with language-minoritized bilinguals, much like they had been with African Americans, to restrict access to voting. The naturalization exam asked language-minoritized bilinguals to answer questions on civics and to demonstrate English proficiency. Tests conducted by the military have had consequences for serving in the military, and therefore also on the pathways to US citizenship available – though not uniformly – to language-minoritized bilinguals. Across all of these uses of tests, the raw numbers of individuals impacted is often small, and thus these tests may be seen has having limited immediate impact. More often, they are a reflection of the white supremacist sentiments of the time during which they were created and implemented. This historical analysis, therefore, focuses on what it means for tests to exist in relation to societal perspectives, and how tests have been used to placate discourses. The importance of using tests in this way is not to be minimized, however, as these tests were put in place often with the intention of harming the lives of language-minoritized bilinguals.

Literacy Testing

Literacy tests and test policies became common around the same time that intelligence tests were being developed – in the late 1910s. Literacy testing presents different controversies in how it was enacted to restrict immigration and voting rights for language-minoritized bilinguals. Literacy tests for immigration were far less controversial and much more detached from the racist, xenophobic rhetoric associated with intelligence testing. Literacy testing for voting, in contrast, was emblematic of anti-immigrant, anti-Puerto Rican, xenophobic and racist discourses, mirroring the racist motivations underlying mandates for literacy testing that restricted voting rights of African Americans in the South (Kates, 2006).

For immigration

In 1917 Congress passed, and bypassed a presidential veto, a law requiring the use of an unnamed literacy test for newly arrived immigrants. There had in fact been four such vetoes – by President Cleveland (1896), President Taft (1913) and President Wilson (1914 and 1917). The law was part of the Immigration Act of 1917, which expanded restrictions on immigrants, with this part of the law being the first that could affect individuals from Western Europe. For the test, immigrants needed to read a 40-word passage in their home language (see Figure 2.1 for a sample test in Italian). Although it has often been argued that this law did little to deter immigration, as most immigrants gained the requisite literacy level to pass the test (Smith, 1995), the data presented in this chapter describe the impacts of failing the test both for those who were denied entry and for those who failed the test but were nevertheless granted admission (for instance for family reasons – see below). The policy for testing home language literacy remained in place for over 40 years, and was one of the last forms of testing used to screen immigrants before they were admitted to the United States.

The estimations of the impact of the test by the government officials who pushed for its use far exceeded the actual reach. Kohler (1912) critiqued the restrictive nature of the test, and to project the potential impact drew data on self-reported illiteracy from immigration reports from 1899 to 1910. Over that period, 2,238,801 or 26.7% of individuals 14 years of age or older reported that they were not able to read or write. Yet once enacted, the policy impacted less than 5% of those arriving who were 16 years of age or older (the age stipulated in the legislation).

In describing how this policy impacted language-memorized bilinguals, this chapter presents data from the annual reports of the Immigration and

---

Io dico: Che cosa è l'uomo, che tu ne abbi memoria? e che cosa è il figuolo dell'uomo, che tu ne prenda cura?
E che tu l'abbi fatto poco minor degli Angeli, e l'abbi coronato di Gloria e d'onore?

—

What is man, that though are mindful of him? and the son of man, that thou visitest him?
For thou hast made him a little lower than angels, and hast crowned him with glory and honor.

(Ps. 8:4,5)

Figure 2.1 Text of an Italian literacy test administered to immigrants arriving in the United States. From the United States Government Printing Office, c. 1920, National Park Service, Statue of Liberty National Monument. Reproduced from https://www.nps.gov/elis/learn/historyculture/history-of-ellis-island-from-1892-to-1954.htm

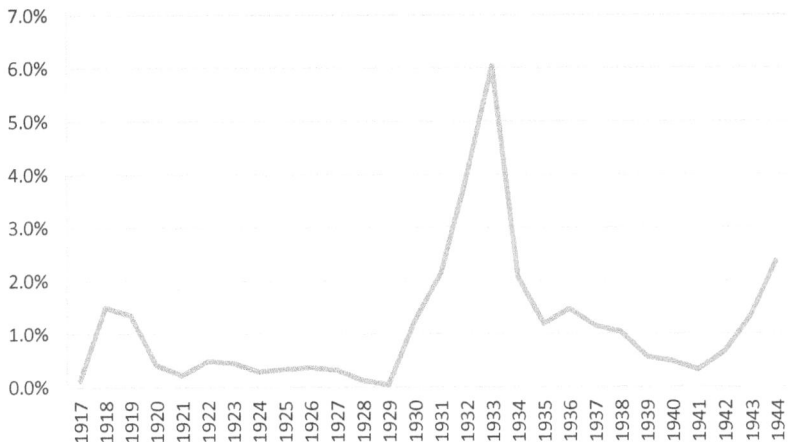

Figure 2.2 Immigrants debarred and deported (combined) on the basis for their performance on the literacy test as a percentage of the total number of immigrants admitted, by fiscal year

Naturalization Service from 1915 to 1944 (published by the US Department of Justice). Figure 2.2 shows the overall percentage of immigrants per year who were either debarred (i.e. not allow entry) or deported as a consequence of literacy testing, as a percentage of all immigrants admitted (rather than as a percentage of the total seeking admission, due to insufficient data) to the United States from 1917 to 1944. Note that the figure for 1917 is low because the admissions relate only to the two months during which the test was used, but this is reported as a percentage of the full year's total of those debarred or deported.

More people who failed the literacy test were debarred than deported from 1917 to 1926, whereas more were deported than debarred from 1927 to 1944. A similar trend is seen for the total group of immigrants debarred and deported (for whatever reason, and not solely on the basis of the literacy test): more individuals were debarred from 1917 to 1929 and more were deported from 1930 to 1944 (Figure 2.3).

In looking at the totals of those debarred and deported (Figure 2.4), the data seem to indicate small proportions of individuals being asked to leave the United States based on their performance on the literacy test.

Figure 2.5 plots the actual percentage of those who were denied entry or removed from the country based on their literacy test performance in relation to the total of individuals debarred and deported, to better illustrate the impact of the literacy test (as opposed to other methods to reject language-minoritized bilingual immigrants). In Figure 2.5, four peaks of impact have been labeled.

48 Part 1: Immigration Policy in the United States

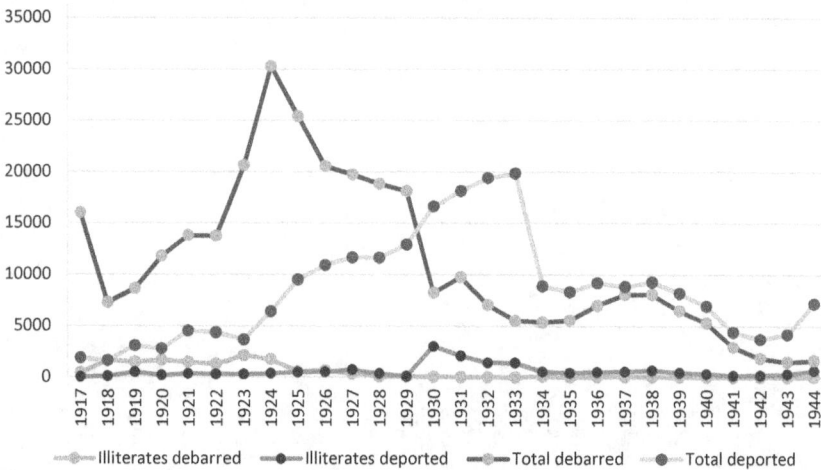

Figure 2.3 Numbers of language-minoritized bilinguals debarred and deported because of the literacy test and in total, by fiscal year

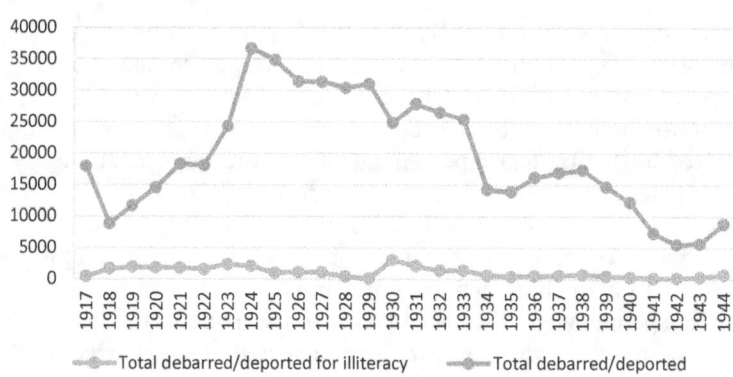

Figure 2.4 Total numbers of language-minoritized bilinguals debarred and deported because of the literacy test and overall, by fiscal year

Compared with the intelligence tests used to screen immigrants (see Chapter 3), the literacy test was much more impactful. Though the raw numbers are far from what those who supported or opposed the policies believed it to be, over the course of 1917–1944 the literacy test remained a relevant means of excluding language-minoritized bilinguals. Yet it should be noted that many individuals were allowed to enter the United States after being classified as illiterate based on this test. The majority were

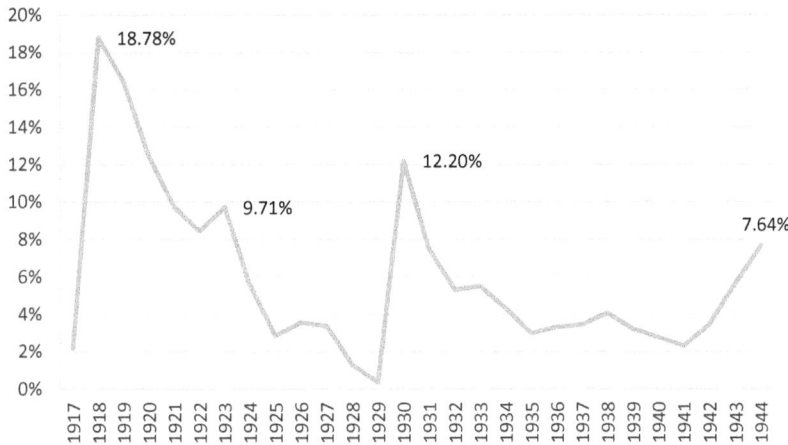

Figure 2.5 Language-minoritized bilinguals debarred and deported because of the literacy test as a percentage of all those debarred/deported, by fiscal year

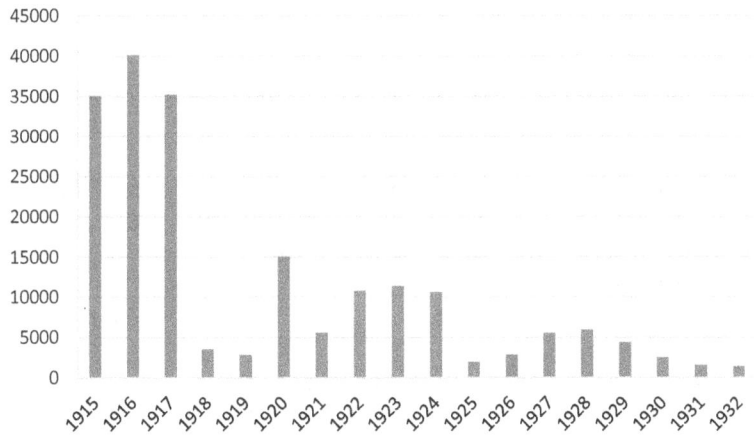

Figure 2.6 Number of language-minoritized bilinguals admitted to the United States who did not pass the literacy test, by fiscal year

granted entrance and permission to stay in order to join a relative. These data are available from 1917 to 1932. In order to see how many individuals were unable to pass the literacy test (were unable to read or write) before the policy went into effect in 1917, Figure 2.6 additionally presents data for 1915 and 1916.

After the literacy test was introduced in 1917, some language-minoritized bilinguals who did not pass the test were nevertheless allowed

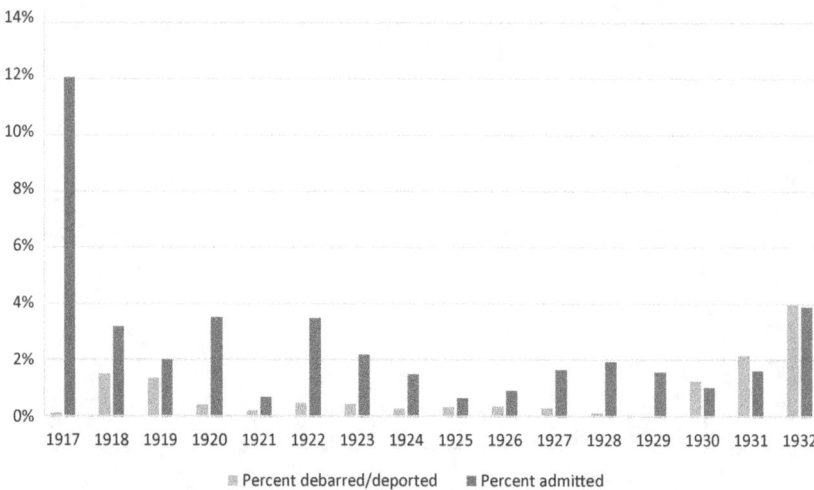

Figure 2.7 Language-minoritized bilinguals who did not pass the literacy test and who were debarred/deported and who were admitted to the United States, as a percentage of the total number of immigrants admitted, by fiscal year

to enter and stay in the United States. The numbers are better understood in relation to overall admission of immigrants to the United States, as presented in Figure 2.7.

These data illustrate how from 1917 to 1929 it was more common for language-minoritized bilinguals to be able to stay in the United States when they did not pass the literacy test than to be sent back to their country of origin. Yet the data from 1930 to 1932 show a dramatic change: in that period, not passing the test more frequently meant that language-minoritized bilinguals would be debarred or deported.

These combined analyses illustrate some of the impact of this test on language-minoritized bilinguals. The data indicate this literacy test was used in 6.01% of debarments or deportations from 1917 to 1944, with a peak of 18.78% in 1918 and a low of 0.35% in 1929 (at the start of the Great Depression). In 1945, the annual reports used in this chapter no longer record the ability to read and write, but instead record the ability to speak English, and it is unclear what role (if any) the literacy test had from 1945 until the repeal of its use in 1952. The annual report for 1947 states that proposals in the Congress would require the ability to read and speak English for naturalization, rather than focusing literacy as a prerequisite for admission. The literacy test used for entrance was replaced formally with naturalization testing requirements in 1952, with the Immigration and Naturalization Act. Literacy tests were used subsequently, however, to restrict access to voting for language-minoritized bilinguals.

For voting

Eligibility for voting presents a very clear case of the use of literacy tests to exclude and deny access (see Shohamy, 2001). Literacy tests for voting were implemented not long after the end of the Civil War and the ratification of the 15th Amendment to the Constitution in 1870, which granted the right to vote to African American men. In 1882, South Carolina introduced an 'eight-box' ballot that required voters to place separate ballot papers in each appropriate box (e.g. the ballot paper for the governor vote in a separate box from the ballot paper for the senator vote) but literate people were not allowed to help illiterate voters to select the right boxes. In 1890, some states began using more formal literacy tests to determine the right vote, but relaxed the requirement with the creation of a 'grandfather' clause that allowed illiterate people to vote if they were descended from someone who had the right to vote in 1867 – who were primarily white illiterate voters. Use of literacy tests – in addition to other deterrents to voting, such as poll taxes – increased at the turn of the century and into the 1900s. In 1959, the Supreme Court ruled that literacy tests were constitutional in *Lassiter v. Northampton City Board of Electors*.

But literacy tests were not purely a Southern practice for discriminating against African Americans. Connecticut used literacy tests from 1865 to restrict the number of eligible Irish voters. New York State created a literacy test in 1921 to discriminate against the large Spanish-speaking Puerto Rican population. Originally, the test consisted of having a voter read aloud from slips of paper that contained extracts of the state Constitution and of writing 10 words from the slips selected by the examiner (Crawford, 1925). The test continued to be developed and remained in place until the passage of the Voting Rights Act of 1965, which Senator Robert Kennedy of New York introduced seeking to put an end to New York State's use of an English literacy test to restrict the right to vote. Section 4(e) of the Act reads:

> No person who demonstrates that he has successfully completed the sixth primary grade in a public school in, or a private school accredited by, any State or territory, the District of Columbia, or the Commonwealth of Puerto Rico in which the predominant classroom language was other than English, shall be denied the right to vote in any Federal, State, or local election because of his inability to read, write, understand, or interpret any matter in the English language.

Backlash against and support for this policy were almost immediate. Court cases were filed both to enforce and to challenge section 4(e). In *United States v. County Board of Elections*, the federal government demanded that use of the literacy test be suspended in New York State and for the Board of Elections to register the previously disenfranchised voters. In the ruling, the court specifically noted that section 4(e) specifically applied to the voting rights of Puerto Ricans (Leibowitz, 1969).

In *Katzenbach* v. *Morgan* (384 U.S. 641, 1966), the plaintiff's complaint stated that the removal of the test would allow more Puerto Ricans who could not read in English the right to vote, and claimed that issues such as voter screening with the literacy test were beyond to scope of the Congress. Two of the three judges on the United States District Court for the District of Columbia who heard the case agreed with the defendant. The case moved to the Supreme Court, where the judges found section 4(e) to be in agreement with the 14th Amendment to the Constitution. They further ruled that Congress had taken appropriate action in adding this provision to the Voting Rights Act:

> 4(e) may be viewed as a measure to secure for the Puerto Rican community residing in New York nondiscriminatory treatment by government both in the imposition of voting qualifications and the provision or administration of governmental services, such as public schools, public housing and law enforcement [...]. This enhanced political power will be helpful in gaining nondiscriminatory treatment in public services for the entire Puerto Rican community. (384 U.S. 641, 1966, at p. 652)

Decided the same day as *Katzenbach* v. *Morgan*, the case of *Cardona* v. *Power* (384 U.S. 672, 1966) ruled against the use of the literacy test. The plaintiff was a woman who had lived in New York since 1946 but who had been born and educated in Puerto Rico. She was literate in Spanish, but could not pass the New York State literacy test for voting. The Supreme Court ruled that the 'New York courts should determine whether the New York English literacy requirement remains valid in light of § 4(e)'. New York State ultimately ended the use of the English literacy test for voting in 1970, when Voting Rights Act of that year put in place a ban on all literacy tests in the country. And the Supreme Court upheld the ban with *Oregon* v. *Mitchell* (400 U.S. 112, 1970).

The end of literacy tests for voting marks a time when government and judicial institutions supported the end of discriminatory practices of testing. The ways in which these tests served as gatekeeping devices – explicitly so in New York State with language-minoritized bilinguals from Puerto Rico – demonstrate the real and intentional misuse of tests to deny language-minoritized bilinguals their voting rights.

Naturalization and Citizenship

Following the Alien Naturalization Act of 9 May 1918, Congress expedited petitions for naturalization for any foreign-born individual who served during World War I. Of the 546,490 individuals who were naturalized from 1918 to 1920, 244,300 or 44.7% had served in the military (Sohoni & Vafa, 2010). Many of these naturalization rulings, however, were publicly contested for non-white foreign-born soldiers. Judge Horace Vaugh, for example, had granted citizenship to approximately 500 Asians in Hawaii by 1921, despite vocal complaints that the 1918 Act did not apply to Asians (Tamura, 1994). Yet these naturalizations were extended to non-white immigrant groups only for a short period of time. The Supreme Court 'racial prerequisite' cases (discussed below) involving Owaza and Thind, both of whom served in the US military during World War I, demonstrated continued exclusion and the role of white supremacy in the treatment of language-minoritized bilinguals.

The racial prerequisite cases

Following the Civil War, national citizenship (in contrast to state citizenship) took on new importance as more rights and decisions were drawn under the purview of the federal government. The abolishment of slavery after the Civil War also meant that the US government revised the racial categories of naturalization; the 14th Amendment to the US Constitution in addition to the Naturalization Act of 1870 stated that both white persons and those of African descent were eligible for naturalization. This change in the eligibility criteria for naturalization coincided with changes in immigration: more immigrants were coming from regions other than Europe (Hing, 2004).[1] The addition of a new racial category for naturalization of African Americans also led to ambiguity about how policies applied to immigrants who were not readily defined as white or of African descent. The 'racial prerequisite' cases from 1879 until 1952 demonstrate a formalized evaluation process where 51 language-minoritized individuals tried to prove that they were white and therefore could be granted citizenship (Haney López, 2006).[2] In explaining how the testing or evaluation of language-minoritized bilinguals moved from *de jure* to *de facto* forms of white supremacy, I discuss one of the most explicit forms of white supremacy in evaluation: the racial prerequisite cases. Although not a traditional form of testing, the evaluations served the same purpose that naturalization tests served, to grant US citizenship. These evaluations centered on definitions of race across the various levels of the judicial system, from state to federal to the Supreme Court. The time period of the racial prerequisite cases coincided with the development of other forms of testing internationally. In this presentation of the racial prerequisite cases, emphasis is given to the ways in which language, specifically English proficiency, was discussed.

In his book *White by Law*, Ian Haney López (2006) detailed the role of the judicial system in constructing race in these racial prerequisite cases. These court cases were heard across the United States, and were brought by people with Afghan, Arab, Armenian, Asian-Indian, Burmese, Chinese, Filipino, Hawaiian, Japanese, Korean, Mexican, Native American, Punjabi and Syrian backgrounds. There were four rationales given to explain whether or not a person would be considered white: scientific evidence, common knowledge, Congressional intent and legal precedence. Of these four, scientific evidence and common knowledge were the dominant reasons given to support rulings. Scientific evidence related to definitions of race from different academic disciplines which defined being white in terms of visible skin color or Caucasian ancestry. Common knowledge, as it implies, meant popular, publicly accepted opinions or beliefs about race.

Haney López (2006) argued that the use of scientific evidence and common knowledge justifications ultimately served to substantiate public beliefs about race. Following a series of inconsistent court rulings over the period 1909–1920 about a petitioner's whiteness, the Supreme Court concluded that common knowledge definitions of race were sufficient to deny naturalization. In 1922 and 1923, unanimous rulings in the Supreme Court rejected, on the basis of their race, the cases of Takao Ozawa from Japan and of Bhagat Singh Thind from India, who both wanted to become US citizens. Not only did these cases make it virtually impossible for any further cases to grant naturalization petitions on the basis of race,[3] but also in the case of Thind, the Court further acted to revoke citizenship for at least 65 individuals. One of those individuals committed suicide after having his citizenship revoked. Indeed, in summarizing the rulings of the racial prerequisite cases of the Supreme Court, Haney López concluded that in trying to explain who was considered to be white or of Caucasian heritage, the Court served 'not to challenge the construction of racial beliefs, but to entrench them even further' (Haney López, 2006: 60).

English proficiency in the racial prerequisite cases

In statements about the role of English in relation to naturalization, courts generally agreed that to have knowledge of English – a requirement of the Naturalization Act of 1906 – was not sufficient for a person to be considered white or eligible for citizenship. In the ruling on *Thind* v. *US*, the Supreme Court ruled quite specifically that a language within the same language family as English, and even English itself, was not equated to the category of whiteness:

> The term 'Aryan' has to do with linguistic, and not at all with physical, characteristics, and it would seem reasonably clear that mere resemblance in language, indicating a common linguistic root buried in remotely ancient soil, is altogether inadequate to prove common racial origin. There is, and can be, no assurance that the so-called Aryan language was not spoken by a variety of races living in proximity to one another. Our own history has witnessed the adoption of the English tongue by millions of negroes, whose descendants can never be classified racially with the descendants of white persons, notwithstanding both may speak a common root language. (US 213–214, p. 214)

Ozawa v. *US* presented evidence not only of Ozawa's knowledge of English but also of his family's. To support his case for citizenship, he wrote that

'Most of the time I use the American (English) language at home, so that my children cannot speak the Japanese language' (Haney López, 2006: 57). The Court offered a positive evaluation of Ozawa's literacy skills and English proficiency: 'the requirement that before an alien can be naturalized he must be able to read, either in his own language or in the English language and to speak or understand the English language' (260 U.S. 178, p. 191), but this did not have any bearing (or further mention) in its decision about his naturalization, which was denied.

Knowledge of English played an important role and was as more definitive than race as evidence that could be used to deny naturalization. A further example is the case of *Ex parte Shahid* (1915):

> According to his statement he is now 59 years of age, and was born at Zahle, in Asia Minor, in Syria, and came to this country about 11 years ago, and is a Christian. He writes his name in Arabic, cannot read or write English, and speaks and understands English very imperfectly, and does not understand any questions relating to the manner and method of government in America, or of the responsibilities of a citizen. His answers to the questions whether he is a polygamist or a disbeliever in organized government were in the affirmative, and he could not be made to understand in English the purport of the questions asked. (Haney López, 2006: 172)

The judge ruled that the personal disqualifications of lack of English proficiency and literacy – rather than race – were the reasons for denying naturalization to Shahid, adding that 'the applicant is not one the admission of whom to citizenship is likely to be for the benefit of the country' (cited in Haney López, 2006: 52).

Naturalization, race and language

The role of English language proficiency gained prominence in naturalization decisions following the racial prerequisite trials. After 162 years, explicit racial exclusions for citizenship were removed in 1952. Language, specifically English language proficiency in reading, writing and speaking, became formalized as a new requirement for naturalization, in addition to tests of civics knowledge. The testing of reading, writing and speaking English was introduced immediately before the removal of race-based restrictions on naturalization. One motivation for the use of an English literacy test within the naturalization process was a fear of communism that equated lack of understanding English with political suspicion (Del Valle, 2003). In 1950, the Internal Security Act amended previous English language requirements for citizenship to include testing literacy, which was later included in the Immigration and Naturalization Act of 1952. Lowenstein (1958) explains how English proficiency became a new prerequisite for citizenship:

> Before its amendment, the 1940 [Immigration and Naturalization] Act required only that a petitioner know how to speak the English language, if physically able to do so. What precipitated these amendments was testimony before a Senate Investigating Committee on the relationship between subversion, non-English speaking aliens, good citizenship and the ability to read, write and speak English. (Lowenstein, 1958: 302)

The development of the naturalization tests is discussed in more detail later in this chapter, but it is worth noting the ways in which English language proficiency was treated before and after the racial prerequisite trials. Pointedly, in the racial prerequisite trials English proficiency was not linked with positive consequences or naturalization, and a perceived lack of English proficiency was linked with negative consequences or the denial of naturalization.

The idea of a perceived lack of English proficiency is not to be overlooked. Ideas about how race or indicators of race such as a Spanish-origin last name, for example, show that it remains commonplace for people to evaluate or to perceive a person to be a language-minoritized bilingual who is lacking English proficiency. Haney López (2006) writes about how questioning of English language proficiency serves as code for race, based on his own experiences:

> To make my Latino identity less easy to disregard, I changed my name by following Hispanic custom and adding my mother's family name to my own. Though I had grown up as Ian Haney, in graduate school I started to go by Ian Haney López. The first paper I turned in under that new name came back ungraded, with the question: 'Is English your first language?' On the cusp between White and non-White, it turned out that achieving a marginalized, suspect identity was surprisingly easy. (Haney López, 2006: Kindle edition location 119)

Haney López's statement about assumptions regarding his English proficiency, though anecdotal, is supported by decades of research on linguistic profiling (Baugh, 2003), match-guise sociolinguistic experiments (Lambert *et al.*, 1960) and directions in research on raciolinguistic ideologies (Alim *et al.*, 2016; Flores & Rosa, 2015; Rosa, 2016).

The racial prerequisite trials stand out as obvious forms of racial discrimination that reflect white supremacy. This history of the racial prerequisite trials has traced entanglements of race and language in forms of evaluating language-minoritized bilinguals. These trials were then followed by the addition of English language testing. In presenting these trials as key historical events, I conclude this section with the two points central to the argument of the book. First, I want to discuss the role of social construction of race and language. Returning to the detail that the racial prerequisite rulings functioned to entrench views about race, note how the racial prerequisite trials presented whiteness as an objective category to support common knowledge or public opinion definitions of race:

> [The] allusion to natural meaning [of race] illustrates the manner in which common knowledge is widely seen as entailing an unmediated (and therefore true) understanding of the world. Locating race in common knowledge suggests that race is part of the external world, and that our perception of race is a matter of its objective existence rather than of its subjective creation. Consequently, races as well as the belief in races are seen as 'natural.' In the face of this type of naturalization, any effort to interrogate Whiteness becomes a doomed battle against received knowledge. The common-knowledge naturalization of Whites deflects and defeats any inquisition of Whiteness by positing that this grouping is an easily identified, commonly recognized truth. Transparency is established and maintained first in the assertion that Whites are a physical grouping and second in the assertion that everyone knows what White is. (Haney López, 2006: 19)

The trials and rulings by judges functioned as authoritative mechanisms to define race. The courts accepted arguments, often contradictory, in order to support their opinions about what it meant to be white. Being white was portrayed as a binary category: a person either was or was not white. The prerequisite trials illustrate the actions taken to try to prove an opinion as a truth, and the repercussions of these choices.

Moving from definitions of race to language, the idea that race is a fixed, nameable, restricted category holds many parallels with well accepted definitions of language. Yet it is important to question the assumptions about language which, just as with race, frame language as a social construct. Makoni and Pennycook have claimed that 'languages do not exist as real entities in the world and neither do they emerge from or represent real environments; they are, by contrast, the inventions of social, cultural and political movements' (Makoni & Pennycook, 2007: 2). Jørgensen elaborated on the social construction of language and the implications for speakers:

> The view of human language which distinguishes between 'different languages' considers language as sets of features which can be separated and counted. This is reflected in the terminology used to describe individual language users. (Jørgensen, 2012: 59)

These social constructions of race and language have ramifications for people, and in particular language-minoritized bilinguals, who are also perceived as non-white at the intersection of two socially constructed identities.

The second point of examining the racial prerequisite trials was to understand the implications for individuals who are said to inhabit (or not) these social constructions. For the prerequisite trials, individuals were given the options of claiming to be white or from African descent, both of which are categories that were often designed to exclude them. The prerequisite trials ultimately defined individuals by what they were not: white. The definition of 'English language learner' also defines individuals by what they are not: English proficient. For the racial prerequisite trials, scientific evidence and common knowledge dominated the rulings by judges to define who these individuals were. To determine which individuals are viewed as lacking English proficiency, scientific evidence and common knowledge remain at the forefront. Scientific evidence from tests and common knowledge in the form of public opinion and beliefs work in tandem, and in conflict, to support the construction of the concept of an 'English language learner'. As Haney López's experiences once he foregrounded his Latino identity illustrated, English proficiency, too, is a social construct or a matter of perception that is closely tied to race and ethnicity, which in turn has been used to (de)legitimize civic participation.

The naturalization test

A civics test for naturalization had been in place in the form of an oral exam since 1802, with practices varying greatly across the United States. Speaking English was established as a prerequisite for naturalization in 1906, and English literacy was mandated in 1950. Yet it was not until the 1990s that standardized tests for English and civics were introduced. Until that time, ambiguities in policies and test practices allowed for highly subjective and idiosyncratic methods for making decisions about naturalization. Even today, recent research points to striking limitations in the current standardized testing methods used for testing English and civics knowledge for language-minoritized bilinguals seeking US citizenship.

The history of testing English and civics knowledge can be traced back to the same period as the creation of literacy tests described earlier in this chapter. Founded in 1894, the Immigration Restriction League lobbied for the use of a literacy test for immigrants (Holt, 1915) in relation to both immigration and eligibility to vote. English literacy testing also informed decisions on citizenship and naturalization (Liebowitz, 1984). Federal policy called for literacy in English as a criterion for becoming a citizen, by demonstrating 'an understanding of the English language, including an ability to read, write, and speak words in ordinary usage in the English language'.[4] Although, as described above, the use of literacy tests was banned in deciding eligibility to vote with the Voting Rights Act of 1965, English literacy testing for citizenship remains.

English literacy and proficiency testing coexists with civic test requirements. English literacy and civics requirements for naturalization were explicitly articulated in 1952 in the McCarran–Walter Act. In addition to other requirements to become a naturalized citizen, language-minoritized bilinguals had to demonstrate 'an ability to read, write and speak words in ordinary usage in the English language, and have a knowledge and understanding of U.S. history and government'.[5] The Bureau of Naturalization and the Immigration and Naturalization Service made efforts to oversee the use of the civics test from 1906 to 1952 and removed questions that were targeted for failure, such as the specific height of landmarks. During the 1950s and through the 1980s, more standardized practices of testing were introduced with the English literacy test, but the civics test had a great degree of variability, with the examiner determining what to ask and how to ask it based on their interactions with the applicant. It was not until 1986 that a standardized set of questions was developed for the civics examination. There is little information on the previous administrations of the civics test (Schneider, 2010; US Citizenship and Immigration Services, 2016).

The secrecy and ambiguity about how language-minoritized bilinguals were assessed in terms of civics knowledge make understanding the history of this use of testing and its consequences challenging. Following a sharp increase in naturalization during World War II, when many immigrants became citizens by joining the military, fewer than 120,000 people became naturalized citizens annually in the 1950s through to the 1970s. The 1980s saw an increase to an average of 210,000 naturalized citizens annually, and 500,000 annually in the 1990s. The increase in naturalized citizens over this period is attributed largely to the amnesty granted with the Immigration Reform and Control Act of 1986, efforts to restrict services to non-citizens and programs requiring replacement of 'permanent resident' cards in 1977. From the 1970s onwards, the majority of naturalized citizens were from Asian countries (Lee, 2012), a reflection of the changes in immigration policies towards this region of the world that were previously restrictive and discriminatory.

Since the standardization of the civics test, problems with the test have persisted. Perhaps most troubling is Winke's (2011) reliability research on the present-day civics exam. In her study, she asked 187 non-citizens and 255 citizens questions from the exam and found that the 100 items did not reliably measure civic knowledge. In a further analysis, she investigated whether particular items favored citizens. Because this is a naturalization exam, it would be expected that all items would favor citizens over non-citizens. However, only 10 items did so; 77 of 100 items did not favor citizens or non-citizens, while the remaining 13 items actually favored non-citizens over citizens. Applicants are asked around 10 questions randomly selected by the test administrator when taking the test for naturalization, which could introduce complications that could be used to advantage or disadvantage the test-taker, given the issues with the test items described above. Thus, this study points to large flaws in the current civics exam. This current, standardized testing form is positioned as an improvement on the civics exams used from the 1950s to the 1980s. Yet, other than the standardization process, it is unclear if this new test has addressed previous issues with the test, or if it has introduced a bevy of new complications.

To test English literacy, language-minoritized bilinguals are asked to read one of three sentences without extended pauses, the omission of small words, and intonation or punctuation errors that interfere with meaning. For the writing portion, language-minoritized bilinguals are asked to write one out of three sentences dictated by the administrator. They pass if the administrator understands the sentence. Spoken English is tested throughout the interactions with the other exams and process of naturalization, including background questions and the civics test – although the civics test can be administered in languages other than English (US Citizenship and Immigration Services, 2015).

The English literacy test, in its previous and its current form, has served as a gatekeeping device despite the biases and improprieties of the test administrator, though that has not been documented or reported to be an issue. There are, however, ways in which language-minoritized bilinguals can be naturalized without taking this test. Individuals are exempted from the tests if they (1) have a documented disability, (2) are over 50 and have lived in the United States for 20 years or are over 55 and have lived in the United States for 15 years, or (3) if the Attorney General has ruled it to be a case of special consideration (under the 1952 Immigration and Nationality Act, Sec. 312, 8, section 1423). One court case has challenged the use of the English literacy test. In 1974 in Brownville, Texas, the court ruled that Congress had the right under the Constitution to set requirements for naturalization (Del Valle, 2003). The use of the test has also been an official English language policy, though on its own the test can produce only weak evidence. Yet the fact that a test exists at all is significant, beyond the added factor of how it may be implemented.

The civics and English proficiency naturalization tests are national attempts to use tests as screening devices. Naturalization tests, in particular English proficiency tests in the United Kingdom and Australia, have been positioned as tools to promote national security as well. Khan explained how the demands of English proficiency tests in the United Kingdom 'are not static but contain within them the capacity to be adjusted and further tightened according to the sociopolitical context' (Khan, 2017: 313). Language proficiency with respect to citizenship 'featured both as the object of regulative intervention and as a prominent medium for the political articulation of security concerns' (Khan, 2017: 315). Khan and McNamara (2017) argue that national security concerns serve as a rationale for connecting immigration, law and testing, with tests being positioned as technical instruments that represent law and are used to implement policies. These policies not only reflect purported security concerns, but have had their roots in overt racist policies in Australia as well. McNamara (2005, 2009) describes how the Dictation Test was implemented to enforce the 'White Australia' policy for entry into Australia:

anyone arriving at an Australian port who was not welcome as an immigrant under this policy was subjected to a 50-word dictation test in a language that it had been ascertained in advance that the person concerned had no knowledge of, and would thus automatically fail. The test gave barely a fig leaf of respectability to the explicitly racist intention of the policy; it acted more as a ritual of exclusion. The test fell into disuse in the 1930s, although the policy was not officially abolished until 1973, when a non-discriminatory immigration policy was introduced. (McNamara, 2009: 106)

The pervasiveness of using naturalization tests as gatekeeping or exclusionary devices historically, currently and in multiple regions of the world begins to illustrate how widespread the negative consequences of these tests are for language-minoritized bilinguals.

The unreliability and potential for administrators' biases are concerns that need to be raised and addressed. At the same time, the tests as they exist now have created barriers for language-minoritized bilinguals that are surmountable. In fact, large percentages of language-minoritized bilinguals pass these tests. The US Citizenship and Immigration Services reports that, as of June 2018, the pass rate was 91%. Higher pass rates are associated with changes that were made to the civics and English tests in 2008, slightly down from the pass rate of 95.8% from the end of the first full fiscal year of administration, 2010, but higher than the pass rate of 87.1% in 2004. ICF International (2011) reported that individuals passed at higher rates in 2010 than from 2004 to 2008 on each test and overall.

Trying to learn more about those who have not passed the test is more challenging. The website of the US Citizenship and Immigration Services reports that the pass rate over the period January 2015 to September 2016 remained 91% and that 5,330,000 individuals had taken the test since it was changed.[6] Thus a rough estimate of the number who have failed the tests is 477,000 from October 2010 to September 2016. This does not factor in the initial pass rate of 95.8% for the 2010 fiscal year, but provides a guiding number to understand how many language-minoritized bilinguals are impacted by failing the test. This number, when compared with Winke's study and a national survey that found that one-third of U.S. citizens did not pass the civics test (Ford, 2012), illustrates the impact that this test may be having on language-minoritized bilinguals. And in looking to the future, the current English proficiency test may be replaced. The RAISE Ac was introduced on 13 February 2017 by Senator Tom Cotton from Arkansas and others, and introduces the use of the TOEFL or IETLS test for citizenship.

Summary

In seeking naturalization or citizenship, language-minoritized bilinguals have faced myriad obstacles. The United States and other regions of the world have readily employed tests and other forms of evaluation in order to further exclusionary agendas, historically rooted in white supremacy. The racial prerequisite trials and English and civics naturalization tests did not affect large proportions of the populations of individuals excluded from the United States, certainly in comparison with the situations in Australia and the United Kingdom, yet the existence of these tests remains significant, as their negative consequences are not to be ignored.

Testing in the Military

Military service has been a way to become a citizen. To serve in the military an individual has to pass initial screenings which generally comprise an interview and/or a pen-and-paper test. When first introduced during World War I, the tests were used to determine whether an individual should be discharged, assigned to non-combat service or development battalions, or deemed ineligible for consideration to hold higher officer ranks. These test uses were entrenched in the eugenics movement and racist, anti-immigrant analyses by leading test developers such as Yerkes more indirectly and Brigham more directly. Such analyses used the test scores to argue for a narrow definition of whiteness as 'Nordic'. Testing in the military has continued although its purposes and consequences have changed. The Army Alpha and Beta intelligence tests from World War I were replaced with the Army and Navy General Classification Tests during World War II, when 15 million took these tests to determine which types of positions or jobs they would be recommended for. Aptitude tests assessed technical or electrical skills, operation tests evaluated people for administrative duties, driving or knowledge of radio codes, and language tests were also implemented. The first large change in military testing came in 1950, when the Armed Forces Qualification Test (AFQT) began to be used. The AFQT was used as a screening device to provide 'a uniform measure of examinees' potential usefulness in the military' (ASVAB, n.d.: para. 7). Additional tests were used to make decisions about the types of positions they would be eligible for. This test was in use until 1972, and was replaced by the Armed Services Vocational Aptitude Battery (ASVAB), which had been introduced in 1968. In 1996 the latter became the first large-scale computer adaptive test (ASVAB, n.d.) but it is currently being phased out: in 2016, actions were put in place to replace the ASVAB with the Prescreen Internet Based Computerized Adaptive Test (PiCAT), which that can be taken on any computer. Those taking the test have 24 hours to complete it, and no official proctors are required (Bock, 2016).

In understanding the role of testing in the military and the implications for language-minoritized bilinguals, what stands out as particularly noteworthy is the disparate impact of negative consequences on groups that, by proxy, are presented here as inclusive of language-minoritized bilinguals, such as minority racial groups or groups defined by citizenship status. Non-English speaking or bilingual status is not a category that appears in US military reports. Further, the military was segregated until 1948, which means that during World War I and World War II there were different training camps for whites and blacks, and that information about language-minoritized bilinguals was reported separately for these categories.[7] Frank (2009) describes a history of bilingual homosexual military staff being ignored, to the detriment of military operations.

Despite these limitations, this section describes the impacts of these initial screening tests, first with a focus on the introduction of testing during World War I, when the tests were largely used to perpetuate negative, racist, anti-immigrant portrayals of language-minoritized bilinguals. I then move to the continued use of testing and discuss more broadly the consequences of access to accelerated paths to citizenship based on service in the military, focusing first on World War I and then on how those who did not take the accelerated path to citizenship were subjected to other consequences, by describing deportations of immigrant veterans.

Testing and test-based decisions during World War I

Chapter 1 highlighted issues around how testing was developed for language-minoritized bilinguals, and this section expands on this information by presenting details on how the test was used and the more immediate consequences for language-minoritized bilinguals in terms of decisions about their placement or rank for military service. In terms of the numbers of those impacted by the recommendations, the documents and records lead to estimates that the total number of individuals administered army intelligence exams before 31 January 1919 was in the range 1,588,904 to 1,726,966.

There were three main outcomes for not performing well on one of the three forms of intelligence test used in the military during World War I: discharge; assignment to a development battalion; or assignment to a non-combat service organization. According to the military, there were in fact four consequences in total:

> As a result of careful psychological examination, the examiner may conclude, (1) that the subject should be assigned or returned to appropriate military organization for regular training; (2) that he should be assigned or transferred to the Development battalion or to a service organization in which simple forms of manual labor are the chief requirement; (3) that he should be recommended to the psychiatrist for discharge by reason of intellectual deficiency; (4) that he should be referred to the psychiatrist for further examination because of peculiarities of behavior of definite psychopathic tendencies. (Yerkes, 1921: 168)

The three tests for intelligence testing were: the Army Alpha test, given mostly to those who were literate in English; the Army Beta test, given to those who were not literate in English and those who came from language-minoritized backgrounds, including non-citizens; and the Performance exam, which was administered individually for recruits who were unable to take or perform well on the other versions in large-scale test administration settings. From 28 April 1918 to 31 January 1919,[8] 483,469 recruits took either the Alpha and Beta or the Beta only, while 83,500 took the individually administered Performance exam in addition to either the Alpha or the Beta. A poor score on the exam meant discharge – no longer serving in the military. Development battalions allowed the military to provide additional training. For example, instruction in English was a common suggestion for work within development battalions, with an emphasis on the language skills related to military duties, such as relay messages and reading documents (Crane, 1927). Special organizations were military posts that at times could lead to combat service overseas.

The specifics are somewhat limited in terms of how discharges were linked to test performance, and in particular test performance by language-minoritized bilinguals. In Yerkes (1921), the Surgeon General of the US Army, D.C. Howard, wrote about psychiatric rather than psychological evaluations, and stated that with these cases there remained little evidence of discharge based on the testing. He wrote that across 34 divisions of the US military, 3,035 men were recommended for discharge based on psychiatric evaluations but that none were actually discharged, and they therefore presumably accompanied their divisions abroad. Paul Giddens, the Adjunct General of the Army, explained that while psychiatric evaluations could result in discharge, psychological (e.g. intelligence testing) could not. Data on the use of the Army Alpha, Beta and Performance tests indicate small percentages of recruits were discharged each month, around 0.5% of all individuals who took the tests, or 7,800. How discharge was decided was subjective, as the score was not the only criterion for the decision:

> It is impossible to state with safety the particular degree of intellectual deficiency which justifies recommendation for discharge. Other factors than intelligence contribute to a man's service ableness in the Army. These must be taken into account. If the officers who are attempting to train a man are satisfied with his responses, the indications are that he should not be discharged, even if very inferior in intelligence. In general, subjects whose mental age is below eight should be seriously considered for discharge or Development Battalion. Those who mental ages range from eight to ten should be considered for use in special service organizations or for assignment to Development Battalion. (Yerkes, 1921: 168)

Looking at the number of individuals with scores that put them within the recommended range for facing these consequences illustrates how far fewer were in fact recommended for discharge or assignment to development battalions or service organizations (see Table 2.1). This information

Table 2.1 Numbers of individuals with intelligence test scores within the recommended range for consequences compared with the total who were selected for discharge, service organizations or development battalions

Intelligence rating (mental age)	Number of individuals	Discharged, service organization, or development battalion
Below age 7	4,780	
Between 7 and 8	7,875	
Between 8 and 9	14,814	
Between 9 and 10	18, 878	
Total number	46,347	27,301

Adapted from Yerkes (1921)

indicates that 19,046 individuals with scores that were recommended to lead to one of the three consequences did not in fact experience discharge or deployment to service organizations or development battalions. Looking at the 27,301 individuals who were discharged or sent to a service organization or development battalion, Table 2.2 shows how there was a slight differences in the proportions of recruits who faced each of these consequences, with deployment to a service organization being selected slightly often more than deployment to a development battalion, and discharge the option least often selected.

Determining how many of these individuals were also language-minoritized bilinguals is complicated by several factors. First, Yerkes (1921) analyzed the scores only of foreign-born recruits who were part of the white draft from the following countries: Austria, Belgium, Canada,

Table 2.2 Percentage of recruits who were not sent for regular service based on their intelligence test score

Month	Discharged	Service organization	Development battalions
May 1918	0.25%	0.52%	
June 1918	0.42%	1%	
July 1918	0.41%	0.77%	0.83%
August 1918	0.6%	0.35%	1.09%
September 1918	0.49%	0.55%	0.67%
October 1918	1.21%	0.94%	1%
November 1918	0.69%	0.75%	0.73%
December 1918	0.13%	0.35%	0.14%
January 1919			
Average	0.5%	0.64%	0.61%
Total number	7,800	10,014	9,487

Adapted from Yerkes (1921)

Denmark, England,[9] Germany, Greece, Holland, Ireland, Italy, Norway, Poland, Russia, Scotland, Sweden and Turkey. Second, he analyzed data from 12,407 individuals who were from a subset from a previous study of approximately 94,000 white recruits. No information was presented on the three consequences, but test scores were. A test-taker's performance was graded A–E. Grade E was recommended as the cut-off score for one of the three potential consequences, but it seems that, in addition, D- grades also had similar consequences. In total, 1,831 individuals were graded D- or E. The average by country varied greatly, with Russia, Italy and Poland having the largest numbers in this category, as well as the largest percentages.

Yerkes's analyses continued for 11,295 language-minoritized bilinguals who also reported their length of residence. As has been discussed by multiple other researchers, and as is detailed in the Introduction and Chapter 1, both Yerkes and Brigham (1923) concluded, on the basis of these data, that increasingly less intelligent individuals were arriving from eastern and southern Europe, further limiting the definition of white to Nordic. Table 2.3 reports the number of language-minoritized bilinguals by test type.

Length of residence was reported in five-year increments, that is, 0–5, 6–10, 11–15, 16–20 and over 20. Scores were reported by those time increments for each test type, as was a score on a combined scale, in order to compare performances on all tests, which reported the score in terms of a mental age (in years). Of this sample, 69.6% had been in the United States 0–10 years. The score reports show differences across each of the groups in terms of their length of residence.

If we use the recommended cut-off score of 10 years of age or less for eligibility for discharge, service organization or development battalion, approximately 4,125 individuals or 36.58% of this sample would be recommended for such consequences. Thus, language-minoritized bilinguals appear to have faced such consequences at a much higher frequency than the general military population. This comparison, albeit crude in

Table 2.3 Number and percentage of language-minoritized bilingual test-takers who were analyzed in terms of their length of residence, by test type

Test type	Number	Percentage
Alpha	3,619	32.1
Beta alone or with Alpha	6,683	59.1
Performance exam	802	7.1
Stanford–Binet	191	1.7
Total	11,295	

Adapted from Yerkes (1921)

its ability to precisely name the specific consequences faced by language-minoritized bilinguals, illustrates how differences in performances on such exams existed when tests were first introduced.

These data were interpreted to support anti-immigrant and increasingly racist perspectives to delineate the boundaries of whiteness to include only those from northern Europe or those characterized as 'Nordic'. The oft criticized interpretation that these data about length of residence represented the new immigrant groups arriving with inherently lower intelligence reflects how ideological consequences substantiated or encouraged similar public and political discourses and anti-immigrant actions. The test results served to support, for example, Terman's thoughts about race and intelligence. In 1916 he wrote:

> The fact that one meets this type [with a low level of intelligence] with such extraordinary frequency among Indians [Native Americans], Mexicans, and Negroes suggests quite forcibly that the whole question of racial differences in mental traits will have to be taken up anew and by experimental methods. The writer predicts that when this is done there will be discovered enormously significant racial differences in general intelligence, differences which cannot be wiped out by any scheme of mental culture. (Terman, 1916: 92)

Terman's prediction came into fruition. His and others' interpretations served to reify social hierarchies and views of white supremacy.

Identifying the origin of the (potential) disproportionate application of consequences from the onset of these uses of intelligence tests further illustrates how continued issues in modern-day testing can be seen as a lasting legacy. The explicit ideologies around the development, use and interpretation of the test scores has changed greatly from World War I, yet the social consequences of taking intelligence tests remain incommensurate for language-minoritized bilinguals in comparison with other groups. One additional concrete consequence that has remained with military service is how these tests can be used to exclude language-minoritized bilinguals who are not citizens, and who would like to serve in the military to have access to accelerated pathways to US citizenship.

Access to military service and accelerated paths to citizenship

One potential positive consequence of passing the military exam and serving is gaining access to accelerated pathways to citizenship. Yet, the issues of who has access to accelerated citizenship and the treatment of veterans who do not receive citizenship – both of which disproportionately negatively impact individuals from anywhere other than northern or western Europe – illustrate the complexities of the social consequences of testing. Those without citizenship have always served in large numbers in the different branches of the US military, and since the Civil War they have been offered an accelerated path to citizenship by the waiving of residency requirements and fees.

Before looking at the history of how the pathway to citizenship has been used, it is important to recognize the shifts in the ways in which language-minoritized bilinguals have had access to military service. Pathways to citizenship have historically been made more available during wartime, when non-citizens were drafted (as well as volunteering) to serve. The armed forces moved to an all-volunteer service in 1973, at the end of the Vietnam War, and since that time there has not been active draft for any conflicts or wars. However, all those aged 18–25, including immigrants and non-citizens, presently must register for selective service, and they may be subjected to military conscription or future drafts.

In moving to an all-volunteer force, the military has also downsized in terms of the number of recruits, which has allowed it to be more selective. Before the PiCAT, the ASVAB was used as a screen to deny eligibility for service. A 2010 report investigated the performance on the ASVAB of 348,203 high school graduates aged 17–20 who applied to enlist from 2004 to 2009 (Education Trust, 2010). Of these individuals, 23% did not achieve the score necessary to enter the military. Whites comprised 57.9% of those who took the test, Hispanics 11.7% and African Americans 18.4%. Yet Hispanics and African Americans were disproportionately represented in the group who failed the test: 19% of whites compared with 29% of Hispanics and 39% of African Americans failed to attain a qualifying score, and mean scores for Hispanics and African Americans were 10 and 17 points lower, respectively, than that of whites (on a scale of 1–99 points). What is also notable is who is not present in these data – Asian Americans, for example. Furthermore, there is no disclosure of the test-takers' socioeconomic backgrounds.

The state-level data describes more differences in performance, with Hawaii, Louisiana, Mississippi and Washington, DC, averaging the lowest performance, and also averaging larger numbers of Hispanic and African American test-takers. The range across states in the proportion of test-takers ineligible for service due to their test score is perhaps the most telling. For whites this spans 16.9 percentage points, from 10.1% in Indiana to 27.0% in Maryland; for Hispanics it spans 26.2 percentage points, from 14.3% in Montana to 40.5% in Massachusetts; and for African Americans it spans 33.7 percentage points from 16.4% in Oregon to 50.1% in Mississippi. For all test-takers combined, it spans 25.3 percentage points, from 13.0% in Wyoming to 38.3% in Hawaii (Education Trust, 2010). The current testing is conducted with the purpose of reducing attrition during the first term of enlistment. Yet in this it is largely seen to be ineffective (Cardona & Ritchie, 2006). Being denied entry to the US military on the basis of performance on the ASVAB, thus, disproportionately impacts Hispanics and African Americans. Being denied access to the military is one clear consequence, yet it is important to note that, historically, serving in the military (i.e. passing this test) has protected some language-minoritized bilinguals from other consequences, such as restricted access to citizenship and the deportation of veterans.

Approximately 18% of all US soldiers who served during World War I were described as foreign born – around 500,000 citizens and non-citizens. Of the non-citizens, many were drafted. They were eligible for the draft either because they had the declared intent of seeking citizenship after meeting the residency requirement or because of a treaty with their country of origin granting the United States permission to draft. Subsequently, 192,000 non-citizen soldiers were awarded citizenship for their service in World War I (Ford, 2001).

During World War II (the last war before desegregation), 306,298 foreign-born individuals entered the armed forces, of whom 109,517 were non-citizens (Miller, 1948). Table 2.4 shows the numbers and percentages

Table 2.4 Numbers and percentages of foreign-born individuals serving in World War II, by country of origin, compared with the total for each subcategory

	Total		Naturalized		Non-citizen	
Canada	55,897	18.25%	36,598	18.60%	19,299	17.62%
Italy	39,256	12.82%	30,343	15.42%	8,913	8.14%
Germany	33,396	10.90%	18,944	9.63%	14,452	13.20%
British Isles	25,036	8.17%	17,131	8.71%	7,905	7.22%
Mexico	19,952	6.51%	4,465	2.27%	15,487	14.14%
Poland	17,513	5.72%	12,590	6.40%	4,923	4.50%
USSR	13,649	4.46%	10,556	5.36%	3,093	2.82%
Irish Free State	13,047	4.26%	9,454	4.80%	3,593	3.28%
China	8,771	2.86%	7,318	3.72%	1,453	1.33%
Austria	7,863	2.57%	4,304	2.19%	3,559	3.25%
Czechoslovakia	6,069	1.98%	4,190	2.13%	1,879	1.72%
Sweden	5,806	1.90%	3,651	1.86%	2,155	1.97%
Greece	5,742	1.87%	3,192	1.62%	2,550	2.33%
Hungary	5,281	1.72%	3,760	1.91%	1,521	1.39%
Norway	4,708	1.54%	2,790	1.42%	1,918	1.75%
Yugoslavia	3,408	1.11%	2,224	1.13%	1,184	1.08%
France	2,749	0.90%	1,894	0.96%	855	0.78%
Romania	2,633	0.86%	1,980	1.01%	653	0.60%
Denmark	2,540	0.83%	1,620	0.82%	920	0.84%
Netherlands	2,321	0.76%	1,440	0.73%	881	0.80%
Cuba	2,249	0.73%	919	0.47%	1,330	1.21%
All others	28,412	9.28%	17,418	8.85%	10,994	10.04%
Total	306,298		196,781		109,517	

Adapted from Miller (1948)

of foreign-born service members by country of origin in total and separated into naturalized and non-citizens. It can be seen in this table that only individuals from Mexico and Cuba had more non-citizens serving than naturalized citizens (77.62% and 59.14%, respectively). And Mexico and Germany were the only countries with substantially larger proportions of more individuals serving with the US military who were non-citizens, and Italy was the only country with a substantially larger proportion of naturalized persons serving. Figure 2.8 shows the percentages of individuals by country of origin who were naturalized or non-citizens in relation to the total foreign-born service members.

Figure 2.8 illustrates how most countries such as Canada, Sweden and the British Isles, had a relatively consistent percentage representation in all three categories. The visualization of the data also presents the striking difference for people from Mexico. Far more individuals from Mexico without US citizenship serve in comparison with those from all other countries. In the data on the naturalization of non-citizens, the differences between those who served and those who were granted citizenship because of their military service are also striking. Figure 2.9 compares the proportion of non-citizens from different countries of origin who served in World War II with the proportion of individuals from different countries who were granted citizenship due to their service in World War II. The proportions are largely similar except for individuals from the British Isles and Mexico. These cases are the inverse of each other, in that a much larger proportion of persons from the British Isles were granted citizenship than the proportion that served (30.65% compared with 7.22%) whereas a much smaller proportion of individuals from Mexico were granted citizenship than the proportion who served (8.91% compared with 14.14%). Although serving in the military did allow many immigrants to become citizens, individuals from Mexico largely were not part of this group. What is also important to understand is that without citizenship, these language-minoritized bilingual veterans were now subjected to increasingly more flexible deportation policies, regardless of service. This has been especially impacting those who served in Vietnam, as well as in the more recent Operations Desert Storm and Enduring Freedom.

Increasingly many of the veterans who do not get citizenship face deportation. There are two factors that are seen as contributing to this. First, the Immigration and Nationality Act of 1996 made it possible to deport legal permanent residents, or those with Green Cards, for committing crimes described as 'aggravated felonies' or 'crimes of moral turpitude'. These categories of crime exist only for immigrants and in relation to deportation. These crimes include violent offenses such as murder, but also drug possession, petty theft and fraud – such as cashing checks illegally. What this means is that any conviction of crime that results in a sentence of one or more years of imprisonment means that a person can face deportation. Second, the Obama administration focused on the removal of

Seeking Access to Civic Participation 71

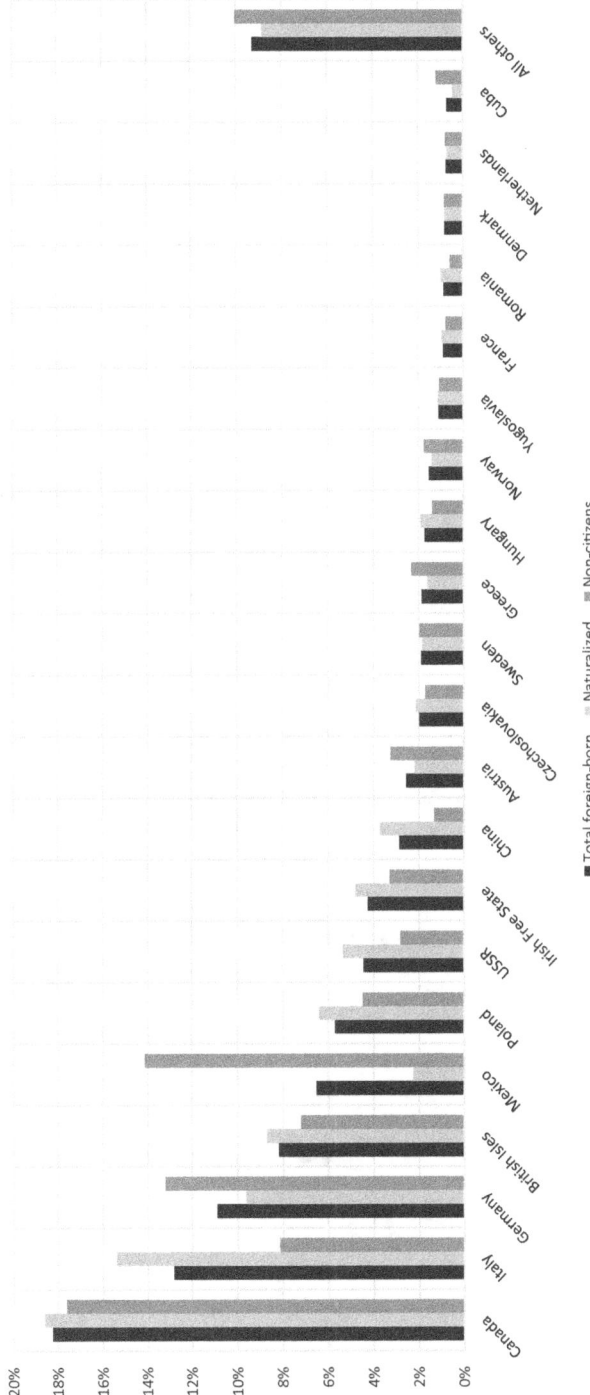

Figure 2.8 Percentage of foreign-born service members by country of origin, comparison of percentage of the total, naturalized, and non-citizens (adapted from Miller, 1948)

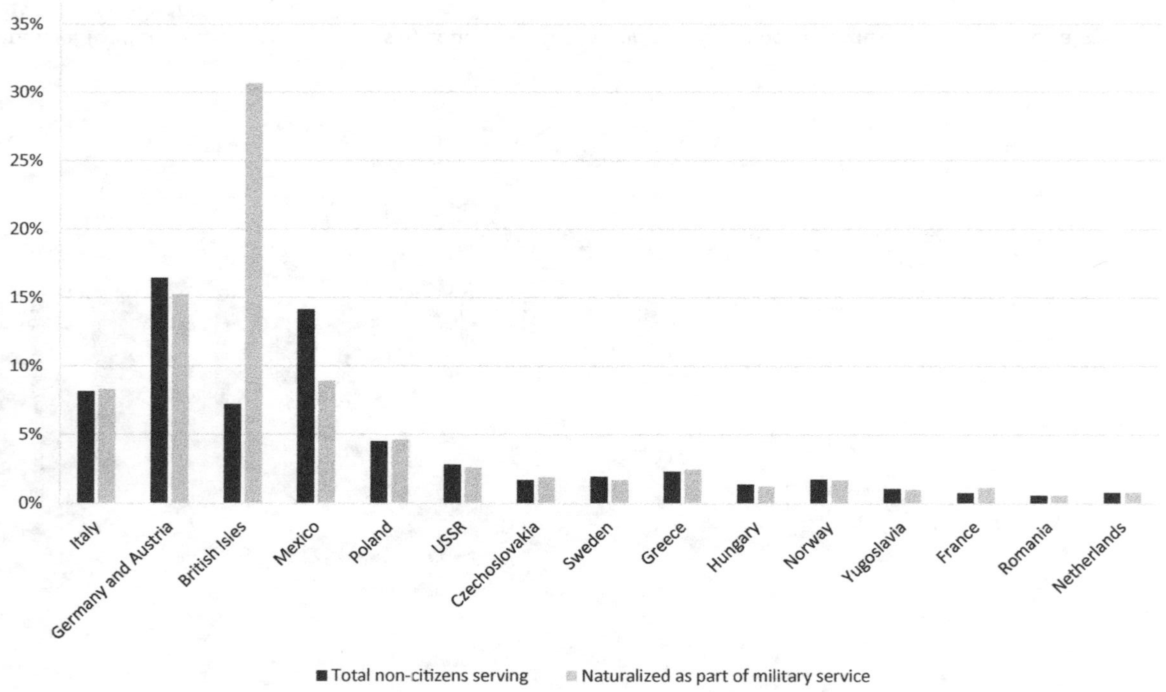

72 Part 1: Immigration Policy in the United States

Figure 2.9 Comparison of the proportion individuals who served in WWII who were non-citizens from different countries of origin with the proportion of individuals from different countries who were granted citizenship due to their service (adapted from Miller, 1948)

immigrants with criminal records. In 2009, 51% of those deported were convicted of what was called a 'serious' crime; this percentage grew in 2016, when more than 90% were reported to have committed a serious crime. In 2014, Obama stated that immigrants who committed aggravated felonies under the 1996 immigration law were part of the 'priority 1' classification, or the most targeted, for deportation. Immigrants were also targeted for committing less serious crimes. Priority 2 focused on immigrants convicted of three misdemeanors or one serious misdemeanor (Chishti et al., 2017). Under the Trump administration, deportations went down, but arrests of immigrants went up. From October to December 2016, there were on average 9,134 arrests per month. From February to June 2017, there were on average 13,085 arrests per month. Immigration courts are experiencing a backlog in processing hearings that could lead to deportation, with each case taking close to an average of 700 days to reach court in 2016 and 2017 – contrasted with around 400 days from 1998 to 2010. Importantly, those deported during 2017 were most often immigrants who were arrested under the Obama administration (Lind, 2017). The impact of these policies in relation to veterans met with a backlash.

The Department of Homeland Security does not keep statistics on the number of deportees who are also veterans. According to the Deported Veterans' Support House (2017), since 1996 over 100 veterans from 30 different countries have been deported. A 2016 report by the American Civil Liberties Union (ACLU) documents 59 cases of veterans who had been deported, or who had received deportation orders. The report (Vakili et al., 2016) details some of the crimes that were committed by the 59 deported veterans, which include more minor, non-violent infractions such as check fraud (theft), perjury, tax evasion and possession of a controlled substance. This intersection of veterans and crime with immigration status is particularly troubling when the general trends around incarceration of veterans in the United States overall are considered. The ACLU reported that 80% of incarcerated veterans had been honorably discharged, yet that veterans were more likely than non-veterans to have been convicted of a violent crime. Seventy-five percent of veterans reported prior drug use. These issues often stem from difficulties that veterans face when returning to civilian life. Yet one additional consequence that deported immigrant veterans face is no access to veteran medical services or support.

Although these consequences cannot be linked to the screening testing, the take-away from the case of deported veterans is that passing a test in order to serve in the military did not necessarily mean that they became citizens, nor that they were able to remain in the United States. It also denotes a very asymmetric relationship between the individual and US government, where language-minoritized bilinguals are willing to sacrifice their lives while the government's positions are changeable, meaning that at any moment these same people can become expendable. These indirect consequences of the intersections of tests, policies and enforcement of policies illustrate how systems put in place to support language-minoritized bilinguals – in this case, the accelerated path to citizenship – can continue to fail due to other structural inequalities.

Summary

The history of testing in the military, and how language-minoritized bilinguals have participated and the consequences they have faced, began with overt racist positioning of immigrants and continues with the disproportionate exclusion of those from Hispanic and Black communities with the screening test. Those who are allowed to serve are not all given equal access to accelerated pathways to citizenship, and those who do not acquire citizenship may be subjected to deportation. These types of consequences, and additional consequences for crimes despite military service, are ways in which language-minoritized bilinguals have a unique and troubled history of seeking participation in the United States through military service, reflective of wider issues but reproduced in the military domain.

Discussion

In this chapter, language-minoritized bilinguals were largely characterized as immigrants seeking admission, voting rights, naturalization or military service. Across all of these different areas to be civically engaged, testing hurdles have been put in place with the potential to discriminate, which creates the preconditions for the discrimination that follows. Literacy tests were seen as somewhat ineffective in restricting immigration, and thus additional policies involving quotas were added to increase restrictions.

Yet the data presented in this chapter also illustrate that literacy tests served to debar a large number of immigrants. For voting, the case in New York demonstrates ways in which testing restrictions that were primarily used on black communities were adjusted to marginalize the voting of Puerto Ricans. For naturalization testing, the move to standardized testing still has not resolved some of the issues with the test, and the unreliability and potential for administrators' biases are concerns that have yet to be addressed. The high pass rate, however, illustrates how this test may not present widespread consequences for language-minoritized bilinguals. Military testing, as detailed in the final sections, has perhaps offered the widest swath of consequences and interactions of tests with other mechanisms, such as designations of criminality.

As a whole, this chapter presents the extremely complex ways in which language-minoritized bilinguals who are seeking to participate in the United States in many civic endeavors face a multitude of barriers. Situating these histories with respect to use-oriented testing, Shohamy argues that 'traditional testing views tests as isolated events, detached from people, society, motives, intentions, uses, impacts, effects, and consequences' (Shohamy, 2001: 4). The multiple roles of the tests presented in this chapter with respect to seeking access to various forms of civic participation need to be understood collectively rather than individually in order to understand the weight of the cumulative consequences of their use. The ways in which language-minoritized bilinguals inhabit intersectional identities are repeatedly ignored. The fact that they inhabit these multiple minoritized identities is leveraged against them, as different tests or policies can be positioned to select the most vulnerable or accessible minoritized identity to implement the consequence. The overarching perspective sheds light on the systematic disenfranchisement of language-minoritized bilinguals in relation to different civic activities in the United States.

Notes

(1) In reflecting on the treatment of the language-minoritized bilingual who petitioned for naturalization, it is important to note that Native Americans were also excluded from citizenship. Although some were granted naturalization rights in 1924 with the Indian Citizenship Act, it was not until the Nationality Act of 1940 that all Native Americans were granted citizenship.

(2) One racial prerequisite case, *Cruz* v. *US* (23. F. Supp. 774), 1938, was the only instance where an individual tried to prove that a person three-quarters Native American and one-quarter African was of African descent for the purposes of citizenship. He was denied naturalization. The stigma and discrimination against being black in the United States also influenced immigrants' decisions to seek white racial classification (Haney López, 2006).

(3) After the Supreme Court rulings, there were 15 more racial prerequisite trials, two ruling that petitioners were white. *United States* v. *Cartozian* (1925) found that Armenians are white, following legal precedent from *In re Halladjiian* (1909). *Ex Parte Mohriez* (1944) found that Arabians are white using 'The Eligibility of Arabs to Naturalization' in the official publication of the Department of Justice, Immigration and Naturalization Service, *Monthly Review*, October 1943, Vol. 1, No. 4, pp. 12–16.

(4) Federal policy 1423, 'Requirements as to understanding the English language, history, principles and form of government of the United States', 8 U.S.C. 1423, 1964, at https://www.gpo.gov/fdsys/pkg/USCODE-2011-title8/pdf/USCODE-2011-title8-chap12-subchapIII-partII-sec1423.pdf (accessed 14 November 2018).

(5) Ibid.

(6) See https://www.uscis.gov/archive/archive-citizenship/applicant-performance-naturalization-test-archives (accessed 14 November 2018).

(7) In World War I, language-minoritized bilinguals served in integrated service units and segregated units. World War I was the last war with a Hispanic regiment. During World War II, language-minoritized bilinguals largely served in the non-segregated units. Individuals of Japanese origin were barred from the draft during World War II.

(8) From 28 April 1918, weekly reports on intelligence testing were required. Although Yerkes also presented estimates of testing from September 1917, those estimates do not differentiate between test type, nor specify how intelligence tests related to recommendations for discharge or assignment to development battalions or service organizations.

(9) English-speaking countries such as England are included in this count of language-minoritized bilinguals because the variety of their English, and how that impacted their performance, was not discussed by Yerkes, and this country of origin is included in the comparative analysis of length of residence. I acknowledge, however, that this stretches the boundaries of what a language-minoritized bilingual was then and is now.

3 Seeking to Enter the United States: A Focus on the Ellis Island and Angel Island Ports of Entry

For those seeking to enter the United States, formal and informal tests have been used to limit access and enforce immigration policies. These policies have been applied differently to individuals based on the person's country of origin, race and age. People from some regions of the world have been welcomed, some have undergone short-term periods of targeted discrimination and others have been subjected to long-term systemically oppressive treatment. At a policy level, children under 16 and adults over 55 have been mostly exempted from immigration restrictions or immigration tests.

In exploring some of the origins of testing with respect to immigration and immigration policies, this chapter focuses on two ports of entry: Ellis Island and Angel Island. Ellis Island is in the Upper New York Bay, near New York City, on the Atlantic coastline of the United States. Presently, Ellis Island is part of the Statue of Liberty National Monument. Angel Island is in the San Francisco Bay, near San Francisco, on the Pacific coastline of the United States and is designated as a California State Park. Both ports served as major immigration stations, but they had contrasting relationships with testing. The prominence of testing with respect to trying to limit immigration at Ellis Island differed vastly from the less formal, less systematized forms of testing used at Angel Island. The interplay of policies with testing is highlighted, with particular attention to how negative testing consequences centered around specific groups, generally those who were non-white and from non-northern European countries.

At Ellis Island, immigrants primarily from Europe were received and screened, and most were given tickets for entry to the United States within hours. The most immediate impact of testing and screening at Ellis Island on the lived experiences of language-minoritized bilinguals came in the form of being debarred or deported. The testing at Ellis Island was also connected with anti-immigrant discourses, policies and actions in the United States. At Angel Island, immigrants primarily from China and other Asian countries were received, screened and held for indeterminate lengths of time. Although the details of many of their experiences were lost in a fire of the administration building on 12 August 1940, the treatment of these immigrants reflected the restrictive immigration policies of the time, which largely barred them from entry and naturalization. The roles of testing in relation to the social consequences for immigrant language-minoritized bilinguals illuminate the complex ways in which testing interacted with policies and public opinion.

Ellis Island

One year after the creation of the Federal Bureau of Immigration in 1891, the federal government opened Ellis Island immigration station. The purpose of this station was to increase the documentation and screening of immigrants, including creating methods for deportation. Although intelligence testing at Ellis Island was not generally used to make final decisions about deportations, the interpretations of these tests contributed to increasingly anti-immigrant, often racist or xenophobic, discourses against language-minoritized bilinguals.

At Ellis Island, language-minoritized bilinguals were evaluated to determine if they could be categorized as 'undesirable' as defined by federal immigration policies. The definition of undesirables expanded in 1903 from what the policy in 1892 called lunatics and idiots, or any other individual who did not appear to be self-sufficient, to include those who were epileptic, seen as beggars or anarchists; its scope increased further in 1907 to include those with intellectual disabilities, categorized as morons, idiots, imbeciles (this terminology was changed in the 1970s to mildly, moderately, severely and profoundly disabled) and a broad category of 'feeble-minded' for anyone with an assumed intellectual disability, often judged on the basis of appearance. The ever-expanding definition of those who could be excluded also targeted specific groups, such as anarchists (who were generally assumed to be from Italy) (Hing, 2004).

The expansion of immigration policies to exclude individuals with intellectual disabilities came at a time when there was new and rapidly growing interest in intelligence testing and establishing a link between inherited intelligence and race or nationality. As discussed in the Introduction and Chapter 1, this early work in developing tests to measure intelligence, in particular when associated with the eugenics movement, was commonly used to promote what Stern (2015) called scientific racism, or the use of evidence presented as objective that was used to substantiate racist claims and ideologies. That tests were the appropriate tool to provide such evidence was a claim made by Francis Galton. In connecting his views of intelligence with genetics in the eugenics movement, he also proposed consequences for those who performed poorly on intelligence tests. These consequences were severe and included institutionalization, forced sterilization and social isolation (Buchanan & Finch, 2005).

Changes were made to US immigration policy at the time when arguably one of the most influential tests was being developed. As part of a government initiative in France, researchers were called to create a mechanism to determine which children were of 'normal' intelligence and which had intellectual disabilities. Alfred Binet and Theodore Simon created the Binet–Simon scale in 1905, and Henry Goddard – whose role in testing immigrants on Ellis Island will be described later – translated the test and began using it in the United States in 1908. Goddard's work on Ellis Island, as understood in this history, made intelligence testing of immigrants on Ellis Island a mechanism to perpetuate the eugenics movement, including restrictive policies to institutionalize and forcibly sterilize those with disabilities. By including intelligence (via feeble-mindedness) as a classification for those deemed deportable, many in the eugenics movement targeted specific ethnicities and races largely through countries of origin, by claiming there was an inherited (i.e. genetic) link between intelligence and race based on the nationality of individuals.

What is not included in this review of testing, largely due to a lack of documentation, are the screening tests conducted onboard the steamboats transporting immigrants. All immigrants at Ellis Island from around 1905 onward were subjected to screening by the steamboat personnel who transported them from their home countries to the United States. Due to the fines of around $100 that steamboat staff would incur for bringing immigrants who were subsequently deported, many more were refused entry to Ellis Island by these personnel before being subjected to any testing on Ellis Island (Boody, 1926).

Ellis Island served as a testing ground, so to speak, for research on intelligence tests which expanded use to military testing (see Chapter 2) and to K-12 schools (see Chapter 4). Table 3.1 shows the number of immigrants by year who were classified as a moron, idiot, imbecile or feeble-minded and subsequently denied entry into the United States, in relation to the total number of immigrant arrivals at Ellis Island and relevant immigration policies. All years represent fiscal years, and therefore are from 1 July of the previous year to 30 June of the year stated.

These deportations represent real, immediate social consequences for language-minoritized bilinguals. Figure 3.1 shows the percentage of immigrants deported from Ellis Island on the basis of their results on intelligence testing. Note the small spike in deportations in 1907/1908, when policies were first put in place to deport immigrants based on intelligence, and the larger spike when intelligence testing was introduced in 1913. The extreme peak of deportation in 1919 has often been overlooked, but compared with the very low number of immigrants during World War I at that time, the dramatic increase in the proportion of immigrant

Table 3.1 Use of intelligence screening on Ellis Island, 1892–1924

Relevant immigration policies	Year	Deported	Arrivals
1812 Ship's captains must provide a list of all passengers, including age, sex, occupation, country of origin and deaths on route 1875 Page Act introduces 'undesirable' category to include prostitutes and criminals, those who would be cared for by public charge 1875 50-cent head tax 1876 US Supreme Court declares state laws on immigration unconstitutional 1882 Chinese Exclusion Act 1888 Provisions added for deportation (first since 1796) 1891 Immigration Act establishes Bureau of Immigration	1892	4	445,987
	1893	3	343,422
	1894	4	219,046
	1895	6	190,928
	1896	1	263,709
	1897	1	180,556
	1898	1	178,748
	1899	1	242,573
	1900	1	341,712
	1901	6	388,931
	1902	7	493,262
1903 Immigration Act expands undesirable category to include anarchists, epileptics, beggars, importers of prostitutes 1906 Naturalization Act requires knowledge of English	1903	1	631,835
	1904	16	606,019
	1905	38	788,219
	1906	92	880,036
1907 Immigration Act expands undesirable category to include those with physical and mental disabilities 1907 Head tax raised to $4 per person	1907	29	1,004,756
	1908	186	585,970
	1909	181	580,617
	1910	181	786,094
	1911	164	637,003
	1912	164	605,151
	1913	555	892,653
	1914	1,077	878,052
	1915	335	178,416
	1916	246	141,390
1917 Immigration Act expands bans on immigration from Asian countries 1917 Literacy testing (in any language) for immigrants aged over 16 1918 Immigration Act strengthens ban on anarchists	1917	252	129,446
	1918	28	28,867
	1919	160	26,731
	1920	78	225,206
1921 Quota Act limits immigration to 3% of that nationality's population in the US in 1910 based on census data, to restrict immigration from eastern and southern Europe 1924 National Origins Act limits immigration to 2% that nationality's population, based on surnames, thereby more tightly restricting immigration from regions other than western and northern Europe, without provisions for refugees 1924 Transfer of intelligence screening responsibilities to country of origin	1921	104	560,971
	1922	112	209,778
	1923	101	295,473
	1924	105	315,587

Adapted from the annual reports of the Commissioner General of Immigration, 1892–1924

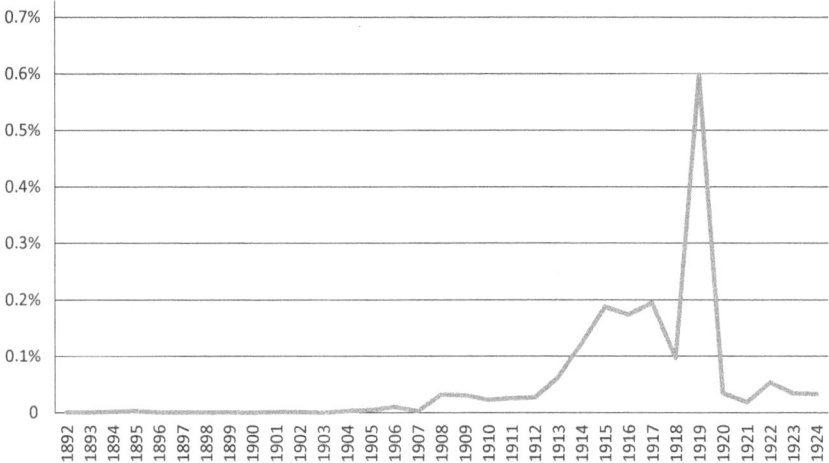

Figure 3.1 Percentage of immigrants debarred from Ellis Island due to intelligence screenings

deportations illustrates the role of intelligence test screenings at a time when military testing of immigrants was being used to fuel anti-immigrant public opinions (see Chapter 2).

Tests played an important role in reifying anti-immigrant public opinion, and further ramifications of the use of intelligence, including forced sterilization, are discussed in Chapter 5. In 1924, the responsibilities of screening immigrants were transferred from US immigration officials to the countries of origin. This created space for the development of country-based policies that explicitly favored English-speaking white immigrants from northern Europe. For example, on 1 August 1925 there was an experiment at Ellis Island to allow English-speaking immigrants from Great Britain and Ireland into the United States if they had passed examinations conducted in their country. On 5 November of the same year Belgium, Germany, the Netherlands, Sweden and Denmark had also suggested (informally) to the State Department that immigrants from their countries should receive the same treatment (Boody, 1926).

The presentation of how language-minoritized bilinguals were screened at Ellis Island begins with children, and the same format is followed for Angel Island, below. I begin with children who were educated at the mostly forgotten school at Ellis Island. The teachers at the school played a role in advocating for children to stay in the United States, and the school was also used in 1922 and 1923 as a site to research intelligence testing of children who were being detained at Ellis Island. This is followed by research on intelligence testing conducted with adults at Ellis Island, and the connection of this research to the eugenics movement. In reviewing these histories of intelligence testing at Ellis Island, I emphasize the different interpretations and responses to or dissemination of findings, and the rejection of evidence that countered the dominant white supremacist lenses applied to analysis of testing language-minoritized bilinguals at the time.

Intelligence testing of immigrant children

The school on Ellis Island was a voluntary program offered to children who were often separated from their family. There is limited documentation of the school, and the majority of the information summarized here is from Gallagher's (2014) research on the kindergarten class, a report from a missionary teacher who worked at the school (Prall, 1922), and Boody's (1926) study of intelligence testing of children at Ellis Island, including the critical reception of her findings.

Although there are photos available – in particular through Getty Images – there is no specific documentation of the number of children at Ellis Island or the school at Ellis Island. The school was also conceived as multiple schools, some run by hospital workers to teach children who were being treated in an infirmary, and others run by volunteer missionaries. In the different schools, children were taught English language and literacy, games and citizenship topics. The schools had playground areas and some toys, although space and resources were limited as Ellis Island was a congested area, and the three playgrounds doubled as instructional spaces. The American Library Association also operated a library on the island, which provided some books and music (Gallagher, 2014).

In describing the conditions as a school on Ellis Island for American missionary audiences, Prall (1922), a missionary herself, reported that around 160 children attended the school each day. She wrote about children by name, describing their experiences at the school. For the children aged two to seven years, she stated that

> Little Moses can sing the song and build houses with the blocks. Esther is happy because she has made a little wagon. Anne, who comes from Palestine, is busy playing with a rag doll. Every nationality is represented in our school. We are all neighborly and kind to one another. There is Lydia from Greece, who is crying for a doll. We have only one doll, and we let each child play with it five minutes. (Prall, 1922: 476)

In describing the older children, she explained

> Over by that blackboard are ten benches filled with boys and girls. This is the English class. How eager they are to learn to read and write English! This is the most encouraging class we have. One of the boys, who is only eleven years old, is going to Akron, Ohio. He has not seen his mother and

father for seven years, and has come from Russia with his three brothers and sisters. (Prall, 1922: 476)

She was also keenly aware of the tenuous circumstances of the children at Ellis Island, and assisted in petitions to help them stay in the United States. She told the stories of several children who were able to stay. For example:

> Two little girls and their mother were put on board the return steamer because one of them had an infected eye. The father was an American citizen and had a home waiting for them. I interested the Italian Society in their case, and new briefs were sent to Washington. The father promised to consult a physician about little Bendetta's eyes and guaranteed that she should not be put in an institution nor become a public charge. The answer came back to admit them. This family is very happy in being united and is very grateful to the school. (Prall, 1922: 477)

The issue with the girl's eyes presumably was trachoma, a common, highly contagious and difficult-to-cure eye disease that was prevalent on Ellis Island. Prall also relayed a story of two sisters who were deported: 'Two girls from Poland, between the ages of fourteen and sixteen, were deported because over the quota. They had attended our English classes and were heartbroken because they could not join their brother in America' (Prall, 1922: 477). Children over the age of 12 could be deported without a parent whereas those under the age of 12 could not.

The personal accounts by Prall were echoed in the research monograph by Boody (1926). Boody visited the school at Ellis Island in the early 1920s to conduct research on intelligence testing, though the bulk of her volume focused on previous research and descriptions of conditions at Ellis Island. Her book includes a lengthy account of the policies and previous research on intelligence testing of immigrants on Ellis Island. She reports deportations made on the basis of policies (described above) about those classified as 'undesirable' from 1907 – the first year with such available information – onward. During the years of her study, for example, she noted that 4,345 people in 1922 and 3,661 people in 1923 were deported. She calls these figures 'appalling' and noted the need 'for infinite care' in screening to reduce these figures (Boody, 1926: 96). I mention this to point to the tone in her research, which contrasts with many of her contemporaries.

Although in presenting her work I am quite cautious in calling Boody an advocate for immigrants, her commentary about human experiences woven throughout the volume countered the dominant framing of 'the immigrant problem' by others conducting similar research. She questioned the rationale of how testing had been applied without necessarily clarifying why testing had been chosen when explaining how intelligence testing became the prevalent mechanism to regulate immigration. That is to say, she indirectly questioned the use of a test that was designed for one purpose being used – with severe consequences – for another purpose, and the historical fear of the 'other' which fueled such decisions. In recounting the history of immigration in the United States, she explained how fear drove policy decisions by quoting government reports from 1819, 1835 and 1845, which all referenced the dangers of immigration. In explaining how the use of intelligence tests with immigrants became of interest, she posited that testing was used because it was an available tool, but does not attribute much more thought to the use of tests beyond convenience and placating fears:

> as these former fears eventually turned themselves into action and legislation, so the fears of today have made men look about them to find what plans may best be made, what tools may best be used. [...] if the immigration of the future must be more highly selective than that of the past had been, what has already been successfully used in making a broad differentiation in large groups, was bound to be thought of. The mental testing in our army camps had done this. Could any such procedure be adopted to help us make decisions in regard to the aliens landing on our shores[?]. With this thought came the fairly little practical suggestion as to how such adaptations might be made. There is little reference as to the difference between the two problems to be solved, the one a successful working scheme for allotting the proper men to the proper grade of usefulness in the army, the other, facing the question not merely of evaluating the immigrants, but also of determining what you are evaluating them for. (Boody, 1926: 6–7)

The question for her study, thus, focused on trying to see how tests could be used to characterize the quality and quantity of immigrants, theorizing that once quality had been defined and identified, quantity would work itself out.

She also described the process by which children gained access to the school at Ellis Island. As stated earlier, participation was completely voluntary, and children were recruited from the detention rooms, where they awaited information about family member(s) who may have been held due to illness or other screenings, family members already in the United States to meet them, financial support, or paperwork for adoption. Most were not awaiting deportation, and therefore the children at the school were largely seen as not requiring further screening to determine their immigration status (Boody, 1926). That is to say, the children included in this testing had already been subjected to, and for the most part had passed, other forms of evaluation of their eligibility for entry into the United States.

In the summer of 1922, Boody used 16 different intelligence tests with around 100 children on Ellis Island. In 1923, she tested another 200–300 children, eliminating some of the previous tests, thus using 12 with younger children and nine with the older children. These were all 'non-language' intelligence tests that were administered individually or to small groups. To ensure what she conceived of as 'fairness' in test administration, she grouped children with different language backgrounds so that they could not discuss the test with each other. In describing the small groups, she wrote:

> It was most interesting to watch at work a group composed of an Arab, a Greek, an Italian, a Welsh boy, an Armenian, and a Russian. The members of such a group do not talk to each other; but they laugh together, and spur each other on. (Boody, 1926: 103)

Results from the tests were first divided by age range, that is, separately for children aged 3–8 and for children aged 9–19. Then, nationalities or race, sex and age were reported for each test, separated by whether or not they passed or failed the test. In reporting a summary of the younger children's performances on the tests, she found no remarkable pattern in terms of passing or failing by nationality. Yet she did not go so far as to claim that her findings discredited others, and concluded that it is important to examine the individual cases, rather than drawing broad generalizations:

> even if to suggest the possibility of little discoverable racial difference here, is but faint, it may not be any less real, and the results showing what these children have actually done may perhaps suggest lines of approach to further study of the smallest immigrant child. (Boody, 1926: 122)

Following the analysis of the older children's test results, she further claimed that the findings spoke more to the children's individual differences than to inherited intelligence related to race or nationality:

> the differences that they [the differences in scores or performance on the test] indicate seem to be in individuals representing a race than in a race or nationality as such [and that] the curve of the scores seems not to differ in any marked degree from race to race. (Boody, 1926: 151–152)

She also addressed the generalizability of the findings, given the randomness of the sampling process at Ellis Island, calling it 'an unusual chance for a typical representation' (Boody, 1926: 151). This is a critique of studies of immigrants outside Ellis Island, where she characterized the sampling as more 'homogeneous' and thus 'less typical'.

The reception of her research was mixed. A review in the *British Medical Journal* (Anonymous, 1926) calls the book a valuable contribution, and in particular emphasizes the contributions in terms of the details about the history and procedures on Ellis Island. In contrast, a review by Taylor states that the book 'is more suggestive of progressive approaches than actually being one or than even being conclusive in the report of its findings' (Taylor, 1926: 571), stating that the book falls short in engaging with racial and national traits and the 'general capabilities and particular abilities of immigrant children' (Taylor, 1926: 573). Pinter's (1927) comprehensive review of over 150 studies on intelligence testing provides no information beyond the title of her book. Thus the contribution of her work, which called for more consideration of the immediate impact of testing on individuals, was relatively small and did little to counter the motivations to use testing to negatively portray language-minoritized bilinguals. In contrast, the testing of adults more clearly indicates which discourses dominated and posed consequences for language-minoritized bilinguals.

Intelligence testing of immigrant adults

As stated at the start of this chapter, the screening at Ellis Island was being conducted while theories of intelligence were still being developed but nevertheless served an important foundational role in leveraging tests to make high-stakes decisions with immediate consequences for immigrants. The intelligence testing on Ellis Island and studies of intelligence testing that included immigrants or children of immigrants already in the United States together were used to support prevalent anti-immigrant discourses that blamed language-minoritized bilinguals for societal issues such as crime, illiteracy and poverty. Although there was debate around definitions and theories of intelligence (Fancher, 1985), the researcher who introduced intelligence testing on Ellis Island – Henry H. Goddard – clearly defined intelligence as an inherited trait, and related intelligence to race, ethnicity and/or national origin. In addition to the specific details of his study, the broader implications of his work are scrutinized in this section. The presentation of Goddard's work focuses on the use of intelligence tests and generalizations about test scores in relation to races, ethnicities or nationalities in the deportation process at Ellis Island. This includes a discussion of the broader impact of his work and the work of others on Ellis Island.

In terms of social consequences for language-minoritized bilinguals, Goddard did not use intelligence tests to directly inform deportation decisions. Yet the ramifications of his work impacted immigrant communities for decades. Later in his career, he questioned his earlier conclusions, but did not directly address the impact on the experiences of language-minoritized bilinguals. Zenderland summarized how Goddard shifted his views on intelligence as he came to support the more common views that intellectual disabilities were not incurable and that institutionalization was unhelpful. When discussing some of his earlier, stronger views on eugenics, he acknowledged that the links between race and intelligence were 'probably negligible' (Goddard, 1928, cited in Zenderland, 1998: 326). Yet this shift in view was not a dramatic one, as he remained silent on the impact and implications of his work. Zenderland explained that

> In Goddard's brave new world, social as well as genetic engineering would produce both a better society and a more intelligent man [...]. [Yet,] Goddard remained completely unconscious both of his own deep class biases and of the dangerous potential for political totalitarianism within his technocratic, eugenic utopia. (Zenderland, 1998: 330)

Throughout his life, Goddard never directly addressed some of the most egregious links between his work and the gross negative social consequences that many others called into question. Goddard's views on eugenics and sterilization were famously discussed in his 1912 book *The Kallikak Family: A Study in the Heredity of Feeble-mindedness*. In this book, he tracked generations of two families that shared a father of 'normal' intelligence. The man fathered children with his wife, also deemed of normal intelligence, and with a barmaid who was classified as having lower intelligence, as indicated by her profession.

In 1942 he seemingly retracted his retractions by defending his inferences from the study of the Kallikaks. This prompted some of his colleagues to rise to the defense of his work as well, declaring his research to be of noteworthy importance and offering anti-Semitic comments about those who critiqued Goddard's work. Zenderland (1998) summarizes how Lewis Terman and Carl Seashore applauded Goddard's restraint in pushing back against his critics. The overtly anti-Semitic statements came from Charles Davenport, whose links not only to the eugenics movement but also to the Nazi party in Germany have been well explored (Kuhl, 2002). About Goddard's defense of his previous book, Davenport wrote: 'I wonder why it is that people with such names as Abraham Myerson and Amram Scheinfeld should think it necessary to attack so much of the work on heredity?' (1942, as cited in Zenderland, 1998: 332).

In discussing his research on intelligence testing, Goddard stated that he had complete faith in the test itself because results were distributed on a normal bell curve, claiming that the tests 'had validated themselves' (Zenderland, 1998: 122). Thus, he felt that the scores were unchallengeable due to the infallibility of the testing instrument. What is also noteworthy about Goddard is the negligence and poor quality of his research work. It has been well documented that his research methods were highly suspect – he sometimes chose not to administer tests at all and instead made judgments about intelligences based on a person's visual appearance, and also made errors in simple math calculations that went unquestioned during his lifetime (Zenderland, 1998). These glaring issues with his research illustrate how his work served more as '*effective* propaganda' (Fancher, 1985: 114, original emphasis) than anything of substance. And yet his efforts are part of the foundations for the widespread use of intelligence testing in the United States.

Goddard was the head of a school for children with disabilities and gained attention for translating and using a version of the Binet–Simon scale in the United States. In 1910 the Commissioner of Immigration at Ellis Island invited Goddard to Ellis Island to pilot intelligence testing as a method for screening immigrants. In doing so, he used a test designed for children with disabilities with adult immigrants, something many of his contemporaries found to be problematic (Richardson, 2003; Zenderland, 1998). The United States was then passing increasingly anti-immigrant policies, and this work by Goddard at the invitation of the Commissioner of Immigration reflected how intelligence test scores were beginning to be positioned as a mechanism to justify racial discrimination. His first visit to Ellis Island was brief, and he did not conduct any testing research at that time.

In 1913, Goddard began his research on Ellis Island by administering a battery of four intelligence tests to a sample of adults he described as 'average immigrants' (Goddard, 1917: 244). To administer the test, Goddard used trained interpreters for Hungarian, Italian and Russian participants and an interpreter/psychologist for Jewish immigrants using an unspecified language, claiming that the use of these interpreters was sufficient both to retain the validity of the test and to make the content accessible to immigrants (Goddard, 1917). He reported finding that the highest mental age of adult language-minoritized persons was 12 and that 79–83% of those tested had developmental disabilities (Goddard, 1917; see also Gelb, 1986). In the write-up of the findings, his tone – in particular when contrasted with Boody (1926) – is flippant and antagonistic:

> What shall we say of the fact that only 45 per cent can give sixty words in three minutes, when normal children of eleven years sometimes give 200 words in that time! It is hard to find an explanation except lack of intelligence or lack of vocabulary and such a lack of vocabulary in an adult would probably mean lack of intelligence. How could a person live even fifteen years in any environment without learning hundreds of names of which he could certainly think of 60 in three minutes? (Goddard, 1917: 251)

His findings increased the negative attention given to immigrants from southern and eastern Europe, who were viewed as 'degenerate individuals responsible for social problems, that endangered the biological fitness of the nation' (Richardson, 2003: 147). Goddard's work was controversial yet highly influential, in particular because he was the first to translate and use the Binet–Simon scale, and the first to use it to test immigrants. Goddard exploited ideologies around testing, which was being readily accepted as a new science, in order not only to substantiate prevalent discourses discriminating against immigrants, but also to argue for social consequences that promoted eugenics, in particular institutionalization, sterilization and more restrictive immigration policies. Yet, on Ellis Island one of the doctors not only took notice of the intelligence tests that were gaining in popularity, but also worked to develop his own tests specifically for immigrants at Ellis Island.

Howard Knox worked at Ellis Island as an assistant surgeon from 1912 to 1926. It is difficult estimate the effect on eugenics theories of his work on intelligence testing. Although he did present his work at eugenics-themed conferences, he was less publicly vocal about eugenics theories than, for example, Goddard. Knox, like most of the doctors on Ellis Island, was a critic of the work conducted there by Goddard. He took contention with Goddard's approach to intelligence testing, in particular because (1) the Binet–Simon scale was developed for children, (2) on-the-spot language interpretation introduced new information within the test administration and (3) the scale had cultural and linguistic characteristics that were not familiar to many immigrants (Knox, 1913). Knox developed 13 mostly non-verbal performance tests to assess intelligence, which he later made commercially available with C. H. Stoelting Co. of Chicago (Richardson, 2003), thus also establishing a link between businesses and testing.

Knox's Feature Profile Test has gained attention by media outlets based on the work of historian Adam Cohen, who described the test as 'kind of like a smooshed up Mr. Potato Head made out of thin wood, seven pieces, an eye, a nose, a mouth, and then an ear that's broken up into four separate pieces' (see Cornish, 2017). This and his other tests were designed to be language-free and less culturally biased; the tests were first described as culture-free and later as culture-fair. Knox (1913) defined intellectual disability as a biological defect: 'a brain with insufficient ability to solve a problem (without previous training) of the proper complexity for its physical age is a defective one' (Knox, 1913: 1017). His tests often contained what can best be described as puzzle pieces, usually made of wood, that the test-taker had to assemble in a certain amount of time (Richardson, 2011). In understanding the implications of his work for language-minoritized bilinguals, his lack of a particular stand in relation to theories of intelligence and eugenics stands out. His research at times engaged with the eugenics movement, but he did not speak out either in support of or against theories of inherited intelligence. Much like Goddard in his later years, Knox did not engage in discussion about the ramifications of his work, which also meant that the use and misuse of his tests were not readily attributed to him during his lifetime.

At Ellis Island, other doctors were competing with Knox to create screening procedures for intelligence. For example, the test developed by Glueck (1913), for administration to all immigrants, comprised a list of questions and math calculations. Bayor explains how screening questions asked by doctors were problematic forms of intelligence testing:

> Even a seemingly simple question asked of a woman, such as 'How many children do you have?,' could be misunderstood as to indicate that the woman was mentally deficient. For example, did the doctor mean how

many children alive and dead did she have, or how many children did she have with her at the moment, or how many did she have including those still in Europe and already in America? As another example, an inspector asked this question of an Irish immigrant: 'If I gave you two dogs and my friend here gave you one, how many would you have?' The immigrant answered 'four.' When asked the same question in regard to apples, he answered correctly. Asked the question about dogs again, the immigration once again said 'four.' The inspector inquired how could that be, and the immigrant answered, 'Why sure, I've got a dog at home myself,' and that made four. (Bayor, 2014: 54)

When these tests were being developed and used, there was contention between researchers and physicians about which types of tests to use, which Goddard discussed:

> Some users of mental tests, notably Healy and the physicians at Ellis Island, have expressed a strong preference for performance tests as against those involving language. With immigrants this at first glance seems particularly reasonable. We were prepared therefore to find the performance tests used in this study of great value. Inspection of results however, whether we regard the time or the resulting mental level according to the standardizations used, shows clearly that the performance tests as often contradict each other as they contradict the Binet. Apparently then the performance tests have not the great value that has been attached to them. (Goddard, 1917: 260)

The issues with these forms of test, though worth critiquing, reflect internal debates around testing that can obscure discussions of the consequences of test use.

Linking scores on intelligence tests to broad claims about groups of immigrants contributed to discussion about proposed deportation policies and practices. Goddard attributed the increase in deportations in 1913 and 1914 to the employment of intelligence tests on Ellis Island. He explained that the increases were 'due to the untiring efforts of the physicians who were inspired by the belief that mental tests could be used for the detection of feeble-minded aliens' (Goddard, 1917: 271). Table 3.1 and Figure 3.1 indicate the increased deportation rates of immigrants from 1914 to 1920, decreasing after the passage of the Quota Act of 1921 to levels similar to those from 1907 to 1913, when policies first articulated the deportation of immigrants based on intelligence. These data indicate an over-identification of language-minoritized bilinguals with intellectual disabilities.

Summary

The examples of the social consequences of testing at Ellis Island have focused on deportation and contributions to anti-immigrant and racist public opinions about language-minoritized bilinguals. Ellis Island was one of the first locations in the United States to use intelligence testing, and the actual number of people tested and deported was just a small proportion of the total number passing through. Yet the limited results met with widespread acceptance – the implications spread quickly, as intelligence testing took hold in the military (see Chapter 2) and soon thereafter in schools (see Chapter 4). In introducing testing, evidence was provided to support existing racist and anti-immigrant ideologies in public opinion. These discourses were then used to support restrictions on immigration. Both Spolsky (1995) and Snyderman and Herrnstein (1983) have argued that there is no clear evidence that those involved in intelligence testing or the eugenics movement aided in the passage of the extremely restrictive Immigration Act of 1924.

It is also worth noting that those individuals did not have to. Public opinion, at that time, was enough to allow US citizenship to be denied or rescinded on the basis of an individual's race (Haney López, 2006). The economic downturn after World War I solidified anti-immigrant sentiment and led to a push to exclude those who did not assimilate. The data from testing did, however, serve to justify fears about language-minoritized bilinguals. Ellis Island was the birthplace of the broad-reaching implications and social consequences of testing faced by language-minoritized bilinguals.

Angel Island

On the Pacific coast, Angel Island, near San Francisco, California, served as the main entry port from 1910 to 1940 for people predominantly from Asian countries, and especially men from China and women from Japan. The immigration station there screened incoming workers, family members and often women preparing to marry a partner in the United States. Because the records for the island were lost in a fire in 1940, much of the information about the numbers of people who were at Angel Island has been estimated from other sources. The conditions at Angel Island were unsanitary, with limited access to clean water and detainments lasting days, weeks, months or, in some cases, years. The deportation rate has been estimated at one in every six people (Daniels, 1997). Immigration from Asian countries was already restricted when the station opened, and policies became stricter up to its closing. The 1875 Page Act banned Chinese, Japanese and other Asian laborers brought involuntarily and women brought for prostitution. The Chinese Exclusion Act of 1882 further strengthened the ban on individuals from China. The Immigration Act of 1917 expanded the ban from China to include individuals from the 'Asiatic Barred Zone', a region that included Afghanistan, Arabia, Burma, India, the Malay States, parts of Russia, most of the Polynesian Islands and Siam (Lee & Yung, 2010).

The bans were applied broadly and were used to revoke past permissions, uproot established residents and target working-class individuals and women. For laborers, the Supreme Court ruled on the constitutionality of the Exclusion Act in 1889, and ruled in support of the policy. Chae Chan Ping was a laborer from China resident in the United States who left before the passage of the Exclusion Act and was denied re-entry upon his return after the Act was passed. The subsequent court case, *Chae Chan Ping v. United States*, solidified the federal government's power to regulate and enforce immigration law. The ruling conclusively stated that 'Congress's decision to deny entry to non-citizens is "conclusive upon the judiciary"' (Villazor, 2015: 137–138).

Census data indicate the low number of Chinese women in the United States. Between 1870 and 1890, women accounted for only 3.6–7.2% of the US Chinese population. Thereafter, the proportion grew, to 12.6% in 1920 and to 30% in 1940, largely due to the number of Chinese American females born in the United States. Factors other than policies also deterred Chinese women from coming to the United States, including cost and the desire to have children educated in China. In terms of policies, Chan has argued that women were targeted for exclusion using moral, racial and class factors:

> Until the mid 1870s, prostitutes among Chinese women were singled out for exclusion ostensibly for moral reasons. But within the expressions of morality there was a hidden racial – or, more accurately, racist – concern. Lawmakers and law-enforcement officers tried to keep out and control Chinese prostitutes not so much because they were prostitutes as such (since there were also many white prostitutes around plying their trade) but because – as Chinese – they allegedly brought in especially virulent strains of venereal diseases, introduced opium addiction, and enticed young white boys to a life of sin. In short, Chinese prostitutes were seen as potent instruments for the debasement of white manhood, health, morality, and family life. Thus their continued presence was deemed a threat to white civilization. (Chan, 1991: 137–138)

The exclusion policies' distinction between working-class laborers and more wealthy merchants also impacted Chinese women. Chinese working-class women suffered some of the harshest treatment, even if they were themselves or were related to citizens of the United States; the wives of merchants were treated much more favorably (Chan, 1991).

In examining the testing and treatment of immigrants at Angel Island, the role of immigration policies in reinforcing racial discrimination is an essential consideration. The motivation for the use of intelligence testing on Ellis Island – increased restrictions and deportation – was moot, as debarring and deporting immigrants from Asia were easily enforced through subjective interpretations of these policies. Instead, testing was used on Angel Island to restrict entry for individuals who were exempted from policies: children and students.

Children at Angel Island

Much has been written about how children, usually boys, were brought from China – the 'paper sons'. These children came to Angel Island and petitioned for entry as relatives of US citizens of Chinese heritage. After a fire in 1906 in San Francisco, the birth and immigration records of many individuals from China in the United States were destroyed, which in turn meant they were granted citizenship and could then sponsor their children to come to the United States. Such ambiguity in records led many families to create false documents, such as doctored photographs, to claim others' children. Children often memorized coaching books during their journey to Angel Island to prepare them for tests of their family knowledge. The intense questioning was such that the coaching books were seen as equally necessary for those who truly had family members to meet as those who did not.

The nomenclature around these children presents a bevy of additional issues. For instance, the literature refers to both those who had legitimate claims to immigrant status and those with false documents as paper sons or paper children (Barde, 2008; Lee & Yung, 2010; Werner, 2009).

There was no standardized process for screening, and thus the preparation materials or coaching books often did not translate to admission into the United States. In a collection of oral histories, Benjamin Choy explained how he and his paper brother were questioned when preparing to meet their paper parents:

> Before we embarked, at the beginning of the trip, they had sent me a booklet; it was filled with questions and answers. You were supposed to learn from these booklets. So when they would ask, 'Who is your father? Who is your mother? And how old are you?' you would know [...] they called the booklet 'the paper.' It takes a long time to memorize all that. You have to be coached, but they didn't ask me anything from what I was coached! They just asked where I lived, how many rooms there were in my house, and where it was located [...]. What I told the examiner my paper brother would not know, because he came from a different family. So during lunch break, very quickly, I went to inform my paper brother about the facts I told the examiner. He said exactly what I said. [...] I don't know how the examiner could tell we were related, because we came with different photographs. [...] I mean, it was ridiculous, but we got away with it! (Werner, 2009: 128–129)

Choy went on to explain the difficulties of preparing to lie to immigration officials as a 13-year-old boy based on the directions of the adults in his life. Albert Kai Wong[1] described some of his frustrations during his process of questioning when he was 12 years old:

> I was interrogated several times. [...] They asked a lot of stupid questions. I remember at my house in the village we had an orchard. The interrogator

asked me, 'How many steps are there going down?' And I didn't know, I didn't count them. And they said, 'you mean you went up and down there every day and you don't remember?' I said, 'you go up and down the stairs here every day. You tell me how many steps there are.' And they cracked up, laughing. (Werner, 2009: 132)

Wong's memories of the questioning on Angel Island speak to the level of specificity in questioning meant to find errors or inconsistencies.

Furthermore, inspectors on Angel Island openly admitted to questioning Chinese immigrant in order to deport more. Lee and Yung explained how an officer was blunt in describing his intention behind questioning the children: 'many of the questions in the interrogations were "not material to the point at issue" but were necessary "to throw [the Chinese] out"' (Lee & Yung, 2010: 86). The Commissioner of Immigration in San Francisco admitted that examiners were ' "reluctant to accept defeat" and would reexamine applicants and witnesses on "every conceivable point" until they had found a discrepancy' (Lee & Yung, 2010: 86).

In addition to questioning the newly arrived children, their relatives residing in the United States were also examined to find inconsistencies in their stories. Jamie Louie arrived at Angel Island when he was 11. His uncle and cousin were also questioned when they came to collect him. When their stories did not agree, he describes the efforts taken by his uncle to get him admitted:

I was questioned three different times. [...] They also always questioned the paper father (my uncle) and my paper brother (my cousin) as witnesses. Whatever was not written down beforehand, whatever was not prearranged, then the answers you gave wouldn't be the same among the three of you. We didn't match up.

They were going to deport me. My paper father (who had been in the United States before) appealed to the court. It cost him a hundred dollars; he had to bribe the immigration officials through a Chinese go-between. Finally, I was admitted. (Werner, 2009: 130–131)

The policies that highly restricted the entrance of immigrants created a situation where small exemptions in the policies were exploited by immigrants, who, notably, did not have other options to enter the United States. The social consequences of being deported – and effectively barred from entry since there were not many other means to be allowed in the country – were extreme repercussions of these examinations. The fact that those who were legitimately using the policy also needed to prepare for these interrogations points to how this form of testing was employed to restrict the numbers of immigrants from China. The second exemption described in this chapter concerns students from Asian countries, who were specifically targeted for additional testing.

University students at Angel Island

Students were an exempted class in the restrictive policies on immigration. Students admitted to US universities needed to present paperwork showing acceptance and proof of financial support. Yung and Lee (2015) note that for non-Asian immigrants at Angel Island, the process was relatively straightforward, even when there needed to be a detainment. They describe how three Russian students, who spent three months on Angel Island in 1923 waiting for entrance due to the quota laws, had a comfortable experience, which included separate quarters from Asian immigrants. That difference in treatment was also realized in testing practices. Although there is limited information about the testing of students seeking entry to US universities from Angel Island, Lee and Yung (2010) present a case of 11 students from Korea who were asked to take math, English, history and geography tests to prove their student status.

The situation of Korean immigrants at Angel Island was unique, as many arrived as refugees living in China, having escaped from Korea during the period of Japanese rule, 1910–1945. Because of Japanese restrictions on providing passports to individuals from Korea, most traveled not only without passports, visas or any documentation of their student status, but also under assumed names, to avoid detention by Japanese officials. The Korean National Association (KNA) in the United States supported many of these refugee students, including paying for medical treatments, providing interpreters or representation in court appeals, while also publicizing the immigration process to Koreans who wanted to travel to the United States, through newspapers such as *Sinhan Minbo* (Lee & Yung, 2010; Nahm, n.d.).

After fears had been raised that the number of Koreans entering as students was increasing with no signs of stopping, and that the KNA was providing 'show money' to prove financial stability, immigration officials instituted additional English and academic content tests to incoming refugee students. Oh Wan Hyung, Lee You Jung, Cho Pyung Mook, In Dyuk Chang, Kiel In Young, Pyung Pong Chick, Chai Il Myung, Kim Kay Chang, Kim Chin Young, Bo Wang So and Lee Hong Nai are the 11 students from Korea who arrived at Angel Island in 1916. They were given a missionary interpreter (rather than an interpreter from the KNA) and were administered English, math, history and geography tests. In Lee and Yung's (2010: 192) description, 'one failed the mathematics test, another failed the history test, and only two of the students could speak English'. The students were repeatedly questioned about finances, and in the end only one, Kiel In Young, was granted admission into the United States, due to his recommendation letters. Nine were deported for not showing they had financial support, and one, Lee Hong Nai, for being suspected of being a laborer, because of the conditions of his hands. In the appeal process, another student, Kim Chin Young, had a brother-in-law who came to show financial support. But after they were questioned – similar to the 'paper children' described above – the discrepancies in their stories led to Kim's ultimate deportation (Lee & Yung, 2010).

After all but one of these 11 students were deported, fewer Koreans made the decision to immigrate to the United States as students. And, due to pressure from Japan, the United States added a passport requirement in 1918, effectively ending the immigration of Korean refugee students. It was not until the Immigration Act of 1924 that students from Korea began arriving again (Lee & Yung, 2010).

The use of testing with these 11 students impacted the standing of the students' claim of student status. Yet, ultimately the tests were not used to support the decisions for deportation, as finances were stated as the rationale. What the experiences of these 11 men illustrate, however, is that when officials were beginning actively to turn against the KNA and Korean immigration, they also turned to tests to help support their case. The role of testing, though small in this case, was part of a larger concern to create an image of Korean refugee students as making fraudulent claims.

Summary

Testing was present in limited ways on Angel Island, and the social consequences of test use were felt most clearly with the interrogations of children. Intensive procedures were put in place with the purpose of restricting the numbers of incoming children, so much so that the title 'paper son' was the default name used to refer to all child immigrants, including those who had family in the United States. The case of testing of the Korean refugee students, though not common, illustrates how testing was introduced for the purpose of restricting immigration when other methods had failed. Ultimately, the uncompromising approach to implementing policies on immigrants from Asian countries proved effective in restricting immigration, making testing much less necessary for such purposes.

Discussion

The two major immigration stations, Ellis Island and Angel Island, provide examples of how testing interacts with policies and public opinion. Comparisons of the role of testing and the social consequences of test use indicate that across both ports of entry testing worked in conjunction with other mechanisms to marginalize language-minoritized bilinguals.

The interrogations of children on Angel Island stand out as egregious evaluations of children. Immigration officials treated all children as though they were making illegitimate claims and even after the fact, children who were making true claims to support their entry have largely also been grouped with those who were not, by also being referred to as 'paper sons'.

The ethical questions that such test use raises point to the dehumanizing racial discrimination against children. On Ellis Island, children were also put in stressful situations to take intelligence tests. Yet they had a school, and possible advocates at the school. Though the role of the school staff as advocates is not well documented, the existence of such services is a stark contrast with the situation on Angel Island.

The immediate impact of intelligence testing of adults on Ellis Island shows in an increase in the percentage of deportations from 1914 to 1920 in comparison with 1913 to 1917. Though the number of deportations decreased over time, the increases in percentages indicate proportionally increased consequences of test use. At Angel Island, formalized testing was used minimally with adults. The example of the Korean refugee students illustrates how testing was added to making a decision about deportation, and was part of a case that marked the downturn in Korean refugee students coming to the United States. Yet, given that decisions were based on other ways of supporting deportation, specifically financial support, those tests seem to have had limited impact. The interrogation of Kim, akin to the treatment of many Chinese children, however, points to how tests served as a mechanism by officials at Angel Island for deportation.

In looking to broader implications, the use of these tests interacted with policies and public opinion. The continued expansion of testing may have occurred with or without the use of tests at these immigration stations. Yet, in tracing how the use of these tests continued to impact language-minoritized bilinguals in the United States, they lay the groundwork for developing a culture that is comfortable using testing as a mechanism within immigration.

Note

(1) Wong's story was written in the children's book *Kai's Journey to Gold Mountain* (Currier, 2004).

Part 2: Educational Trends

Part 2 provides an overview of educational events leading up to and informing the social consequences of testing for language-minoritized bilinguals seeking K-12 and higher education opportunities in the United States. The emphasis on K-12 policies is seen as necessary as myriad events merit discussion. Comprehensive reviews of educational policies for language-minoritized bilinguals have been undertaken by scholars in the fields of applied linguistics and bilingual education (e.g. Crawford, 2002; García, 2009; Wiley, 1998; Wright, 2005). Similar to these previous works, Part 2 focuses on education policies after 1965, though it also includes brief overviews of major court cases impacting education prior to 1965.

Early Court Cases About Language Education

Nebraska presents a case of extreme shifts in educational policies: in only six years the state move from mandating support for the use of students' home languages in schools (e.g. German) to outright banning them. The 1913 Mocklett law 'required authorities to inaugurate foreign language instruction on an elective basis in urban schools if the parents or guardians of fifty pupils above the fourth grade requested it' (Luebke, 1968: 117). The law was upheld in 1916 by the Nebraska Supreme Court (Luebke, 1968). Yet as World War I intensified, Americanization policies began to influence state-level policies. The Nebraska State Council of Defense publicized the names of foreign-born residents in 1918, in particular those from Germany, to increase scrutiny of these individuals. In 1919 the state legislature banned instruction in languages other than English in private schools. A teacher at a Lutheran school, Robert T. Meyer, continued to teach religion using German as the medium of instruction and was arrested and fined. In challenging the law, his case reached the US Supreme Court. In 1923, the Court ruled in *Meyer v. Nebraska* that it was unlawful to prohibit teaching children in any language other than English. Citing the 14th Amendment, the ruling sated that not only was it within the rights of the teacher to teach in a language other than English – in this case German – but also that it was within the rights of the parents to make decisions about language for their child's upbringing. This included protecting parents and communities who organized language instruction outside of public schools, while also maintaining the right of the government to determine the medium of instruction inside public schools (Del Valle, 2003; Menken, 2008). In describing the prejudicial motivations for the language ban, the lawyer in the case, Arthur Mullen, concluded his closing statements with these telling comments:

> the nations who used prohibitions [sic] laws and verboten signs to limit and deny the rights of their citizens passed out of existence the most odious form of prohibition appeared in the United States under the guise of 'language prohibition.' [...] This intolerant act grew out of the hatred, national bigotry and racial prejudice engendered by World War. (Cited in Hanley, 1969: 155)

In reading transcripts of Mullen's arguments to the Supreme Court from the 1920s, what is particularly striking is how much of what he says resonates today. Often, historical evidence is presented as representative of a specific time or place, and also often to minimize xenophobic, racist and other prejudicial discourses. Yet Mullen's statement shows how during this time people also spoke out against 'bigotry and racial prejudice' in laws that target bilingual language use and language-minoritized bilinguals.

During this period, educational policies also were enacted to impact Japanese-speakers in Hawaii. In 1925 and again in 1943, the legislature in Hawaii enacted policies designed to restrict instruction in foreign languages. The Supreme Court overturned the policy in 1927 with *Farrington v. Tokushige* and in 1947 with *Mo Hock Ke Lok Po v. Stainback*. In both cases, the Court emphasized that these policies would ostensibly make illegal all education delivered in a foreign or second language. As with the case in Nebraska, the Court ruled against these policies because they limited parents' choice in deciding how (and in which language) their child would be educated (Del Valle, 2003).

Beginning in the late 1960s, state-level policies and legislation gave way to a much more active role of the federal government in creating policies specifically for language-minoritized bilinguals in K-12 schools, especially in the development of the Department of Education, Elementary and Secondary Education Act of 1965, and the Bilingual Education Act of 1968.

Legislation on Bilingual Education

The increased focus on the educational attainment of language-minoritized bilinguals coincided with the development of the US Department of Education and the passage of the Elementary and Secondary Education Act of 1965. The National Education Agency (NEA) played a key role in drawing attention to the educational attainment of language-minoritized bilinguals, which led to the creation of federal oversight and funding for bilingual education programs with the Bilingual Education Act of 1968 (BEA, Title VII of the Elementary and Secondary Education Act). The passage of the Act and the subsequent reauthorizations reflected wavering support for and changing definitions of bilingual education.

The BEA has its origins in a strong focus on Mexicans or Mexican Americans. The board members at the NEA analyzed of the 1960 census data on achievement inequalities within US public schools among the self-reported categories of whites and Mexican Americans. In this analysis, the NEA referred to the Mexican American students as Spanish-surnamed students and focused primarily on this group of emergent bilinguals. The NEA reported that white students averaged approximately nine more years of education than Spanish-surnamed students (Schissel, 2009).

In 1966, the NEA held a conference in Tucson, Arizona, which addressed these findings from the census data to make policy changes for Spanish-surnamed students in US public schools. Publicizing this inequity helped to protect the rights of all emergent bilingual students to education (Moran, 1988; Schissel, 2009; Wright, 2005). Senator Ralph Yarborough, a Democrat from Texas, was invited by the NEA to attend, and at the conclusion of the conference he became a vocal proponent of bilingual education. Following the conference, he began work on legislation to help raise the academic achievement of students who did not have high proficiency in English. Senator Yarborough served as the chief sponsor of S. 428, an amendment to the Elementary and Secondary Education Act, better known as Title VII, the Bilingual Education Act. The BEA introduced new perspectives in educational policy, changing pedagogical approaches to meet the needs of emergent bilingual students (Crawford, 1998, 2002; Schissel, 2009). Language-minoritized bilingual students who fell into this classification were first referred to as 'limited English speakers' in the policy. In 1978 the label changed to 'limited English proficient' (Wright, 2005).

During the debate over the BEA, there were factors both inside and outside education affecting the reach of the Act. To meet the linguistic needs of language-minoritized bilingual students, top-down federal policies such as the BEA were enacted. The BEA followed the trends of changing orientations in educational policy set by the ESEA, which challenged and questioned state and local education agency decisions, ultimately giving more control to federal education policies (Crawford, 1998; Moran, 1988). During the Congressional hearings for the BEA, Senator Yarborough made this explicit when he pointed out the faults of the states to meet the needs of emergent bilingual students: '[w]e [Texans] have been doing less to see that our Spanish-surnamed citizens got a fair education' (Congressional Record, 1967: 325, as cited in Schissel, 2009). The way in which language-minoritized bilingual students were included in schools and given access to education was through the federal funding of bilingual education programs. In the initial 1968 passage of the Act, bilingual education models and evaluation of the programs' effectiveness were not specified. The 1968 BEA did not provide much guidance to local or state education agencies.

Each reauthorization of the BEA in 1974, 1978, 1984, 1988, 1994 – including the end of the BEA in 2002 with the passage of the No Child Left Behind Act – reflected changing orientations to and public support for bilingualism. In 1974, the reauthorization added legislation on models of bilingual education. This reauthorization provided support for bilingual education, which in turn would allow emergent bilinguals to 'progress effectively through the educational system [using] the native language' (Sec 703[a][4][A][i]). However promising such language may have seemed for providing language-minoritized bilingual students with education in languages other than English, the reauthorization did not allow funding for the maintenance of bilingualism (Wright, 2005).

After this reauthorization, additional guidelines from *Lau v. Nichols* in 1974 and the Lau Remedies in 1975 were put in place that supported language-minoritized bilingual students. The 1974 *Lau v. Nichols* ruling clarified that providing language-minoritized bilingual students with the same instruction afforded to English monolingual students did not constitute fair or equitable education. And in conjunction with the US Office of Civil Rights, these rulings led to the Lau Remedies in 1975, which outlined key requirements to meet the educational and linguistic needs of language-minoritized bilingual students (Crawford, 1998, 2002; Menken, 2008; Wright, 2005). The Lau Remedies also began to address fairness in assessment, in that they called for schools to have professionals trained in the assessment of students in both English and their home language, in addition to training in cognitive and motivational learning styles (Baker & de Kanter, 1983).

In 1974 the reauthorization of the BEA had called for research projects to determine the effectiveness of bilingual education programs. Two influential studies were conducted following this that greatly shaped the 1978 reauthorization. The American Institutes for Research (AIR) and the Comptroller General of the US Government Accountability Office provided findings that clearly did not support the continued use of bilingual education. Congress members used the reports of both studies as program evaluations to inform the direction of the 1978 reauthorization. The reports played a major role due to the lack of other large-scale evaluations of bilingual education programs.

The AIR study that was presented to Congress was conducted during the 1977–1978 academic year and contrasted two groups of students in grades 2–6: those in Spanish/English bilingual programs and those with a comparable background receiving English-only instruction. It was the fourth report in a series on the impact of bilingual education. Although the previous study conducted by AIR in the 1975–1976 academic year had concluded that 'Title VII Hispanic students [...] performed better in Mathematics computation than would have been expected in the absence of a program' (Danoff, 1978: 7), this favorable tone was absent in the Congressional hearings. The final report concluded that there were no discernable differences between the students enrolled in bilingual education and those not, in terms of their scores on the mathematics exam and in comprehension of English, but that the students in English-only classrooms scored higher on the English language exam. The report was also critical of the cost of bilingual education. It stated that bilingual education yielded little benefit, in contrast to the academic achievements seen with the lower-cost English-only education. Limitations of the AIR study, addressed by Crawford (2002), include the fact that around two-thirds of the students in the English-only classrooms had previously been in bilingual programs.

The US Government of Accountability Office conducted a smaller study, looking at 16 bilingual programs that were making progress but scoring below national norms. Its report, titled *Bilingual Education: An Unmet Need* (Controller General of the Unites States, 1976), pointed to limitations such as a lack of trained bilingual education teachers. Although the study found that student achievement was not meeting national norms, the report interpreted these findings as the result of in-appropriate assessments of student achievement and language proficiency. It called for the creation of

> (1) specific project goals consistent with the intent of title VII and (2) clear, measurable performance objectives to achieve the goals. To be consistent with program intent, project goals and objectives should address the levels of progress desired for the participants in English proficiency and academic achievement in both English and the other language.

It further said there was a need to examine

> the appropriateness of testing instruments available for children with limited English-speaking ability and, if needed, take action to have better ones developed at the earliest possible date. (Controller General of the Unites States, 1976: 42, 43)

Following the recommendations of these reports and other testimony, the reauthorization of 1978 reflected a backlash against bilingual educational programs. The reauthorization added language focusing on developing English proficiency and transitional English programs, and this increased the attention given to evaluation and assessment systems. The subsequent reauthorizations continued to support English transitional programs, but in 1984 and 1988 the reauthorizations moved away from the need for what would be defined as an effective program in a broad sense, and instead allowed for communities to develop special programs that met the needs of language-minoritized bilingual students in their schools (Crawford, 2002; Menken, 2008; Wright, 2005).

At the state level, there has been mixed reception of bilingual education. In the late 1990s and early 2000s, state initiatives in California, Massachusetts and Arizona banned bilingual education and promoted English-only education. However, at the same time, efforts were being taken to expand heritage language programs such as Spanish for Spanish speakers (Hornberger, 2005). In 2016, California passed proposition 58, which brought back bilingual education in schools. Massachusetts similarly repealed its ban in 2017. It is within this somewhat bifurcated climate that testing has come to take a central role in K-12 education, in particular for language-minoritized bilinguals. Before discussing the federal policy changes introduced by the No Child Left Behind Act of 2001 (NCLB) and the most recent policy, the Every Student Succeeds Act (ESSA, 2015), the next section discusses a key critique of bilingual education, namely the ways in which bilingual education was seen as a form of segregation in schools.

Bilingual Education and Segregation

Holding educators accountable for providing support in languages other than English while also having language-minoritized bilinguals in mainstream classrooms proved challenging for bilingual educators. The ruling from *Brown v. Board of Education* and the Civil Rights Act of 1964 ended school segregation and criminalized discrimination based on race, ethnicity, religion and national origin. Although language was not explicitly listed, language-minoritized bilinguals were protected against segregation and discriminatory practices by these policies. Holding educational institutions accountable for meeting these definitions of equity in relation to inclusion and access had a mixed reception in bilingual education.

Legislation had been used to segregate language-minoritized bilinguals in schools before the 1968 BEA. Japanese students were placed in separate schools from the 1900s (Hing, 2004), as were Latino students (see *Independent School District v. Salvatierra*, 1930). Yet not all language-minoritized bilinguals felt integration was their best educational option after the passage of the BEA. In San Francisco, the Chinese community fought desegregation in 1971 with *Guey Heung Lee v. Johnson* on the grounds that their culture and language could not be maintained if language-minoritized bilinguals were educated in a different community. The Supreme Court ultimately denied the option to remain separated and further elaborated that bilingual education classes in general should not 'create, maintain, or foster segregation' (U.S. 1217, p. 404). Also in 1971, *United States v. Texas* required bilingual and bicultural faculty and curriculum to foster positive relations among Latinos and Anglo-Americans after desegregation. These programs were meant to aid Latino students by helping them address and overcome any culture or linguistic shock and for Anglo-American students to understand and appreciate the culture and language of Latino students (Sneeringer, 1974).

In Colorado in 1973, *Keyes v. School District Number One* asked Denver schools to address segregation. Schools with student populations that were mostly Latino and African American were seen as educationally inferior to the schools in areas of the city with predominately white student populations. The ruling expanded beyond the desegregation of African American students to include Latino bilinguals by clarifying that the ruling from *Brown v. Board of Education* did not apply to blacks alone (National Archives, 2016).

Combined, these cases show strong judicial support for desegregation at the school and district level for language-minoritized bilinguals. Segregation has continued to be debated not just for language-minoritized bilinguals, but for school populations nationwide. A survey by the US Government Accountability Office (2016) reported growing segregation of Latino and African American student populations. Comparing enrollment data from 2000–2001 with data from 2013–2014, the report documented that the percentage of concentrated high enrollment of these minority groups grew from 9% to 16 % of schools. This racial segregation also correlated with socio-economic status: most racially segregated schools were classified as 'high poverty', where high poverty is defined as 75–100% of students qualifying for free or subsidized lunch. School districts have implemented a variety of measures to reduce segregation, but with limited results, and the Government Accountability Office recommends continued data tracking and monitoring by the Department of Justice.

Federal Policy Shifts with NCLB and ESSA

The two most notable changes with the passage of NCLB were: (1) replacing the BEA with Title III: English Language Acquisition, Language Enhancement, and Academic Achievement Act; and (2) inclusion of language-minoritized bilinguals in annual testing for academic content and English proficiency. What is important to note is that the changes in the testing of language-minoritized bilinguals was largely led by the policy shifts with NCLB. Previous federal policies, starting with the Improving America's Schools Act (IASA, 1994), had mandates for including language-minoritized bilinguals in testing, but many states created exemptions for these students. Notably, this systematic exemption of language-minoritized bilinguals helped to lay the groundwork for NCLB (Kopriva, 2008; Rivera & Collum, 2006). Thus, NCLB intensified the testing mandates of the IASA.

When NCLB became law, however, many states did not have a plan drafted to include language-minoritized bilingual students in standardized testing. Additionally, most states had faltered in developing tests that met the federal guidelines set forth in the IASA. While NCLB was being written, only 11 states had federally approved assessment systems (Rigney *et al.*, 2008). Testing of language-minoritized bilinguals remained an issue that states did not know how to address. ABC News reported this: 'students learning English [...] were an afterthought when the No Child Left Behind law was being written' (Zuckerbrod, 2007). Thus, different sources point to the problem that the policy of NCLB was put in place before researchers and state education agencies knew how to implement it appropriately.

The development of standards during this time – though not part of NCLB – was in response to the Race to the Top initiative, which provided funding for states to create plans to emphasize college and career readiness in education. After initial discussions and meetings starting in 2007, in 2009 various state leaders from 48 states, two territories and Washington, DC, began the process of developing the Common Core State Standards (CCSS). Race to the Top assessment grants from the US Department of Education led to the development of two testing consortia that would create content tests in mathematics and language arts based on the CCSS (Common Core State Standards Initiative, n.d.).

Under NCLB and moving into ESSA, the education and testing measures for language-minoritized bilinguals have continued to be an area of focus. Rather than the emphasis on program models in BEA, changes to NCLB and ESSA have largely concerned the ways in which testing is used. For example, NCLB allowed for newly arrived language-minoritized bilinguals to be exempted during their first year in US schools from taking an English language arts annual standardized achievement test. It also provided additional monitoring, for the first two years, of students who had exited ESL programs by using test scores to identify an 'English learner' subgroup. NCLB specified that all four language domains (speaking, listening, reading and writing) needed to be tested annually if student gains in English language proficiency were to be documented.

ESSA has changed terminology, so that 'language-minoritized bilinguals' are referred to as 'English learners' rather than 'limited English proficient students'. In terms of testing, much remains the same in terms of annual testing of content areas and English proficiency. Some notable changes, however, relate to the choices that states have in their approach to testing recently arrived language-minoritized bilinguals. For one option, states may exempt the students from content testing in English language arts and mathematics as well as English proficiency. Then, in the students' second year, they must take all of these tests and their scores are reported with respect to a predetermined scale that is used for accountability purposes. For the second option, states give language-minoritized bilinguals tests of content and English proficiency in their first year, and then their scores are reported in terms of the growth in scores from year 1 to year 2 (Linquanti & Cook, 2017). For reclassified language-minoritized bilinguals, their test scores can still be aggregated with the scores of the classified 'English learners' for 0–4 years for accountability purposes. In terms of bilingual testing options, in certain states language-minoritized bilinguals continue to be able to take content tests in a language other than English if they have been in US schools for less than three years, and may be able to have access to tests in this other language for two additional years if that is seen as more illustrative of their learning. ESSA has intensified the provision of language proficiency testing, putting it under greater scrutiny by placing it under Title I in federal policy, which includes holding states accountable for reporting how many students attain English proficiency or are reclassified (Llosa *et al.*, 2016; Wright, 2016).

However, the ways in which these test scores were used in school, district and statewide accountability measures has changed more drastically. States have some additional flexibility in determining which indicators of learning progress can be submitted annually as evidence of growth. They must still include both content and English language proficiency test scores, but ESSA places less weight on test scores because the policy has added two criteria: one additional academic factor, such as graduation rates, and one non-academic factor, such as school safety (Llosa *et al.*, 2016; Wright, 2016).

Another change with ESSA is the increased attention to classification and reclassification and the role of testing in making these decisions. States must now report their procedures for classification and reclassification, and must also document how many students are being reclassified each year. States must also begin to report how many 'English learners' have been identified as having disabilities (Llosa *et al.*, 2016; Wright, 2016). The implications of these changes will reveal themselves over time. Most state-level plans were reviewed by the US Department of Education during the summer of 2017.

Summary

As testing developed nationally, it seemed almost inevitable that it would expand to become prominent in the education of language-minoritized bilinguals. Although policies still often discuss merely allowing bilingual education at the state level, at the federal level the focus has been on increasing the number and variety of tests. The greater attention given to the education of language-minoritized bilinguals is defined by this increase in testing.

4 Seeking Education in K-12 Schools

Testing in K-12 schools is common for all students, yet the situation differs for language-minoritized bilingual children. Intelligence testing was first developed in France to identify children with disabilities. In the United States, these tests were first used with adults for a variety of purposes related to immigration and the military, and then were quickly adapted for use in with children in schools. The performance of language-minoritized bilingual children on intelligence tests was used to identify their disability status in school. The applicability of these tests for language-minoritized bilinguals has persistently been linked to both the over- and the under-identification of language-minoritized bilinguals' disability status. In addition to using these test results to inform decisions around disability status, performance on intelligence tests was used to make broad claims not only about children's intelligence, but also about the intelligence of their parents and other language-minoritized bilinguals with similar national origins and language, racial or ethnic backgrounds. Intergenerational application of test performance, that is to say using children's scores to make inferences or inform decisions about the treatment of their parents and other adults, introduces severe social consequences of testing: restrictive immigration policies and forced sterilization.

For content and English proficiency tests, the social consequences of performances on these tests connect with access to educational services, which then link to high school graduate rates, pathways to higher education and different career opportunities. Largely, however, intelligence testing, content area testing and English proficiency testing are used to make decisions about the teaching and learning opportunities made available to language-minoritized bilinguals. Across all these forms of testing, additionally, is an erasure of the bilingualism that these children have, and of how that could be utilized in schools. To understand the erasure of bilingualism in K-12 schools, this chapter begins with an overview of educational trends and policies developed for language-minoritized bilinguals.

Intelligence Testing

Intelligence testing in K-12 schools has played a prominent role since the inception of intelligence tests. As stated in the Introduction, the first tests were designed in France for children with disabilities, then used with children with disabilities in the United States by Goddard, who subsequently applied these tests to adult immigrants. The development of large-scale intelligence testing began with the Army Alpha and Beta, and Frederick J. Kelly's multiple-choice format created an efficient method of evaluating intelligence. These approaches, combined with 'culture-free' or 'culture-fair' approaches, or performance-based, largely non-verbal tests started by Knox on Ellis Island and others, coalesced to create evaluations of students that, though often questioned, were readily accepted. The analyses of results from individual students were used to draw conclusions or generalizations about groups of people based on race, ethnicity and language, which had ramifications for the children taking the tests and their families as well.

In the 1920s, researchers using intelligence testing began to move from explicitly talking about race to discussing national origin and language. Kirkpatrick, for example, framed his study of intelligence and the children of immigrants in Massachusetts in relation to national origin and non-English language use because 'the concept of race is vague at the present time and most peoples are racially very much mixed' (Kirkpatrick, 1926: 53). In summarizing the debates by researchers from the 1920s to the 1950s about intelligence testing of language-minoritized bilingual children and their low scores, Hakuta (1986) explains how researchers remained steadfast in their conclusions that the tests were indeed detecting a lower intelligence, because of either inherited intelligence or what was referred to at the time as 'the language handicap'. For those who felt that intelligence was inherited, and therefore language was not a factor, he explains that they claimed that 'even if the language handicap does impede performance, that does not belie the validity of the tests, because the language handicap is itself a result, rather than a cause, of inferior intelligence' (Hakuta, 1986: 27).

For Kirkpatrick and others who continued to posit that intelligence was an inherited trait, test results were not just about the children, and he argued the results were indicative of broader immigration trends:

> The differences between the immigrant stocks themselves are significant as suggesting that mental inferiority to American children is not merely environmental in origin. [...] the writer is inclined to the view that probably the effect of immigration from 1900 on has been to lower the level of American intelligence. (Kirkpatrick, 1926: 107)

His research was conducted with the children of immigrants, many of whom were born in the United States. The design of his study, premised on the assumption that intelligence is inherited, raised the stakes and social consequences of these children's performances on these exams from decisions that impacted their educational trajectories to immigration policies.

In what follows, I explore how language-minoritized bilingual children's lives have been shaped by taking intelligence tests. It begins with the more immediate consequences of limited educational and vocational opportunities through these children's over- and under-representation in disability services as a result of their scores on intelligence tests. I then turn to how children's intelligence test scores were one of several factors used to support immigration restrictions and the sterilization of language-minoritized bilinguals, what I describe as intergenerational social consequences of tests. This problematic positioning of language-minoritized bilingual children's test performances in relation to larger conclusions about immigration and reproduction rights presents as a grossly unethical use of test scores that merits closer examination, despite the limits of data currently available.

Disability diagnoses and services

Intelligence testing in schools is done for the purported practical purposes of identifying intellectual differences among learners to determine who may need additional or alternative teaching methods. These tests identify not only those with disabilities, but also those of above-average intelligence, according to the test scores. Data about how or how many language-minoritized bilinguals are identified on either end of this continuum remain scant. In the early 2000s, around the passage of NCLB, when language-minoritized bilingual children were becoming more of a priority at the federal level, language-minoritized bilingual children with disabilities also were gaining more national attention, including how testing was used for identification or reclassification procedures. Yet schools and districts had not been required to report data on language-minoritized bilinguals with disabilities until the passage of ESSA in 2015. As such, some of the most comprehensive historical information rests on the efforts of individual families who brought cases against school districts using policies such as the Bilingual Education Act of 1968 and the Education of the Handicapped Act of 1966 (which was amended to the All Handicapped Children's Act of 1975) and the Rehabilitation Act of 1973. In doing so, they contested the consequences of intelligence testing in schools, namely being over-identified with learning disabilities or have learning disabilities ignored through under-identification (August & Hakuta, 1997; Valdés & Figueroa, 1994). Information about language-minoritized bilinguals being over- or under-identified as having above-average intelligence points almost overwhelmingly to under-representation of language-minoritized bilinguals in these programs (US Department of Education, 2015).

Language-minoritized bilingual children in US public schools commonly took intelligence tests for identification for special education and gifted programs. In the late 1960s, language-minoritized bilingual children took intelligence tests that were administered in English, with inconsistent use of interpreters. These students generally performed poorly on such tests, which led to them being over-represented in special education programs. These low scores are not surprising, however, as the tests were not designed for multilingual students and privileged monolingual perspectives (Baca & Cervantes, 2004). Yet exclusion from testing presented the opposite problem – that language-minoritized bilinguals with disabilities were not identified, and were thus under-represented in special education.

State courts are where language-minoritized bilinguals began to challenge the consequences of their performance on intelligence tests. The rulings in these cases centered on creating additional or alternative assessment processes for identifying disabilities in language-minoritized children, such as classroom performance and teachers' observations, but the rulings had little impact on the development of holistic assessment systems for language-minoritized children (Baca & Cervantes, 2004; for detailed descriptions of such court cases, see Valdés & Figueroa, 1994). Overall, the decisions resulting from the court cases supported the inclusion of these children in testing, while also trying to introduce tests that could be more applicable to, though not necessarily developed specifically for, language-minoritized bilinguals. Looking more specifically at the court cases illustrates how the challenges to negative test consequences resulted in new tests, and repeated similar consequences.

With *Arreola v. Santa Ana Board of Education* (1968), *Diana v. State Board of Education* (1970) and *Covarrubias v. San Diego Unified School District* (1971), plaintiffs challenged the over-representation of language-minoritized bilinguals in special education programs. The ruling from the *Diana* case added visually based, as opposed to verbally based, tests and stipulated that schools needed to collect data from multiple sources rather than relying heavily on one test score (Baca & Cervantes, 2004; Valdés & Figueroa, 1994). Following these rulings, the next set of petitions to the courts addressed the inverse issue: that few, if any, language-minoritized bilinguals were being identified as having disabilities. To address the under-representation, two cases in 1979 advocated for language-minoritized bilinguals with disabilities who were being denied services: *Jose P. v. Amback* and *Dyrcia S. et al. v. Board of the City of New York et al.* The cases in 1979 clarified procedures for identifying disabilities in language-minoritized bilingual children. The following recommendations were to be implemented to the extent possible by local school districts: (1) identification of children with outreach and bilingual resources; (2) bilingual, non-discriminatory evaluation with school-based teams in a supportive environment; (3) placement in appropriate programs, in the least restrictive environment (following the Education for All Handicapped Children Act); and (4) due process and the support of parental and student rights via facilitating community and parent participation in evaluating and determining an individualized educational program (Baca & Cervantes, 2004; Valdés & Figueroa, 1994). The issue of how to evaluate and understand language-minoritized bilingual children's potential disabilities drew attention from bilingual education advocates, who set out to make sense of the intelligence test results in relation to language learning.

In Canada and California, Cummins investigated how teachers and administrators interpreted intelligence tests scores from language-minoritized bilingual children. Cummins (1979) closely examined the test results and reports of approximately 400 children who were recommended for special education services in Canada. The teachers often reported cases of students who had high proficiency in contexts when they answered questions orally and in conversations but who struggled with writing. They saw this discrepancy in students' performances as a possible indicator of a cognitive disability. Cummins (1979, 1981b) used these findings to develop theories about language learning, such as the distinction between social and academic language skills and uses, and later a four-quadrant model that describes language use in schools in terms of the context embeddedness of the cognitive demands (Cummins, 2000). Cummins's work has a continued legacy in the education and testing of language-minoritized bilingual children more generally, with continued emphasis on academic language proficiency.

It is worth noting the critiques of these theories as oversimplifying bilingualism (Valdés, 2004) because 'language skills cannot be neatly compartmentalized' (Martin-Jones & Romaine, 1986: 29). Though there are limitations to Cummins's work, when looking at testing this perspective aids in understanding how views of language as compartmentalized are related to the social consequences of tests, in that tests serve as a reflection and reproduction of these perspectives on bilingualism. Though not in these exact same terms, Cummins has defended his previous work by explaining that these concepts help to clarify 'how schools construct academic failure among subordinate groups' (Cummins, 2008: 78), which in turn highlights the consequences that language-minoritized bilingual children face because of their performance on tests. Cummins has argued that intelligence tests specifically 'not only fail to sample the culturally-specific skills and knowledge of the minority child, they frequently penalize children for demonstrating this knowledge' (Cummins, 1986: 196). This insight about the social consequences language-minoritized bilingual children face in having their knowledge or understanding either erased or demonstrated in tests illustrates aspects of assessing and identifying disabilities in language-minoritized bilinguals that are absent from new efforts to create tests for this same purpose.

Sustained issues in disabilities identification for language-minoritized children illustrate how social consequences from these previous court cases remain relevant today, that is to say, over- and under-representation in special education programs remain an issue in schools. In addition, recent research has described the pattern of over- and under-representation as being more as indicative of the number of language-minoritized bilinguals in schools and districts than of the test methods used. When looking at the proportions nationally, a study by the US Department of Education (2003) found that 357,300 language-minoritized bilingual children were identified with disabilities, or 9% of all language-minoritized bilinguals, or 8% of children identified with disabilities. The national average of students identified as having disabilities has been generally consistent at 13.5%. In the early 2000s, district- and school-level data revealed that over-representation of language-minoritized bilingual children who are identified with disabilities is concentrated in districts that have large populations of language-minoritized bilingual children; and under-representation is concentrated in areas with low numbers of these children. This 'dual identification' also means that most children receive special education services, but not language-related support (US Department of Education, 2003).

Performing poorly on an intelligence test and potentially being (mis)identified as having a disability has many consequences in relation to access to educational opportunities. Current research has found patterns of restricting language-related services for language-minoritized bilinguals who are also identified as having disabilities. Kangas (2014) has documented how elementary classroom teachers and administrators favor special education services over language-related services. In understanding additional complications not only of over-identification but also of the lack of reclassification criteria, Kanno and Kangas (2014) demonstrated how being a language-minoritized bilingual child who was also identified with disabilities in high school connected to limited access to college-preparatory classes. The US Department of Education's Office of English Language Acquisition (2017) used data for the 2013–2014 school year to describe how language-minoritized bilinguals with disabilities are over-represented in the following ways: (1) identification of specific learning disabilities; (2) high school drop-out rates when compared with those of non-language-minoritized bilinguals with disabilities; and (3) out-of-school suspensions/expulsions when compared with language-minoritized bilinguals without disabilities. They were also under-represented in rates of high school graduation with a regular diploma when compared with non-language-minoritized bilinguals with disabilities. Yet drawing broad conclusions about these trends in terms of consequences does not capture the district-level or school-level practices that are obscured in these averages. For example, Arkansas, Delaware, Idaho, Indiana, Iowa, Minnesota, Missouri and New Hampshire had graduation rates of over

80%, more than 30% higher than the national average of 48.2% (Office of English Language Acquisition, 2017).

The above concerns about misidentification echo those made by researchers in special education that mislabeling students can have long-lasting and harmful effects such as limited, simplified curriculum, lower expectations, fewer post-secondary opportunities, social stigmatization and less access to non-identified peers – all exacerbated by the fact that once a student is classified as having a disability, that classification is very rarely removed throughout their educational trajectory in US schools (Harry & Klingner, 2006; Losen & Orfield, 2002; National Research Council, 2002). It could be argued that a language-minoritized bilingual who is accurately identified with a disability may face the same consequences. Data on the accuracy of identification for language-minoritized bilingual children, however, are not available, and therefore it is difficult to speculate. Yet, given the consistent historical trends of social consequences faced by language-minoritized bilingual children from the use of intelligence testing in relation to disability identification, it is within the realm of this analysis to point to persistent issues that require more attention than they have received in the course of 50 years of changing educational policies and testing procedures.

In examining the disability diagnoses and services for language-minoritized bilingual children, there are questions left unanswered about the testing practices. The lack of data describing these issues comprehensively or qualitatively to include the perspectives of language-minoritized bilinguals within this historical analysis make more urgent the call for empirical work in such areas to better understand the function and consequences of testing.

Intergenerational social consequences

The performance of language-minoritized bilingual children on intelligence tests can also have consequences that potentially impact their parents. Although intergenerational consequences are typically conceived as how the life or treatment of a parent impacts children, this examination of intergenerational social consequences describes how children's test results can have consequences for adults, as well as for the children themselves when they become adults.

Immigration policies

In conjunction with policies, discourses, ideologies and adult test scores, the scores of these children were part of a larger tapestry of evidence used to support actions rooted in white supremacy and the delegitimizing participation in the United States. Multiple scholars have discussed how the intelligence test scores of immigrants – adults and children – were part of a larger argument presented to enact restrictive immigration policies, in particular the Immigration Act of 1924 (Hansen & King, 2001; Kelves, 1995; Kraut, 1995; Ludmerer, 1972; Ngai, 1999, 2005; Roberts, 1998; Thielman, 1985; but see also Snyderman & Herrnstein, 1983, for the counterargument). A recent way in which these discourses have been recirculating is through the controversies related to Jason Richwine's dissertation at Harvard University in 2009, which largely used historical intelligence testing data of language-minoritized bilingual children to make broad claims about the intelligence of those he categorized as Hispanic and to recommend immigration restrictions.

Although Richwine stayed away from arguing pointedly for a genetic basis of intelligence, he posited that the test results presented the sufficient and necessary evidence not only to make overarching claims about the intelligence of language-minoritized bilinguals, but also to call for restrictive immigration policies specifically targeting them. His work met with a widespread backlash, yet his dissertation advisor, Murray (co-author of *The Bell Curve*, 1994), stood behind the analyses:

> I had disagreements then and now about his policy recommendations, but not about the empirical accuracy of his research or the scholarly integrity of the interpretations with which I disagreed. (Murray, 2013: para. 4)

This support for Richwine's methods and interpretations includes, then, support for Richwine's use of first- and second-generation Mexican heritage children's test scores to make claims about overall intelligence across age groups within a group of individuals he referred to as Hispanic.

The public largely rejected these findings (Beauchamp, 2013; Matthews, 2013; Wiener, 2013), and Richwine also lost his position at the Heritage Foundation, an organization which is widely known for supporting conservative views on immigration. His use of testing data to support racist, anti-immigrant positions, and in particular his overwhelming use of children's intelligence test scores to make generalized claims about adults, illustrates ways in which the social consequences of tests can be presented intergenerationally.

Sterilization

In unpacking the relationship between children's test scores and the implications for others, forced sterilization presents as a severe social consequence of testing. Forced sterilization was a practice steeped in eugenics that carried on, in particular for language-minoritized bilinguals, into the 1970s. In this case, scores on intelligence test were used as one piece of evidence to support the view that language-minoritized bilinguals should not be able to have children. This argument was used in California in particular to support sterilization laws and practices. Although documentation of the specifics of forced sterilizations in relation to the eugenics movement is challenging to locate (many records have been destroyed and many of those impacted have since passed away), the description below presents an important synthesis of the currently available research based largely on Alexandra Minna Stern's scholarship.

When making the link between children's intelligence test scores and the recommendations for sterilization of adults, testing is just one of a set of factors used. Information about the eugenics movement and sterilization is documented in California by Stern, who in 2007 uncovered microfiche records of 19,000 sterilization recommendations with information about nine state institutions from 1919 to 1952. Her work has focused on California, which had sterilization laws in place from 1909 to 1979. Her analyses of these records highlighted how Mexican Americans, Mexican immigrants and Native Americans were disproportionally subjected to forced sterilization. In this short section, I discuss the problematic role that children's intelligence test scores played in these decisions about sterilization. Although not the only reason used to support or move forward with these sterilizations, they were a component of what Stern described as the merging of 'scientific racism and intelligence testing' (Stern, 2015: 96), or the use of intelligence test scores to substantiate racial categories and reify discriminatory social hierarchies.

In providing the background on how forced sterilizations were occurring in California, Lira and Stern presented a report by the department in charge of psychiatric and mental hospitals from 1920 that describes the inferences made about their intelligence, citing unnamed research study findings. They quote from the report as follows:

> Children of Mexican and Indian descent constitute one of the most important educational and social problems in Southern California. The exact proportion of these persons in the population is not known, but it is known that delinquency is common among them. The Mexican standards of living, of course, do not accord with ours, but it is more likely that intellectual differences account for most of their unsocial conduct. Mexican children do not learn readily at school, and few of them ever pass above the third grade. Recent studies have indicated that this failure to learn is not because of language difficulties, but is more likely due to low intelligence. Apparently, the average intelligence of Mexican children in Southern California is not greater than three-fourths that of American children. If this is true, nearly one-half of the Mexican children in our schools are feeble-minded according to the standards which we apply to our own people. (Whittier State School, 1920, as cited in Lira & Stern, 2014: 15)

These views about children's intelligence were juxtaposed with discriminatory caricatures of Mexican-origin women as hyper-fertile and sexually promiscuous people who were 'dependent on welfare handouts and medical care' (Stern, 2015: 114), and thus not only giving birth to children who would be of lower intelligence, but also living a life that was a financial burden to the state. These two views were self-perpetuating. The scientific racist view that persons who had some type of intellectual disability or other marker of deviancy would only be able to have children with similar 'issues' meant that children with lower than average scores on intelligence tests were seen to be indicative of their parents' intelligence. The circular logic about mothers and children was one of multiple ways in which those in California with Mexican heritage could be explicitly targeted. The room to challenge such allegations was slim, as the generalizations about children's intelligence and the sexual deviance of women were inescapable for the language-minoritized bilinguals of Mexican heritage in California.

Youth of Mexican heritage were explicitly targeted for admission to state hospitals, which in turn made their sterilization almost a certainty during this period. Lira and Stern (2014) synthesize multiple sources of these sterilizations conducted at the Pacific Colony state hospital that illustrate disproportionately high numbers of admissions of individuals of Mexican heritage. The ages of those approved for sterilization ranged from 9 to 58, with mean age of 18, which indicates a larger proportion of those who were younger. Women represented 61.3% of these sterilizations. Though throughout this time these decisions about sterilization were challenged, mostly by parents, Californian law was written so that physicians did not need consent or permission to sterilize, thus making any arguments against sterilization moot until the legislation was changed in 1963. And yet sterilizations continued until the 1970s, as illustrated in the case *Madrigal v. Quilligan*.

Stern has argued that *Madrigal v. Quilligan* is the 'concluding link in the history of forced sterilization in California' (Stern, 2005: 1128). During a period when the Civil Rights Movement and female reproductive rights (e.g. the development of birth control, the legalization of abortion with *Roe v. Wade* and the American College of Obstetricians and Gynecologists' removal of prohibitory rules regarding women's options to choose sterilization in the form of elective hysterectomies or tubal ligations) were gaining national attention and protection, discourses continued about the low performance of 'Spanish-surnamed' students in schools and there was a backlash against women of color, in particular those with more than two or three children. *Madrigal v. Quilligan* was brought in 1978 by 10 women of Mexican heritage to challenge sterilizations that they said occurred without their consent between 1971 and 1974 at one hospital in California. Despite testimony and evidence that supported the women's assertions that they did not willingly give consent, the judge ruled that the case presented an example of a communication error because the women did not speak English and no one had presented the information in Spanish. Although the ruling was in favor of the doctor, it led to new policies which required consent forms to be bilingual (Stern, 2005, 2016).

In trying to piece together the role of intelligence testing in these forced sterilizations, I add to the discussion on intergenerational social consequences of test scores. Fortuna Valencia's case stands out because her intelligence test score was relatively high, and therefore she was not clearly seen as having below-average intelligence. Further, she was a married woman and thus did not fit into the stereotypical definitions of sexual promiscuity. Yet authorities deemed her eligible for sterilization by expanding the definition of feeble-minded, such that it the group 'is defined by any sort of [undesirable] social orientation' (Sterilization Authorizations, 1945, reel 124, as cited in Lira & Stern, 2014: 26). Lira and Stern (2014) conclude that she was sterilized because she was of Mexican heritage, poor and had a large family (six children with her first husband who passed away, and five with her second husband). Her relatively high score on the intelligence tests was not sufficient to save her from sterilization. Though only one case, it illustrates how individual test scores could be put aside when making a decision about forced sterilization. The same individuals who were using low performance on intelligence test scores to support forced sterilization actively rejected her high performance on those tests. This is not to say that tests overall were irrelevant, but rather it points to the ways in which people dismissed test scores that did not align with prevalent racist ideological perspectives that dehumanized language-minoritized bilinguals. When test scores supported the social consequence of forced sterilization, then tests were used, but when test scores did not support the social consequence, then tests were rejected.

Summary

In understanding the role of intelligence testing of language-minoritized bilingual children, this section has presented the myriad consequences of being identified as having a disability, and the ramifications of these consequences when disability is inaccurately identified. The policies and practices of identifying disabilities has faced scrutiny in state courts and by federal policy-makers, and despite proposed changes, the consequences that language-minoritized bilingual children face have remained largely consistent. In addition, the continued confusion around identification procedures means that many children may not be identified and thus denied services that could help their educational endeavors. And in broadening the scale of consequences beyond the children to include how their scores were used to argue for immigration policy changes and the sterilization of individuals of Mexican heritage in California, the intergenerational social consequences of intelligence test scores are indicative of the systemic, inescapable nature of consequences related to intelligence testing. Also contributing to deficit narratives about language-minoritized bilingual children in US schools are the practices around academic achievement or content area testing and English proficiency testing.

Standardized Testing of Content and English Proficiency

Standardized tests of academic achievement or content areas are ubiquitous within modern, compulsory schooling in the United States. Indeed, the first state to mandate compulsory schooling, Massachusetts, was also the first documented as moving to oral testing to early 'standardized' written achievement testing in the 1800s (Office of Technology Assessment, 1992). For language-minoritized bilingual children, the documented history of inclusion in standardized tests at a national level is much more recent. NCLB, which came into force in 2002, was the first federal policy to mandate inclusion in standardized testing of the content areas of language arts and mathematics (and later science) as well as exams to measure academic English language proficiency. These testing practices have been contributing to different sets of consequences for language-minoritized bilingual children, including the continued deficit positioning of bilingualism (i.e. the folk versus elite bilingualism divide – see de Mejía, 2002, 2012; Romaine, 1999) typified by the push to perform in a monolingual, English-only learning environments.

Using the testing data following NCLB, researchers have worked to understand the achievement gap for language-minoritized bilinguals (Abedi & Dietel, 2004; Fry, 2007, 2008; Hemphill & Vanneman, 2011), or reasons why language-minoritized bilinguals, on average, get lower scores on tests than their non-language-minoritized bilingual peers. Mandates about English proficiency testing have led to increasing attention on English language proficiency scales and reclassification policies (Park *et al.*, 2016; Schissel & Kangas, 2018). Critical examination of the testing practices used with language-minoritized bilinguals (e.g. Menken, 2008) points to issues with the deficit positioning of bilingualism in test accommodations for content tests and English proficiency testing.

Test accommodations

Accommodations are being portrayed by critics of the current testing practices of NCLB as measures that are 'at least palliative, which can ameliorate inequitable assessment practices' (García & Kleifgen, 2010: 112). Test accommodations or changes in the test administration, test response or test itself have been developed specifically in recent years for language-minoritized bilinguals in K-12 schools taking academic content area achievement tests (e.g. language arts, mathematics). Yet, as a testing practice, they stand out as a recently new development, specifically for language-minoritized bilinguals. Accommodations introduce a new bevy of issues as well. Shohamy has pointed out that 'accommodations need to reflect the wealth of factors that play a role in academic processing', and should not be seen 'as temporary help' (Shohamy, 2011: 425). Researchers who have worked in the development of test accommodations also caution against their widespread use, because accommodations 'are not a solution to the larger issues of promoting the academic skills of ELLs [English language learners/language-minoritized bilinguals]' (Kieffer *et al.*, 2009: 1190). These critiques aside, test accommodations are used in all 50 states and are being further developed with each new content area test.

The Improving America's Schools Act (IASA, 1994) made the first mention of test accommodations for language-minoritized bilinguals. Yet the concept of test accommodations first appeared in federal education policy in 1973, with section 504 of the Rehabilitation Act. This policy dealt with test inclusion for students with disabilities. Although the Equal Educational Opportunities Act of 1974 and the Education for all Handicapped Children Act of 1975 had further provisions to include students with disabilities in all facets of education, most states continued to exempt them from testing (Richards, 2003). This systematic exemption of language-minoritized bilingual students and students with disabilities laid some of the groundwork for the IASA (Elliot & Roach, 2002; Kopriva, 2008; Richards, 2003; Rivera & Collum, 2006; Thurlow & Bolt, 2001).

To begin researching the use of accommodations with language-minoritized bilinguals for large-scale standardized tests, the US Department of Education funded pilot studies of accommodations with the National Assessment of Educational Progress (NAEP). Introduced in 1969, the NAEP is the largest ongoing test used to report on students' performance in subject matters such as mathematics, reading and science across the United States. Yet the NAEP exempted language-minoritized bilinguals from participation. In 1996, the NAEP piloted test accommodations for language-minoritized bilinguals in addition to the piloting of accommodations for students with disabilities. Choosing the NAEP to pilot accommodations was important for several reasons. Although the results of the NAEP do not have a large impact on US education policies (as a low-stakes test), the practices used by the NAEP traditionally have influenced state practices (Rigney *et al.*, 2008). Given the limited research done on accommodations, recommendations based on research on the NAEP were generally adopted by state education agencies. Importantly, NAEP's first pilot studies did not distinctly parse use of accommodations for students with disabilities and language-minoritized bilinguals. The first studies of accommodations with the NAEP drew upon the body of research available at the time – research on test accommodations with students with disabilities (Rivera & Collum, 2006).

The conflation of language-minoritized bilinguals with students with disabilities in the use of test accommodations also connects to federal policies. NCLB intensified the testing mandates of the IASA, ending most means of exempting language-minoritized bilinguals from testing. Without many options available, state education agencies followed the practices of the NAEP and applied the policies on accommodations for students with disabilities directly to language-minoritized bilinguals. Rivera (2008) reported that, as recently as 2007, 18 states did not distinguish their test accommodations policies for these two populations.

The broader context in which these policies and research about accommodations were being developed and conducted complicates matters, but comparing the broader context of when accommodations came into practice for language-minoritized bilinguals and students with disabilities can provide valuable insights. For students with disabilities, this inclusion also has some positive implications for classroom practices. Although there is some debate, research has shown that inclusion in mainstream classes or the least restricted environment has positive learning effects on students with disabilities (Crockett & Kauffman, 1999). Further, accommodations for students with disabilities were made at a time when improving education was characterized by trying to meet the learners' specific needs. This is typified by the passage of the Equal Educational Opportunities Act of 1974 and the Education for all Handicapped Children Act of 1975. The policies and practices surrounding the development of test accommodations for language-minoritized bilinguals, however, were less attuned to trying to meet students' individual needs.

The introduction of accommodations for language-minoritized bilinguals came at a complicated time when multilingualism in the classroom was losing support. Policies from 1990s to the early 2000s in California, Arizona and Massachusetts mandated English-only instruction (Menken, 2008; Wright, 2005). From the 1980s through to the 2000s, 26 states passed English-only legislation. Before 1980, only three states had similar legislation. In addition, the testing protocols put in place focused on achievement in an English-only environment.

By definition, test accommodations aim to reduce construct-irrelevant variance due to English language proficiency for bilingual students taking tests of mathematics, language arts and science content that were originally designed for non-multilingual populations (Rivera & Collum, 2006). On a math test, for example, language-minoritized bilinguals should be able to demonstrate their knowledge of a particular math operation rather than their ability to parse the linguistic complexity of a question. Despite the succinctness of the definition of reducing construct-irrelevant variance, this approach to assessing language-minoritized bilinguals is complex. In research on test accommodations, access presents another layer of complication. Accommodations are available to bilinguals who are classified as 'English learners'. If students are reclassified as 'fluent English proficient', all accommodations are generally rescinded and they are tested using the same procedures as their monolingual peers (Rivera & Collum, 2006; Schissel 2010, 2012). Thus, bilingual learners are positioned as working towards a goal of receiving the same treatment during testing as monolingual English speakers, disregarding their bilingualism.

Complicating matters further for language-minoritized bilinguals, 'test items are generally not developed with test accommodations in mind' (Faulkner-Bond & Forte, 2015: 406); nor have tests historically been designed with bilingual test-takers in mind. The US Department of Education has explicitly acknowledged this limitation:

> most conventional tests have been normed on native English speakers. As a result, tests that have not been designed to include LEP [limited English proficient, or language-minoritized bilingual] students may not yield accurate and reliable information. (US Department of Education, 1999: 59)

These test design issues have consequences for language-minoritized bilingual students. Abedi (2011) argued that their performance is impacted by more sources of bias than is monolinguals' performance and that scores from tests developed for monolingual English speakers are less valid for bilinguals.

The lack of consensus on the effectiveness of accommodations exacerbates these questions of bias and validity. A meta-analysis by Kieffer *et al.* (2012) found limited support for the use of simplified English, English glossaries, giving the test in the language that matches the medium of instruction, and extended or untimed tests. Pennock-Roman and Rivera (2007) found some support for the use of accommodations when test-takers' English language proficiency level is taken into account. Faulkner-Bond and Sireci (2015) called for an increased focus on fairness in their review of test translations, dual-language test versions, glossaries, linguistic simplification, extended time and reading items or directions aloud. Yet, these recommendations do not directly address underlying deficit views of bilingualism at the root of test accommodations. This research points to many issues in the implementation and use of accommodations, demonstrating that it is inherently difficult to capture, in an English-medium test, what a language-minoritized bilingual learner can do. Thus, the limited evidence on test accommodations as a means of reducing construct-irrelevant variance due to language does not seem sufficient to warrant any claim of erasing (or even minimizing) the impact of bilingualism on test results. With these issues unresolved, the continued testing of language-minoritized bilinguals, with important decisions being made on the basis of their test scores, in itself represents a negative consequence. These testing practices, coupled with the changes that have been made in relation to English proficiency testing, reflect educational consequences of how learning is measured with a focus on English rather than bilingualism.

K-12 English proficiency testing

Federal policies that began to address the teaching and learning of language-minoritized bilinguals did not address English proficiency testing directly until 1975, and did not become part of federal policy until 2001. *Lau* v. *Nichols* in 1974 challenged unequitable teaching practices in public schools and, in conjunction with the US Office of Civil Rights, the Lau Remedies in 1975 outlined key educational recommendations (Crawford, 1998; Menken, 2008; Wright, 2005) that for the first time addressed test use for language-minoritized bilinguals. The Lau Remedies called for schools to have an individual with some proficiency in the student's home language to assess the proficiencies in that language and English (Cardenas, 1976; García & Baker, 2006).

In 1980, the Notice of Proposed Rule Making (NPRM) from the Department of Education provided more specific guidance on assessment of English language proficiency by placing more emphasis on reading achievement test scores (Levin, 1982). The Office for Civil Rights withdrew the NPRM in 1981 and in 1990 wrote of continued ambiguity about how tests were to be used with language-minoritized students: 'the mere absence of formal identification and [language] testing procedures and of a formal program does not, per se, constitute a violation of [federal policies]' (Smith, 1990). With these guidelines, states were given leeway in deciding whether or not to use English proficiency tests, how to use the scores and the consequences attached to score use. In 2001, with the passage of NCLB, policy shifts, continued under ESSA, required states annually to test, and to document gains in, English proficiency for language-minoritized students.

Yet a critical examination of the implications of assessing language-minoritized English proficiency is lacking. Performance on tests of English proficiency has consequences that relate most closely to classification and reclassification of ELL status. Reclassifying, or exiting, occurs when the official status changes to 'English proficient student'. To determine eligibility for reclassification, federal policies require schools to use language-minoritized bilingual students' scores from annual standardized tests of English language proficiency (ELP). Yet there is variability at the state level in the enactment of this federal policy. For example, the threshold for which proficiency levels are deemed sufficient and necessary for reclassification varies across the states (Liquanti & Cook, 2015; Wixom, 2015).

The majority of states employ one reclassification criterion: performance on the ELP test (Liquanti & Cook, 2015; Ragan & Lesaux, 2006). Reclassifying language-minoritized bilinguals on the basis of an ELP test with four domains (reading, writing, listening and speaking) requires the use of a cut-off score based on an overall average (i.e. a composite score) or scoring at a proficient level across those four domains. States have also broadened the scope of reclassification criteria beyond the mandated composite English proficiency score, including as many as four reclassification criteria, such as state and district tests, academic grades, teacher evaluation or recommendation, teacher agreement and parent consultation (Liquanti & Cook, 2015). Regardless of the number of criteria, ELP tests are at the core of the reclassification process, the basis of which is embedded in federal policies.

If language-minoritized bilingual students are categorized as 'reclassified-fluent English proficient' (R-FEP), this introduces a shift in their educational programming and support, as they are no longer in need of tailored language services (Liquanti & Cook, 2015; National Center for Research on Evaluation, Standards, and Student Testing, 2010). As summarized earlier, Kanno and Kangas (2014) documented how classification can impact access to grade-level and upper-level courses, making English language status synonymous with remedial courses, conflating language-minoritized status with disability status. Knowles and Carlson (2016) have discussed how, after reclassification, grade-11 students in Wisconsin generally improve their college entrance exam score (i.e. on the ACT) by one point, graduate high school at higher rates and enroll in different post-secondary education options at higher rates. This aligns with reports about inverse trends for language-minoritized bilinguals: if they remain classified, they have a disproportionately high dropout rate from high school (National Center for Education Statistics, 2016). Kieffer and Parker (2016) conducted a longitudinal study with seven cohorts of students, followed at school for two to nine years, to understand the patterns of reclassification in New York City public schools. In summarizing their key findings, they described how students who entered kindergarten were generally reclassified within four years, and students who entered in grade 6 or 7 took about one extra year to be reclassified, and that language-minoritized bilinguals who were identified as also having learning disabilities generally took four years longer, or two years longer if identified as having speech and language disabilities.

In a follow-up analysis of language-minoritized bilinguals who entered New York City schools in grades 5 or 6, Kieffer and Parker (2017) reported that only 64% of students graduated from high school on time – seven percentage points lower than the city average. Another 15% graduated high school one to two years after the expected graduate date, with a higher proportion of these students being classified as an English learner for longer than six years. Significantly more of these students received a high school diploma than did language-minoritized bilinguals who were reclassified in less than six years. Similar disparities around reclassification were found in the percentage of language-minoritized bilinguals who did not receive a high school diploma: 26% of those classified for more than six years did not receive a diploma compared with 13% of those classified for less than six years. These findings present the potential consequences that language-minoritized bilinguals face in relation to reclassification with regard to graduation and potential access to post-secondary education. Many of the indicators used in these studies to describe the impact of reclassification use performance forms of test (e.g. the ACT, high school exit exams in New York City). This indicates that reclassification provides information about potential performance on other forms of tests that are required for access to post-secondary education.

Yet the landscape of reclassification is complex when looking beyond these indices and when comparing districts across states. Cimpian *et al.* (2017) have completed some of the most comprehensive research on reclassification, using longitudinal data from over 100,000 language-minoritized bilinguals in two states. In addition to addressing the different criteria for reclassification at the state level, they more importantly examine the 'heterogeneity of effects across districts – with some districts having negative effects, and others having positive ones' (Cimpian *et al.*, 2017: 271S). In relation to negative effects, they discuss how courses for language-minoritized bilinguals may be less rigorous. Thus, remaining classified may restrict access to courses that are connected with the general trend of higher graduation rates for reclassified students. The implications of their work point to the need to understand how states not only set cut-off scores for reclassification on tests, but also make decisions about instruction and services made available to language-minoritized bilinguals who both are and are not reclassified. Thus ELP tests and their role in reclassification are only part of the picture when understanding the consequences that language-minoritized bilinguals face in relation to reclassification and the correlations with reclassification and social consequences such as graduation rates.

Testing agencies undergo a process of standard-setting, or aligning ELP tests with standards used for instruction. The US Department of Education recommended that states to develop ELP tests that are aligned with the Common Core State Standards (CCSS). Yet the effort to integrate language-minoritized bilinguals into the CCSS in 2011 occurred over a year after work and feedback groups were formed for the English language arts and mathematics standards in November 2009. In a written statement to *Education Week*, Kenji Hakuta characterized this delay in asking for English proficiency standards in this way: 'I guess we are once again in a situation where the train has left the station, and here we are again (now with 5-plus million students) watching it leave and trying to jump on' (quoted in Zehr, 2011). This case of the CCSS illustrates how the needs of language-minoritized bilinguals are often ignored or overlooked.

In looking at the current landscape of ELP tests, two testing consortia play prominent roles. The development of ELP tests has been led largely by the WIDA consortium, which comprised 39 member states and US territories as of mid-2017. The English Language Proficiency Assessment for the 21st Century (ELPA21) has seven participating states. Other states, such as New York and California, have created their own ELP tests. When looking at these tests in relation to the CCSS, ELPA21 created its first operational test in the spring of 2016. The development of its test, therefore, was completed after the development of the CCSS. WIDA's ELP test was first used in three states in the spring of 2005, expanding to 12 states in the spring of 2006. In 2007, WIDA conducted standards setting for this test, updated in 2017. The 2017 changes reflected an alignment with the CCSS, and were projected to mean that language-minoritized bilinguals' scores may go down and that fewer may meet the criteria for reclassification. In response, Colorado, Maine, Massachusetts and Tennessee lowered their criteria for reclassification (Mitchell, 2017).

The consequences that language-minoritized bilinguals face in relation to these ELP tests connect with previous discussions of reclassification of language-minoritized bilinguals identified as having disabilities. Thompson (2017) identified the inflexibility of an ELP test being necessary for reclassification. She documented how it took four to seven years for reclassification, but how after nine years reclassification was rare. In such instances, language-minoritized bilinguals cannot generally contest a test score, and instead are often left with a stigma of not being able to be reclassified from a categorization from which they are expected to leave. As with the over- or under-representation in special education services, the ramifications of early or late reclassification based on these scores rests not only on the accuracy of the tests, but also on the services and instruction made available with respect to these scores.

The ELP tests remain an area that has varied impacts on language-minoritized bilinguals' educational experiences, while also contributing to the erasure or deficit positioning of bilingualism. The policy requirements have removed much flexibility around the use of ELP tests for reclassification. Yet they are part of a larger picture of tests that include high school graduation exams or college entrance exams. The admission requirements involving English proficiency testing for individuals who have not been reclassified as English proficient or fluent are less clear. There are no policies to date that require language-minoritized bilinguals to provide information about classification status at high school, or for high schools to provide it, for universities (e.g. on transcripts). Robertson and Lafond (2008) claim that non-reclassified applicants to universities most likely would be required to take ELP entrance tests (e.g. TOEFL), but there remains little documentation of ELP testing of non-reclassified language-minoritized bilinguals. The situation may be different based on citizenship, as individuals need to disclose their citizenship on applications and English proficiency is required for all non-US citizens – though graduating from a high school in the United States is often seen as sufficient evidence of English proficiency. There are options to enroll in university English bridge programs, or English courses that are taken before students enroll in other university programs, without taking ELP tests. The University of Colorado at Boulder, for example, offers an ESL bridge program as part of conditional admission (see https://iec.colorado.edu/programs/eabp).

Summary

The deficit positioning of bilingualism in content area and ELP tests presents uses of tests with consequences that often impact the day-to-day educational experiences of language-minoritized bilinguals. Often these tests are used make decisions about classification or access to different educational opportunities. How these decisions impact language-minority bilinguals is highly dependent on the classrooms, schools and district contexts. Yet the lingering disregard for the bilingualism of language-minoritized bilinguals, and often the ideas, experiences, knowledge, skills and perspectives they hold, can be seen as a consequence of using tests that also do not recognize these views.

Discussion

Intelligence testing and content and ELP tests have a multitude of consequences for language-minoritized bilingual school children s and their families. There can be severe intergenerational social consequences around immigration policies and sterilization as well as consequences for decisions around access to learning opportunities for disability, language, content and college and career-readiness courses. Across these different forms of testing, bilingualism has been discussed as a problem. Some researchers felt that bilingualism was the cause of lower performance on intelligence tests, and that language-minoritized bilinguals were therefore of lower intelligence. Hakuta explained that such researchers viewed these children as 'deficient in both languages' (Anastasi & Cordova, 1953, as cited in Hakuta, 1986: 32). As language-minoritized bilinguals did not perform as well as their peers on intelligent tests, content tests and language proficiency tests, researchers have looked into concepts such as semilingualism or limited bilingualism (Cummins, 1979, 1981b; Martin-Jones & Romaine, 1986), non-nons (MacSwan, 2000) or languagelessness (Rosa, 2016).

In the 1960s into the 1980s, researchers in Canada (Cummins, 1979, 1981b) and Scandinavia (Hansegård, 1968; Skutnabb-Kangas & Toukomaa, 1976; Toukomaa & Skutnabb-Kangas, 1977) noted the 'poor performance of minority children [...] on verbal tests' (Martin-Jones & Romaine, 1986: 27) as evidence of semilingualism. Claims of semilingualism were based on test scores that indicated that language-minoritized bilinguals lacked proficiency in the national language and their home language. In the 1990s, states began to refer to these students as 'non-nons'. Non-nons was an abbreviation of 'non-English speaking and non-Spanish speaking', and was applied overwhelmingly to Latino students based on their scores English and Spanish proficiency tests the Language Assessment Scales in English and Español (MacSawn, 2000). Rosa (2016) points to 'ideologies of languagelessness' that have continued or sustained consequences for language-minoritized bilinguals. 'For various racialized groups, neither the use of a particular "national" language nor the standardized variety of that language alone can ensure societal inclusion' (Rosa, 2016: 177). These debates among scholars – though important for understanding the ways in which bilingualism has been researched in the United States – have had little impact on the negative social consequences that language-minoritized bilinguals have faced based on their performance on tests. Despite criticism that many tests are not developed with language-minoritized bilinguals in mind, use of the scores has been accepted and defended. The view that language-minoritized bilinguals do not possess a legitimate language remains a legacy in this history of the social consequences of testing.

5 Seeking Higher Education

Currently, many four-year colleges or universities require applicants to take an admissions exam, the Scholastic Achievement Test (SAT) or the American College Testing Program (ACT). For graduate studies, most programs require applicants to take the Graduate Records Exam (GRE). There are also tests specific to particular areas of study, such as business, medical or law. In looking at the history of university admissions testing, one notable absence is attention to creating instruments that are inclusive of language-minoritized bilinguals from either the United States or other regions. Further complicating the creation and use of admissions tests has been the simultaneous increased attention to evaluating the English language proficiency of applicants coming from outside the United States, and the continued testing of non-US citizens in graduate programs who are working as teaching assistants.

For language-minoritized bilinguals from the United States, their bilingualism is often ignored or erased by the testing instruments. Accommodations that are made to tests in K-12 schools (see Chapter 4) are not available for most of these tests, and in some instances language-minoritized bilinguals who graduated from high school in the United States may be required to take an English proficiency exam or to complete an intensive English program in order to enroll in college (Robertson & Lafond, 2008). For language-minoritized bilinguals from outside the United States, their bilingualism is continually the subject of attention and testing. The consequences of not performing well on these exams are quite clear and are generally irreversible: being denied admission to a university or being denied teaching assistantships, the latter of which can have the additional consequence of not being able to remain in a graduate program. Though there are some universities that do not require tests for admission (see Introduction), the treatment of language-minoritized bilinguals from within and outside the United States serves to (re)privilege English dominance.

The first section of this chapter provides a historical overview of how the SAT, ACT and GRE have been developed and used in general, with a discussion of the blanket erasure of bilingualism. The second section looks at English language proficiency testing and the requirements for language-minoritized bilinguals both from within and outside the United

States. This includes providing details about the two most common English proficiency entrance exams: the Test of English as a Foreign Language (TOEFL) and the International English Language Testing System (IELTS), as well as post-admissions English proficiency testing of international teaching assistants.

College Admissions Testing

Universities in the United States have a long history of using admissions exams. Barker (1967) reported that universities in those British colonies that are now the United States already required entrance exams. Most of these early tests were oral exams, though some colleges, such as Harvard, also required essay writing in Latin. In general, these tests asked applicants to demonstrate their knowledge of Latin and/or Greek, as most scientific writing used these languages until the mid-1700s. These early tests, therefore, were also tests of the multilingual language skills of applicants. Eventually, they were replaced with testing more like that used the K-12 education system of today (e.g. in mathematics and history), though Harvard also introduced tests of modern language in 1875. After much debate about what should be included in entrance exams, and about the different requirements across universities, the College Entrance Examination Board – or College Board – was formed on 17 November 1900 (Angoff & Dyer, 1971). This was indicative of the trends in the development of testing from the late 1800s. After the US Army exams were created and used from 1917 to 1919, the College Board expanded work in testing in this direction to create what was then called the Scholastic Aptitude Test (SAT), an intelligence test for college applicants.

The SAT

The College Board turned to Carl Brigham to create this test. Brigham was known at the time for his analysis of the Army exams in his 1923 book *A Study of American Intelligence*. In Chapters 1 and 2, and widely critiqued by others, Brigham presented an analysis that served to promote white supremacist and racist ideologies that were also anti-immigrant. He narrowed definitions of whiteness to focus on those of 'Nordic' heritage, and leaned into the Army tests' tendency to separate test-takers into officer and infantry pools largely on the basis of their racial backgrounds. Shortly after publishing this volume (and before he renounced this writing in 1930), Brigham created an admissions test for Princeton University. He adapted this test to create the SAT, which was administered to 8,040 high school students for the first time in 1926. The use of the SAT steadily grew during the 1930s, and was generally employed by elite colleges to screen for scholarships. In the 1940s and during World War II, the use of the SAT was less prominent, and the College Board instead focused its efforts on creating the V-12 Testing program to identify high school students who could serve as officers. In 1947 it prepared a test to screen veterans returning from World War II who would be enrolling in universities (Angoff & Dyer, 1971). The concerns of the military have been a consistent influence on the development of tests (Stewart & Johanek, 1996).

After World War II, the College Board increased in size. The Carnegie Foundation had expressed an interest in expanding the testing aspects of the organization and asked the president of Harvard University to chair a committee to create a unified testing agency. In 1947, after much negotiation, the Educational Testing Service (ETS) was created. The College Board remained to focus on issues related to admissions and the ETS headed all tests. The ETS was and remains a non-profit company and was established with grants from the Carnegie Foundation, the American Council on Education's testing funds and the College Board's assets (Spolsky, 1995). In the postwar era, the College Board has been further developing and expanding the use of the SAT. The test underwent major revisions in 2000 and 2015.

The College Board has reported limited information about test-takers who are not US citizens. For example, during the 2016 academic year, 1,637,589 individuals took the SAT. Of this total, 49,304 or 3% were permanent residents or refugees and 116,636 or 7% were non-US citizens. The College Board also reports on test-takers' first language. Of the test-takers in 2016, 308,356 or 19% reported having English and another language as a first language, while 208,519 or 13% reported having a language other than English as their first language, and 1,078,298 stated that English was their first language. In many ways, the individuals who may be conceived of as language-minoritized bilinguals are outperforming US citizens with English as a first language. Table 5.1 presents the mean scores and standard deviations of scores for the three SAT tests by first language and citizenship. The data for those who did not respond to the questions are not included in Table 5.1. The highest mean score for each test and mean composite score are shown. Those who reported having English as their first language performed, on average, 51–60 points overall higher than those who could be characterized as language-minoritized bilinguals. However, using non-US citizenship as a proxy to identify language-minoritized bilinguals, that group performs 85–191 points overall higher than US citizens or permanent residents or refugees.

In looking at overseas administration of the SAT, test security has been a major concern. Thomas Reuters New Agency conducted an investigation of various forms of cheating, largely in China (Reuters, n.d.). In circumventing the gatekeeping mechanisms of the SAT as an admission test through fraudulent means, language-minoritized bilinguals are often banned from ever taking the test again. Yet embedded in these efforts to perform well on these tests is an overwhelming desire to gain admission to US universities. The SAT generally serves one function related to

Table 5.1 Performance on SAT sections by first language and citizenship for the 2015–2016 academic year

	Critical reading		Mathematics		Writing		Mean composite
	Mean	SD	Mean	SD	Mean	SD	
First language							
English	508	110	508	113	490	109	1,506
English and another	476	121	499	130	471	121	1,446
Language other than English	465	124	525	141	468	128	1,458
Citizenship							
US	500	113	503	116	485	111	1,488
Permanent resident or refugee	450	127	485	137	447	129	1,382
Non-US	490	124	583	122	500	127	1,573

Adapted from College Board (2016a)

admission to US universities: to support or restrict. The high stakes attached to these tests can be seen as disproportionate in relation to how students fare during their first year of college. The College Board found that the 2015 revision of the SAT did not change how well the scores could predict performance during a student's first year, though the writing test was a better predictor than the other two sections (College Board, 2016a).

It should be noted that the College Board has created separate tests specifically designed for language-minoritized bilinguals already in the United States and those seeking to come to the United States. It created a test for students from African countries seeking to study at the African Scholarships Program of American Universities from 1961 to 1970. In 1964, it developed the Prueba de Aptitud Academica™, a set of aptitude and achievement tests in Spanish for Spanish speakers in the US territory of Puerto Rico and those in other areas of the United States. This test remains in use today, as reported by the College Board:

> Se utiliza en prestigiosas instituciones de educación superior, tanto públicas como privadas, en once países latinoamericanos: Bolivia, Costa Rica, Ecuador, El Salvador, Guatemala, Honduras, México, Panamá, Puerto Rico, República Dominicana, Uruguay y en varias universidades de los Estados Unidos para evaluar a los candidatos de origen hispano. (College Board, 2016b: section 6)

> It is used at prestigious institutions of higher education, both public and private, in eleven Latin American countries: Bolivia, Costa Rica, Ecuador, El Salvador, Guatemala, Honduras, Mexico, Panama, Puerto Rico, the Dominican Republic, Uruguay and in several universities of the United States to evaluate candidates of Hispanic origin. (Translation mine)

It is important to note the error in listing Puerto Rico as a country in Latin America, as it is a territory of the United States and therefore those taking the test are US citizens. This association of the language of the test with geographic regions, and the misidentification of a place because of the language of the test, represent modern-day obfuscation of the citizenship and rights of residents of Puerto Rico.

The other common college admissions test is the ACT or American College Test program, which does not offer the tests in languages other than English, but its developers are making steps to develop and implement test accommodations for language-minoritized bilinguals.

The ACT

In 1959, Everett Franklin Lindquist and Ted McCarrel developed the ACT based on the Iowa Test of Basic Skills, a standardized achievement test that has been used in K-12 schools. At the time the test was developed, the SAT was used by only a few select colleges in the north-east of the United States and the ACT saw room to expand into the marketplace. In the first year, approximately 75,000 students took the ACT. In 1968, almost 950,000 students took the ACT, and the popularity of this test has continued to grow. Depending on how one calculates the academic year, in either 2011 or 2012 more individuals took the ACT than the SAT (Jacobsen, 2017). The number of students taking the ACT has remained higher than the number taking the SAT, with 2,090,342 taking the exam during the 2015–2016 academic year (ACT Inc., 2016). Increasingly, students have been taking both the ACT and the SAT to maximize their chance of matriculation (Lewin, 2013). Unlike with the SAT, ACT Inc. is taking steps to modify its exam specifically for language-minoritized bilinguals in the United States.

In a 2016 press release, Marten Roorda, ACT Inc.'s chief executive officer, explained how the ACT was planned to be more responsive to the increased numbers of students classified as English learners in US public schools by offering test accommodations for the ACT:

> To enable more students to demonstrate their abilities, starting in the fall of 2017 ACT will offer supports for qualified English learners in the United States taking the ACT. These supports will include limited additional time to take the test, the use of an approved word-to-word bilingual glossary (containing no word definitions), test instructions provided in the student's native language (limited languages at first), and testing in a non-distracting environment. (Roorda, 2016: para. 14)

ACT Inc. takes the position that it is not trying to test knowledge of English, and instead would like to know how students understand the content of the test. Roorda continued:

> To do well on the math test, students will still need to know math. Similarly, they will also need to need to know English, Reading, and Science, the other subjects covered on the ACT.

In English, the test measures usage, mechanics, and rhetorical skills; it's not a vocabulary test. A bilingual glossary helps even the playing field, but does not define the words on the test.

For example, if you were a Spanish speaker learning English you may not understand the word 'rhetorical' but you would likely understand the Spanish word 'retórico.' The glossary doesn't define 'rhetorical.' It only clarifies the word is one you already understand in your native language. (paras 16–18)

Roorda concludes by stating the company is proud to have developed the first test for college admissions to offer such supports (see also ACT Inc., 2018). One may predict that changes to the SAT will also follow this shift in the ACT.

Additional data about language or national origin of those taking the ACT, however, are not available. And similar to the SAT, ACT Inc. has been challenging testing procedures abroad, and even canceled test results in Asian countries after an essay question was leaked (Stecklow, 2016) ; it consequently raised testing fees outside the United States to pay for increased test security measures (Harney & Stecklow, 2016). This differentiated treatment of language-minoritized bilinguals in the United States and those not in the United States speaks to the complications in how test developers view test-takers, with additional ramifications for those taking the tests.

Like the SAT and ACT, use of the common graduate school admissions test, the GRE, has increased dramatically and it is now used by most graduate schools in the United States. In contrast to the SAT and ACT, the GRE reports more specific information about international test-takers.

The GRE

The GRE began following a project in the 1930s that studied the outcomes of college education. After World War II and increased applications to universities for graduate courses, the GRE was used more widely and further developed after the creation of ETS in 1947. The GRE was designed to evaluate the knowledge and skills of students who had studied at a variety of undergraduate institutions (Educational Testing Service, 2008).

In the 2015–2016 academic year, 252,488 non-US citizens took the GRE. This accounted for 43% of all test-takers. The number of test-takers is reported by country of citizenship for any country that had more than 30 individuals take the test, and also separating US territories from the general US population. The top five countries are presented in Table 5.2. In terms of performance, the highest mean score for verbal reasoning (on a scale of 130–170) achieved by students from a country outside of those seen as predominately English speaking or 'inner-circle' (cf. Kachru, 2006) English-speaking countries (i.e. Australia, Canada, Ireland, New Zealand

Table 5.2 The five countries with highest numbers of GRE test-takers

Country	Number	Percent
India	99,376	39.36%
China	45,777	18.13%
Korea	5,826	2.31%
Iran	5,319	2.11%
Canada	5,108	2.02%
Total	161,406	63.93%

Adapted from Educational Testing Service (2016a)

and the United Kingdom) was by those from Singapore – where English is a co-official language and is used in multiple public and private spheres – with a mean score of 157.8; for quantitative reasoning (again on a scale of 130–170) China had the highest mean score, of 164.4, and for analytical writing (on a scale of 0–6) Singapore again had the highest mean score, of 4.3. These scores are all higher than the mean scores of test-takers with US citizenship (Educational Testing Service, 2016a).

Yet many international applicants face additional scrutiny in relation to cheating scandals. There have been allegations of cheating and of hiring proxies to take the GRE, SAT, ACT and English proficiency tests for international applicants. In 2015, 15 students from China were arrested in the United States for being part of plan to pay or be paid to take these tests for others. The punishment for being involved included expulsion from the universities and deportation to China (Redden & Jaschik, 2015). As with other high-stakes tests, the types of cheating speak to the lengths to which individuals are willing to go in order to be able to study at US universities, as well as their views of tests as a hurdle to reach that goal.

Summary

The SAT, ACT and GRE represent different forms of college admissions testing, but all were created with the explicit purpose of serving as a gatekeeping device for those applying to college. For language-minoritized bilinguals in particular, there are the additional hurdles of being required to take an exam that has been not been developed with them in mind. The recent change of adding test accommodations to the ACT illustrates a shift in perspective and begins to address the reality that language-minoritized bilinguals have different testing needs. Yet, as described in Chapter 4, test accommodations fall short of substantively addressing concerns about the testing of language-minoritized bilinguals.

International college applicants have to take English proficiency tests in order to be admitted to US universities, adding another layer of testing, which amplifies the different treatment to which this group of language-minoritized bilinguals is subjected.

English Proficiency Testing

Although there are some reports that students who are classified as English learners and who graduate from US high schools may have to take English proficiency tests for admissions to US universities (Robertson & Lafond, 2008), tests of English proficiency for college admissions are predominately required for international applicants. Many universities, such as the CUNY (City University of New York), have a well established tradition of accepting students who are classified as English learners (Lay *et al.*, 1999). Thus, this section focuses on the use of English proficiency tests for university admissions and post-admissions testing for non-US citizens.

The TOEFL and IELTS

After World War I – and in conjunction with increasingly restrictive immigration policies (i.e. the quota system of the Immigration Act of 1924) – the Commissioner General of Immigration required universities to document the English proficiency of international students. Formal steps were taken to create a test for this purpose because the Commissioner had noted an increased number of applications for student visas. At this time, there were not many English proficiency tests available and the College Board was commissioned to create a test. However, with worsening worldwide economies in the late 1920s and early 1930s, the number of international applicants dropped dramatically, and testing and further test development ended in 1936. The economic climate did not improve for over 10 years, and therefore the development of an English proficiency test for incoming international students to US universities was put on hold until the early 1960s (Spolsky, 1995).

The idea for a new test, the Test of English as a Foreign Language (TOEFL), was taken up again in earnest in 1961 at a meeting at the Center for Applied Linguistics in Washington, DC. There was a general belief that current tests of English proficiency were insufficient. In 1962, a national council on the testing of English as a foreign language was formed with members who represented over 30 different organizations and government agencies. The council funded the first iteration of the TOEFL and, after two years of planning, much negotiation and some disagreement, the TOEFL was created, piloted, revised and printed within a very short period of time. The leadership of David Harris and Leslie Palmer is credited with meeting what was considered to be a very tight deadline. In 1964 the TOEFL was administered worldwide. During this first year, 80 colleges agreed to require the TOEFL for foreign applicants. Since then, the test has transitioned to an internet-based form, or the TOEFL iBT. Today, the TOEFL iBT is accepted by over 10,000 universities and businesses in 130 countries, and it is claimed that 30 million people

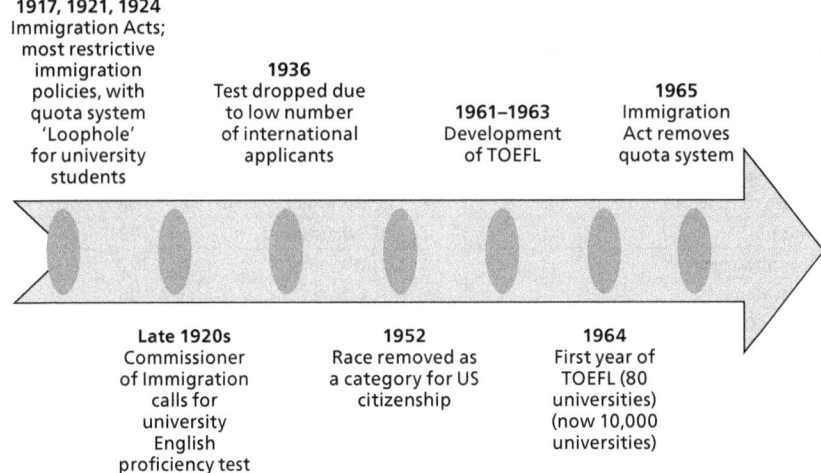

Figure 5.1 Timeline of TOEFL development and immigration policies

have taken a version of the TOEFL (Educational Testing Service, 2016b; Spolsky, 1995).

Figure 5.1 presents a timeline of the origins of the TOEFL together with the immigration policies initiated during this period. When looking and the socio-political contexts surrounding the development of the TOEFL, it is important to note the historical connections to anti-immigrant and racist immigration policies that were prevalent throughout this period.

The ways in which these policies motivated the first attempts to develop an English proficiency test, in the 1920s and 1930s, were not explicitly repeated or evoked in the development of the TOEFL. Instead, there was a lack of engagement with the early origins of English proficiency testing. This is not to over- or under-state the relationships between the periods in which English proficiency tests were generated. Instead, a historical lens introduces a complicated, somewhat uncomfortable conversation topic on the origins of the TOEFL, and one that does not need to be avoided or minimized, nor amplified. Looking at performances on the TOEFL today introduces other complexities into the discussion. The highest scores by language and country show that individuals from western and northern European countries are the top performers. Another group comprises individuals from the former British colony of India. The Educational Testing Service reports the performance on the test by native language of the test-taker. Table 5.3 reports the top composite scores by native language and country (excluding English-dominant countries, as was done for the GRE in Table 5.2) in 2016 (on a scale of 0–120).

Table 5.3 Top mean TOEFL composite scores by language and country

Language	Score	Country	Score
Dutch	99	Austria	99
Estonian	98	Netherlands	99
German	98	South Africa	99
Konkani	98	Belgium	98
Danish	97	Denmark	98
Galician	97	Switzerland	98
Luxembourgish	97	Germany	97
Malayalam	97	Estonia	96
Assamese	96	Iceland	96
Icelandic	96	Luxembourg	96
Kashmiri	96	Singapore	96
Hindi	95	Finland	95
Oriya	95	Slovenia	95
Slovenian	95		

Note: English has a mean composite score of 93; the United States 89
Adapted from Educational Testing Service (2016b)

In looking at the languages and countries of origin of test-takers, there are some clear correlations between the score of 99 for Dutch and the Netherlands, or 96 for Icelandic and Iceland, or 97–99 for German and Austria or Germany. The less common languages, such as Konkani, Assamese, Malayalam, Kashmiri and Oriya are spoken in India. Galician, in contrast, is spoken in north-west Spain. Countries such as South Africa and Singapore also have English as an official language along with multiple other languages. The numbers or percentages of test-takers from these language backgrounds is not reported, but even with this information it is important to note the prominence of European countries and languages.

Language-minoritized bilinguals also have the option of taking other English proficiency tests, such as the IETLS. Early versions of the IELTS focused on creating an English proficiency test for universities in the United Kingdom, around the same time as the TOEFL, in 1965. In the 1980s, the International Development Program of Australian Universities and Colleges joined the British Council and Cambridge English Language Assessment to expand the international reach of the test. By 1995, about 43,000 individuals took the IETLS test worldwide. More than 3 million individuals took the test during the 2016–2017 academic year (IELTS, 2017a), and 2.9 million during 2016 (IELTS, 2017b). In addition to being a test for university admissions, IELTS has a general test version often used for employment. The organization has also been developing tests for immigration purposes, including various visa requirements for Australia, Canada, New Zealand and the United Kingdom (IELTS, 2017b).

Students do not always need to take the TOEFL or IELTS for admissions. If, for example, language-minoritized bilinguals do not achieve a high score on an English proficiency test, they may be able to attend an intensive English program at a US university, and gain admission after successful completion of that program. If they come from a country with English as an official language, they most likely will not be required to take an English proficiency test. At the University of North Carolina at Greensboro, for example, we exempt students from taking an English proficiency test if they are a citizen of a country or a graduate of a university in a country where English is an official language, and currently have 68 countries listed as eligible. Universities can also make exceptions when a student holds a degree from a university that has English as the medium of instruction. Yet, it should be noted that many graduate and some undergraduate students are subject to post-admissions English proficiency testing in order to serve as international teaching assistants (ITAs).

Post-admission testing: Focus on ITAs

Many language-minoritized bilinguals who have been admitted to US universities must pass additional English proficiency tests or screenings before being awarded positions as teaching assistants. For some, especially individuals in graduate programs, serving as a teaching assistant is a requirement of the degree, and therefore this testing can determine whether a student is eligible to continue in a program of study. States and universities set and enforce these policies, which can require additional coursework and the use of different English proficiency tests. In Wisconsin, for example, the Board of Regents created a policy in 1991 on the selection, training and evaluation of ITAs, stating that 'Non-native English speakers must be required to demonstrate proficiency in spoken English before they are assigned classroom duties as teaching assistants' (section 1.B, as cited in University of Milwaukee, n.d.). The University of Minnesota (2012) provides a rationale for its policies by positioning them as evidence of its commitment to high standards of English communication:

> In support of high quality undergraduate education, the University requires of its nonnative speakers of English employed as TAs evidence of English language proficiency. This policy also serves as a response to a request, to ensure that classroom TAs for whom English is a second language are proficient in speaking, reading, and writing English, from the Minnesota Legislature in their 1985 First Special Session Laws/ Chapter 11, Section 7 subdivision b.
> This requirement engenders continuing cooperation of each academic department in maintaining high standards of English language communication skills for all nonnative speakers of English who provide instruction at the University of Minnesota.

The Pennsylvania State University conducted a study and published a report on the policies and practices for ITAs in 1999 to 'to address concerns expressed by undergraduates that English language deficiencies of International Teaching Assistants (ITAs) were inhibiting student learning' (Cahir *et al.*, 1999: para. 1). Across these different policies and practices of ITA testing there is a general portrayal of deficiencies on the part of ITAs as judged by undergraduate students, as stated in the report from the Pennsylvania State University.

Focus on ITAs includes a special interest group for the TESOL International Association. In its July 2017 newsletter, Chen, Hung and Takahashi, who were all former ITAs, discussed challenges they identified as unique to their experiences as first-year ITAs. First, they discussed rapport in the classroom. They named the discrimination they faced as ITAs: 'For ITAs who are more likely to face negative judgments because of their accents, the issues of trust and authority seem to be more crucial' (Chen *et al.*, 2017: para. 3). In terms of materials, they worked with texts that were US-centric, which often prompted them to collaborate with American colleagues to understand the context of the material, while also adding material to the classroom that drew from their own experiences. In addressing their own self-doubts, they reported spending extra time preparing and practicing lessons because they were 'especially conscious of our students' perceptions and prejudices, and we [felt] the responsibility (or burden) to perform in a way that [would] win their respect and appreciation' (para. 7). Their reflections illustrate some of the pervasiveness of the deficit positioning of ITAs.

This focus on ITAs also is connected to the development of and research on different testing programs. These approaches generally do not question the necessity of ITA programs or testing, but instead seek to refine programs and testing. Wagner (2016) examined the TOEFL iBT test, which is used by many universities in testing their ITAs, and reported that the listening subscore correlated with and predicted various measures of teaching competence. Kang (2012) examined how undergraduate students rate ITAs' speech in comparison with prosodic measurements of speech rate, pausing, stress and intonation. She noted that undergraduate students were sensitive to these traits of oral proficiency, but also demonstrated personal biases.

Recently, there has been more research that is critical of the positioning of ITAs as lacking English and the privileging of complaints by undergraduate students. Subtirelu (2017) applied a critical sociolinguistic lens to critique the overall deficit framing of ITAs, and the ways in which the policies and practices applied to ITAs at universities often are incongruent with the explicit comments supporting cultural and linguistic diversity. Meyer and Mao (2014) turned their attention to the pervasiveness of undergraduate students' negative evaluations of ITAs in their survey of student attitudes. In doing so, they pointed to the ethnocentrism underlying these negative evaluations – rather than a more reflective assessment of ITAs' teaching – and called for more intercultural training of undergraduate students, who seem poorly prepared to engage with the increasing international nature of communication. That study addressed the issues that prompted the introduction of many ITA testing programs in the first place, and can be used to seriously question the utility of such policies and testing practices. Manohar and Appiah (2016) have extended this work to develop an intervention program to improve undergraduate students' perceptions of ITAs. They found that a program that emphasized having undergraduate students imagine how ITAs feel improved their perceptions of ITAs better than a comparable program where they put themselves in the shoes of the ITA – so to speak – and imagined how they would feel if they were the ITA. In working with ITAs, Zheng (2017) described how two ITAs used a link between identity and pedagogy to engage in translingual practices in the classroom, but that developing an orientation that was inclusive of multilingualism was often challenged by perceptions of linguistic membership and competence. This study in particular illustrated some of the ways in which ITAs can also reframe themselves and their practice in a manner that reflects an asset-based view of linguistic diversity.

In these interactions, the students of the ITAs are being socialized within a deficit framing of language-minoritized bilinguals. In trying to understand more critically the experience of language-minoritized bilinguals who are ITAs, it is important to note that when they are in the classroom teaching, as Chen *et al.* (2017) stated, the burdens of making the communication meaningful is largely placed on them, with little reflection on the roles or responsibilities of their interlocutors. And as Subtirelu (2017) pointed out, such treatment of ITAs is antithetical to many universities' statements on equity, diversity and inclusion. Taken as a whole, the post-admission testing of ITAs serves to reproduce inequities and perpetuate deficit positioning of language-minoritized bilinguals.

Summary

English proficiency testing in higher education presents another burden for language-minoritized bilinguals. In addition to being tests of English proficiency for college admissions, the TOEFL and IELTS exams intersect with historical and current immigration policies in the United States and other regions of the world. In gaining broader understandings of these tests with respect to immigration, measurements of English proficiency take on additional ideological positionings not unlike other, more controversial forms of testing, such as intelligence testing, that have been used in relation to immigration. This section has also explored how, when used for college admissions, these tests do not preclude language-minoritized bilinguals from being subjected to additional tests in order to serve as ITAs. Thus, even the positive consequences of passing the TOEFL or IELTS and being admitted to a program do not preclude additional testing with additional potential negative consequences.

Discussion

This chapter has presented the different forms of testing that language-minoritized bilinguals face when seeking access to higher education in the United States. It has presented the differentiated treatment of language-minoritized bilinguals who are in the United States and those arriving from other regions of the world. Those within the United States are subjected to fewer forms of testing, and with changes to the ACT are also eligible for test accommodations that are currently used in K-12 schools (see Chapter 4). Those from outside the United States are subjected to multiple forms of testing. They must take not only the SAT, ACT and/or the GRE, but also an English proficiency test. And once admitted, they may face additional testing in order to serve as ITAs. These additional testing burdens mean that language-minoritized bilinguals have more chances to be excluded from or denied educational opportunities at a US university. It is worth noting that although most language-minoritized bilinguals do not need to take an English proficiency test in addition to the SAT, ACT or GRE, this double testing burden mimics the testing policies they are subjected to in K-12 schools.

The consequence that language-minoritized bilinguals face for poor performance across the tests discussed in this chapter is fairly consistent: denial of admission or removal from a program. The need to pass these tests for admission has meant that cheating has become an issue. Testing companies are working against such cheating, which can result in criminal charges and deportation. The actions that some language-minoritized bilinguals are taking speak to the positioning of testing for university admissions as gatekeeping devices, or hurdles to overcome. In examining the roles of these tests, their contribution to the deficit positioning of bilingualism may be exacerbated by the additional testing requirements for language-minoritized bilinguals.

Concluding Thoughts

Throughout this book, I have worked to provide a history of the social consequences of testing faced by language-minoritized bilinguals. The use-oriented testing view (Shohamy, 2001) aided in constructing a narrative that presented the cumulative experiences of language-minoritized bilinguals, rather than test score inferences in isolation, in order to contribute to validity approaches for the testing of language-minoritized bilinguals. In moving away from approaches that organize these consequences or that disentangle how they are aspects of validity, the overall picture and overarching impacts of these consequences have been presented in a manner that aims to illuminate the profound weight of these consequences.

The historical narrative began with accepting the premises that language-minoritized bilinguals (1) constitute a group of individuals who are seen (by others) as not possessing a particular type of English, (2) inhabit multiple minoritized categories as intersectional individuals and (3) can be unified as a group because of shared minoritized bilingual *and* intersectional individual positionalities. These understandings of who language-minoritized bilinguals are have been constructed in relation to broader socio-historical structures, policies and institutions, as being minoritized is construed with respect to different power relationships, in particular those related to histories and legacies of white settler colonialism and white supremacy in the United States. Critically examining these histories and legacies with respect to the social consequences of testing for language-minoritized bilinguals has served to illustrate that their collective experiences of historic and systemic discrimination are profound. By viewing these experiences with respect to consequential validity, those involved in testing are called to task not only to acknowledge these histories, but actively and explicitly to incorporate work in their testing efforts to dismantle these legacies of discrimination. In this conclusion, I return to the conceptual framework of the book to synthesize the historical narrative constructed. From this, I discuss how the use-oriented testing view can inform future work in testing, arguing that historical narratives are an essential aspect of consequential validity. I end the chapter with questions to move forward, framing this historical narrative as just the beginning of a necessary, continued discussion.

Language-minoritized Bilinguals as Intersectional Individuals

The Introduction began with the definition of English language learners from *The Standards* (AERA, APA & NCME, 2014). In doing so, I contrasted the test developer perspective of an English language learner as 'An individual who is not yet proficient in English' (AERA, APA & NCME, 2014: 218) with the term 'language-minoritized bilingual' to critically engage in perceptions of and ideologies around language proficiency. Language-minoritized bilinguals have also been seen in this book as intersectional individuals who inhabit multiple minoritized categories. Integrating an intersectionality framework served to facilitate the documentation of historical accounts and the forces that perpetuate the oppression of language-minoritized bilinguals.

Understanding language-minoritized bilinguals to be intersectional individuals has been key in showing how they are subjected to social consequences of tests. Crenshaw's (1989, 1991) work examined how different forms of oppression were brought with the specific ways in which inhabiting these multiple minoritized categories experienced forms of oppression different from the categories in isolation. For language-minoritized bilinguals, their multiple minoritized identities are sometimes muddied by the use of tests to construct a minoritized identity – as has often been the case with intelligence tests. Further complicating matters is that by inhabiting multiple minoritized identities, any one of these identities may be foregrounded, calling for the test consequence to be more readily applied, focused solely on one of these identities while not taking into account others. The racial prerequisite trials illustrated some of the ways in which different racial identities could be foregrounded to deny citizenship, and the deportations of veterans illustrated how different criminal convictions could void military service in terms of eligibility for citizenship.

What comes up throughout this history is that the intersectional identities complicate the construction of a narrative, but are also necessary to more fully understand the collective experiences of language-minoritized bilinguals. Recognizing intragroup heterogeneity is not meant to divide or subcategorize, but rather points to the need for frameworks such as intersectionality that can value and make visible these differences. Across the various experiences presented – seeking civic participation, entry into the United States or access to different educational opportunities – the consequences of testing rarely impacted individuals because of their language-minoritized bilingual identity alone. Solano-Flores (2011) and Solano-Flores and Nelson-Barber (2001) have argued for cultural validity in testing, which positions cultural and linguistic diversity as integral to test design. In addition to this work, an intersectionality lens provides for nuanced conceptualizations of cultural and linguistic diversity.

Language-minoritized Bilinguals and Histories of Discrimination

Similar to the way multiple identities interact in creating this narrative, tests and their related consequences have not operated in isolation. They co-occur with policies, laws, legislation and other institutional and structural forces that exert power and influence in imposing or enforcing social consequences of testing. Embedding these actions within histories of white settler colonialism and white supremacy serves to contextualize the profoundness of the systemic oppression language-minoritized bilinguals have faced. In commenting on the histories of discrimination connecting race and language-minoritized bilinguals with testing, Menken (2008) has described how:

> the testing movement has historically been tied to racism and linguisticism, rising in response to the record rates of immigration to this country. Tests are presented to the public as objective and their power is largely unquestioned, yet historically they have served to legitimize the marginalization of racial and ethnic minorities. (Menken, 2008: 19)

In working towards finding a pathway for testing to grapple with these social consequences, Omi and Winant's (1993) work on racial projects undergird the connections between historical events to everyday practices. Understanding that language-minoritized bilinguals are seen by *The Standards* as 'not yet proficient in English' serves as a link between monolingual or native-speaker ideologies about English proficiency and views of white supremacy (Flores & Rosa, 2015; Sledd, 1969). In working with these concepts, this narrative of the social consequences of testing has traced the ways in which historical, political, social and economic influences and events are encompassed within enduring legacies of white supremacy in the United States.

Chalhoub-Deville's (2016) contributions to consequential validity has introduced ways in which professionals in the testing field can begin to grapple with how tests co-occur with factors such as policies and she has worked to conceptualize how roles and responsibilities in testing can change over time. Tracing how historical events connect with current practices by adding a historical lens to these works on consequential validity in Chalhoub-Deville's work has the potential to create efforts to work purposefully and actively to dismantle the systemically oppressive forces that have (re)circulated in the field of testing. Using a historical narrative as an aspect of consequential validity means interrogating the many aspects of testing which may be taken for granted. It also means working *with* those communities with whom tests are being used, to better understand how test use impacts test-takers. By folding historical perspectives into the conceptualization of social consequences, the historical narrative becomes an aspect of the validity evidence of the test, a core element of the test development and test score interpretation.

Thoughts Moving Forward

In trying to understand the scope of the social consequences of testing faced by language-minoritized bilinguals, in particular negative consequences, I return to the question: *do tests represent inequities or do they reproduce them?* There is no simple answer to this question, but this historical narrative has described how language-minoritized bilinguals have faced repeated, often severe, consequences linked to tests and other mechanisms which have exacerbated existing and introduced new inequities. In this book, I have highlighted how *testing* or *test use* foregrounds the experiences of language-minoritized bilinguals, which allows for a more comprehensive understanding of the complexities of the social consequences of testing faced by language-minoritized bilinguals. Intensifying efforts that continually question the histories and legacies of discrimination are essential to change testing such that it actively confronts and dismantles inequities.

At the start of this work, I argued that testing professionals and other stakeholders account for test-taker goals that are attuned to the different ideological belief systems and the historical influences that may impact their work. *Collaborating with the communities that will be impacted by the social consequences of testing* is key in accomplishing some of these changes. This needs to be done with the understandings that sometimes tests may not be a viable option and that ongoing involvement in the community is necessary to ensure that the test continues to meet their needs. A series of framing questions based on Fishman's (1965) seminal question about language planning and policy – which was later revised by Solano-Flores (2008) with respect to testing of language-minoritized bilinguals – can serve as entry points to apply a use-oriented testing approach:

- *Who has been asked to take what test(s) in which language(s), when, where and how? That is, what communities do these test-takers belong to?*
- *Why are these communities being asked to take what test(s) in which language(s), when, where and how?*
- *What are the historical experiences and treatments of these communities in relation to **who** they are and **why** they are being asked to take test(s)?*
- *What are the related political, structural, economic, social and/or discursive histories and present concerns circulating around this test use?*
- *What actions are being taken to address the historical experiences and treatment of these communities with respect to related political, structural, economic, social and/or discursive histories and present concerns circulating around this test use?*

Test misuse and negative consequences may persist, but if counter-perspectives become part of the purview of those in the field of testing, then it is possible that there could be a change in the historical narrative of social consequences of testing faced by language-minoritized bilinguals.

References

Abedi, J. (2011) Assessing English language learners: Critical issues. In M. del Rosario Basterra, E. Trumbull and G. Solano-Flores (eds) *Cultural Validity in Assessment: Addressing Linguistic and Cultural Diversity* (pp. 49–71). New York: Routledge.

Abedi, J. (2017) Utilizing accommodations in assessment. In E. Shohamy, I.G. Or and S. May (eds) *Language Testing and Assessment* (pp. 303–322). New York: Springer International.

Abedi, J. and Dietel, R. (2004) Challenges in the No Child Left Behind Act for English-language learners. *Phi Delta Kappan* 85 (10), 782–785.

Abedi, J. and Linquanti, R. (2012) Issues and opportunities in strengthening large scale assessment systems for ELLs. Paper presented at the Understanding Language Conference, Stanford University, CA.

ACT Inc. (2016) *The ACT Profile Report – National Graduating Class 2016 National*. Iowa City: ACT, Inc., at http://www.act.org/content/dam/act/unsecured/documents/P_99_999999_N_S_N00_ACT-GCPR_National.pdf (accessed 29 October 2018).

ACT Inc. (2018) *ACT Policy for English Learner Supports Documentation*. Iowa City, IA: ACT, at https://www.act.org/content/dam/act/unsecured/documents/ACTPolicyforEnglishLearnerSupportsDocumentation.pdf (accessed 14 November 2018).

AERA, APA and NCME (2014) *The Standards for Educational and Psychological Testing*. Washington, DC: American Educational Research Association.

Alim, H.S., Rickford, J.R. and Ball, A.F. (2016) Introducing raciolinguistics. In H.S. Alim, J.R. Rickford and A.F. Ball (eds) *Raciolinguistics: How Language Shapes Our Ideas About Race* (pp. 1–30). Oxford: Oxford University Press.

Allen, R.L. (2001) The globalization of white supremacy: Toward a critical discourse on the racialization of the world. *Educational Theory* 51 (4), 467–485.

American Educational Group (2010) Universities in USA without TEOFL, IELTS/Admissions in USA without TEOFL, IELTS', blog post, 27 November, at http://aegedu.com/blog/universities-in-usa-us-without-toefl-admission-in-usa-without-toefl-ielts (accessed 20 June 2014).

Angoff, W. and Dyer, H. (1971) The admissions testing program. In W. Angoff (ed.) *The College Board Admissions Testing Program: A Technical Report on Research and Development Activities Relating to the Scholastic Aptitude Test and Achievement Tests*. Princeton, NJ: Educational Testing Service.

Anonymous (1926) A psychological study of immigrant children at Ellis Island. *British Medical Journal* 3, 482–485.

Ansley, F.L. (1989) Stirring the ashes: Race class and the future of civil rights scholarship. *Cornell Law Review* 74 (6), 993–1077.

Anthias, F. (2012) Transnational mobilities, migration research and intersectionality. *Nordic Journal of Migration Research* 2 (2), 102–110.

ASVAB (n.d.) History of military testing, at http://official-asvab.com/history_rec.htm (accessed 1 February 2016).

August, D. and Hakuta, K. (eds) (1997) *Improving Schools for Language Minority Children: A Research Agenda*. Washington, DC: National Academy of Education.

Baca, L. and Cervantes, H. (2004) *The Bilingual Special Education Interface* (4th edn). Columbus, OH: Merrill.

Baker, K.A. and de Kanter, A.A. (1983) *Bilingual Education: A Reappraisal of Federal Policy*. Lexington, MA: D.C. Heath.

Barde, R.E. (2008) *Immigration at the Golden Gate: Passenger Ships, Exclusion, and Angel Island*. Westport, CT: Praeger.

Barker, D.G. (1967) The history of entrance examinations. *Improving College and University Teaching* 15 (4), 250–253.

Baugh, J. (2003) Linguistic profiling. *Black Linguistics: Language, Society, and Politics in Africa and the Americas* 1 (1), 155–168.

Bayor, R.H. (2014) *Encountering Ellis Island: How European Immigrants Entered America*. Baltimore, MD: JHU Press.

Beauchamp, Z. (2013) The inside story of the Harvard dissertation that became too racist for heritage, 22 May, at https://thinkprogress.org/the-inside-story-of-the-harvard-dissertation-that-became-too-racist-for-heritage-3a14238f662e (accessed 1 June 2016).

Berliner, D. (2011) Rational responses to high stakes testing: The case of curriculum narrowing and the harm that follows. *Cambridge Journal of Education* 41 (3), 287–302.

Binet, A. (1911) *Les Idées Modernes sur les Enfants*. Paris: Flammarion.

Bock, F. (2016) Recruiter journal: Updates to PiCAT implemented, 28 January at http://www.usarec.army.mil/hq/stories/20160128_10.html (accessed 31 July 2017).

Boody, B.M. (1926) *A Psychological Study of Immigrant Children at Ellis Island*. Baltimore, MD: Williams & Wilkins.

Brigham, C.C. (1923) *A Study of American Intelligence*. Princeton, NJ: Princeton University Press.

Brigham, C.C. (1930) Intelligence tests of immigrant groups. *Psychological Review* 37 (2), 158–165.

Buchanan, R. and Finch, S. (2005) History of psychometrics. In B. Everitt and D. Howell (eds) *Encyclopedia of Statistics in Behavioral Science* (pp. 875–886). Oxford: Wiley-Blackwell.

Buchmann, C., Condron, D.J. and Roscigno, V.J. (2010) Shadow education, American style: Test preparation, the SAT and college enrollment. *Social Forces* 89 (2), 435–461.

Cahir, J., Adegoke, J., Brownawell, D., Crane, R., Cunning, T., Enerson, D., Gallagher, S., Hecht, M., Hendrickson, L., Kayal, D., Turns, S. and Xi, X. (1999) Reports on policies and practices related to the English proficiency of international teaching assistants, at http://gradschool.psu.edu/faculty-and-staff/faculty/english1 (accessed 4 September 2017).

Carbado, D.W. and Harris, C.I. (2012) The new racial preferences. In D. Martinez HoSang, O. LaBennett and L. Pulido (eds) *Racial Formation in the Twenty-First Century* (pp. 183–212). Berkeley, CA: University of California Press.

Cardenas, J. (1976) *Lau Remedies Outlined*. San Antonio, TX: Intercultural Development Research Association.

Cardona, R. and Ritchie, E.C. (2006) Psychological screening of recruits prior to accession in the U.S. military. In B. DeKoning (ed.) *Recruit Medicine*. Washington, DC: Office of the Surgeon General.

Chalhoub-Deville, M. (2016) Validity theory: Reform policies, accountability testing, and consequences. *Language Testing* 33 (4), 453–472.

Chan, S. (1991) *Entry Denied: Exclusion and the Chinese Community in America, 1882–1943*. Philadelphia, PA: Temple University Press.

Chen, X., Hung, J., Park, Y. and Takahashi, J. (2017) How we survived our first year teaching as new ITAS at http://newsmanager.commpartners.com/tesolitais/issues/2017-07-18/3.html (accessed 1 October 2017).

Chishti, M., Pierce, S. and Bolter, J. (2017) The Obama record on deportations: Deporter in chief or not?, at http://www.migrationpolicy.org/article/obama-record-deportations-deporter-chief-or-not (accessed 4 August 2017).

Cho, S. (2013) Post-intersectionality: The curious reception of intersectionality in legal scholarship. *Du Bois Review: Social Science Research on Race* 10 (2), 385–404.

Cho, S., Crenshaw, K.W. and McCall, L. (2013) Toward a field of intersectionality studies: Theory, applications, and praxis. *Signs: Journal of Women in Culture and Society* 38 (4), 785–810.

Cimpian, J.R., Thompson, K.D. and Makowski, M. (2017) Evaluating English learner reclassification policy effects across districts. *American Educational Research Journal* 54 (suppl. 1), 255S–278S.

Cizek, G.J. (2016) Validating test score meaning and defending test score use: Different aims, different methods. *Assessment in Education: Principles, Policy and Practice* 23 (2), 212–225.

Cizek, G.J. and Wollack, J.A. (2017) *Handbook of Quantitative Methods for Detecting Cheating on Tests*. New York: Routledge.

Clarke, M.M., Madaus, G.F., Horn, C.L. and Ramos, M.A. (2000) Retrospective on educational testing and assessment in the 20th century. *Journal of Curriculum Studies* 32 (2), 159–181.

College Board (2016a) *2016 College-Bound Seniors Total Group Profile Report*. New York, NY: College Board, at https://reports.collegeboard.org/pdf/total-group-2016.pdf (accessed 29 October 2018).

College Board (2016b) PAA – Prueba de Aptitud Académica, at https://latam.collegeboard.org/page/paa (accessed 4 June 2017).

Colvin, S.S. and Allen, R.D. (1923) Mental tests and linguistic ability. *Journal of Educational Psychology* 14 (1), 1–20.

Commissioner General of Immigration (1892–1924) *Annual Reports. US Immigration Statistics: Immigration Station at Ellis Island, NY*. Washington, DC: Commissioner General of Education.

Common Core State Standards Initiative (n.d.) Development processm at. http://www.corestandards.org/about-the-standards/development-process (accessed 24 July 2018).

Congressional Record (1967) Debate on the Elementary and Secondary Education Amendment Act of 1967 (H.R. 7814), May–July', 1–681.

Controller General of the Unites States (1976) *Bilingual Education: An Unmet Need*. Washington, DC: Office of Education, at http://gao.gov/assets/120/116035.pdf (accessed 24 July 2018).

Cooper, B. and O'Neill, K. (2005) Lessons from the Immigration Reform and Control Act of 1986, at. http://www.migrationpolicy.org/pubs/PolicyBrief_No3_Aug05.pdf (accessed 31 July 2016).

Cornish, A. (2017) This simple puzzle test sealed the fate of immigrants at Ellis Island, at https://www.npr.org/templates/transcript/transcript.php?storyId=528813842?storyId=528813842 (accessed 14 November 2018).

Crane, A.G. (1921) *Education for the Disabled in War and Industry*. New York: Teachers College, Columbia University.

Crawford, F.C. (1925) New York State literacy test. *American Science Political Science Review* 19 (4), 788–790.

Crawford, J. (1998) Language politics in the USA: The paradox of bilingual education. *Social Justice* 25 (3), 50–69.

Crawford, J. (2002) The Bilingual Education Act, 1968–2002: An obituary, at http://www.languagepolicy.net/books/AEL/Crawford_BEA_Obituary.pdf (accessed 24 October 2018).

Crenshaw, K. (1989) Demarginalizing the intersection of race and sex: A Black feminist critique of antidiscrimination doctrine, feminist theory and antiracist politics, *University of Chicago Legal Forum* 140, 139–167.

Crenshaw, K. (1991) Mapping the margins: Intersectionality, identity politics, and violence against women of color. *Stanford Law Review* 43 (6), 1241–1299.

Crenshaw, K. (2014) The structural and political dimensions of intersectional oppression. In P.R. Grzanka (ed.) *Intersectionality: A Foundations and Frontiers Reader* (pp. 17–22). Boulder, CO: Westview Press.

Crockett, J.B. and Kauffman, J.M. (1999) *The Least Restrictive Environment: Its Origins and Interpretations in Special Education*. London: Lawrence Erlbaum Associates.

Cronbach, L.J. (1971) Test validation. In R.L. Thorndike (ed.) *Educational Measurement*. Washington, DC: American Council on Education.

Cummins, J. (1979) Linguistic interdependence and the educational development of bilingual children. *Review of Educational Research* 49 (2), 222–251.

Cummins, J. (1981a) *Bilingualism and Minority-Language Children: Language and Literacy Series*. Toronto: Ontario Institute for Studies in Education, at http://files.eric.ed.gov/fulltext/ED215557.pdf (accessed 24 October 2018).

Cummins, J. (1981b) The role of primary language development in promoting educational success for language minority students. In California State Department of Education (ed.) *Schooling and Language Minority Students: A Theoretical Framework.*. Los Angeles, CA: Evaluation, Dissemination and Assessment Center, California State University.

Cummins, J. (1986) Empowering minority students: A framework for intervention. *Harvard Educational Review* 71 (4), 649–676.

Cummins, J. (2000) *Language, Power, and Pedagogy: Bilingual Children in the Crossfire*. Clevedon: Multilingual Matters.

Cummins, J. (2008) BICS and CALP: Empirical and theoretical status of the distinction. In N. Hornberger (ed.) *Encyclopedia of Language and Education, Vol. 2: Literacy* (2nd edn) (pp. 71–83). New York: Springer.

Currier, K.S. (2004) *Kai's Journey to Gold Mountain: An Angel Island Story*. San Francisco, CA: Angel Island Association.

Daniels, R. (1997) No lamps were lit for them: Angel Island and the historiography of Asian American immigration. *Journal of American Ethnic History* 17 (1), 3–18.

Danoff, M.N. (1978) *Evaluation of the Impact of ESEA Title VII Spanish/English Bilingual Education Program. Overview and Study Findings*. Palo Alto, CA: American Institutes for Research in the Behavioral Sciences.

de Mejía, A.M. (2002) *Power, Prestige, and Bilingualism*. Clevedon: Multilingual Matters.

de Mejía, A.M. (2012) Elite/folk bilingual education. In *The Encyclopedia of Applied Linguistics*. Hoboken, NJ: Blackwell.

Del Valle, S. (2003) *Language Rights and the Law in the United States: Finding Our Voices*. Clevedon: Multilingual Matters.

Department of Justice (1943) *Immigration and Naturalization Service Monthly Review* 1 (4), 12–16.

Deported Veterans Support House (2017) 'About Us', at http://www.deportedveteranssupporthouse.org/about-us(accessed 20 June 2016).

Doane, A.W. and Bonilla-Silva, E. (eds) (2003) *White Out: The Continuing Significance of Racism*. London: Psychology Press.

Duran, R.P. (1989) Testing of linguistic minorities. In R.L. Linn (ed.) *Educational Measurement* (pp. 573–587). New York: American Council on Education and Macmillan.

Education Trust (2010) Shut out of the military: Today's high school education doesn't mean you're ready for today's army, at https://files.eric.ed.gov/fulltext/ED514183.pdf (accessed 14 November 2018).

Educational Testing Service (2008) Factors that can influence performance on the GRE General Test 2006–2007, at. https://www.ets.org/Media/Tests/GRE/pdf/gre_0809_factors_2006-07.pdf (accessed 2 October 2016).

Educational Testing Service (2016a) *A Snapshot of the Individuals Who Took the GRE General Test*. Princeton, NJ: Educational Testing Service, at https://www.ets.org/s/gre/pdf/snapshot_test_taker_data_2016.pdf (accessed 29 October 2018).

Educational Testing Service (2016b) *Test and Score Data Summary for TOEFL iBT® Tests January 2016–December 2016 Test Data*. Princeton, NJ: Educational Testing Service, at https://www.ets.org/s/toefl/pdf/94227_unlweb.pdf (accessed 29 October 2018).

Elliott, S.N. and Roach, A.T. (2002) The impact of providing testing accommodations to students with disabilities, paper delivered to the 'Symposium on How Federal Requirements are Affecting Inclusion of Special Needs Students on State Assessments' at the Annual Convention of the American Educational Research Association, New Orleans, LA, 3 April.

FairTest (2016) More than 670,000 refused tests in 2015, at http://www.fairtest.org/more-500000-refused-tests-2015 (accessed 15 December 2015).

FairTest (2017) Just say no to standardized tests: Why and how to opt out, at http://www.fairtest.org/get-involved/opting-out (accessed 16 May 2017).

FairTest (2018) More than 1000 accredited colleges and universities that do not use ACT/SAT scores to admit substantial numbers of students into bachelor-degree programs, at https://www.fairtest.org/university/optional (accessed 14 November 2018).

Fancher, R.E. (1985) *The Intelligence Men: Makers of the IQ Controversy*. New York: W.W. Norton.

Faulkner-Bond, M. and Forte, E. (2015) English learners and accountability: The promise, pitfalls, and peculiarity of assessing language minorities via large-scale assessment. In C.S. Wells, M. Faulkner-Bond and E. Hambleton (eds) *Educational Measurement: From Foundations to Future*, (pp. 395–415). New York: Guildford Press.

Faulkner-Bond, M. and Sireci, S.G. (2015) Validity issues in assessing linguistic minorities. *International Journal of Testing* 15 (2), 114–135.

Fishman, J.A. (1965) Who speaks what language to whom and when? *La linguistique* 1 (2), 67–88.

Flores, N. and Rosa, J. (2015) Undoing appropriateness: Raciolinguistic ideologies and language diversity in education. *Harvard Educational Review* 85 (2), 149–171.

Ford, M. (2012) Civic illiteracy: A threat to the American ream, at http://xuamericandream.blogspot.com/2012/04/civic-illiteracy-threat-to-american.html (accessed 22 October 2018).

Ford, R. (2001) City-states and citizenship. In T.A. Aleinikoff and D. Klusmeyer (eds) *Citizenship Today: Global Perspectives and Practices* (pp. 226–253). Washington, DC: Carnegie Endowment for International Peace.

Frank, N. (2009) *Unfriendly Fire: How the Gay Ban Undermines the Military and Weakens America*. Basingstoke: Macmillan.

Fry, R. (2007) *How Far Behind in Math and Reading Are English Language Learners?* Washington, DC: Pew Hispanic Center.

Fry, R. (2008) 'The role of schools in the English language learner achievement gap, at http://www.pewhispanic.org/2008/06/26/the-role-of-schools-in-the-english-language-learner-achievement-gap (accessed 21 May 2017).

Gallagher, C.B. (2014) 'I was so glad to be in school here': Religious organizations and the school on Ellis Island in the early 1900s. In J. Marten (ed.) *Children and Youth During the Gilded Age and Progressive Era* (pp. 81–101). New York: New York University Press.

Galton, F. (1909) *Essays in Eugenics*. London: Eugenics Education Society.

García, O. (2009) *Bilingual Education in the 21st Century: A Global Perspective*. Oxford: Wiley-Blackwell.

García, O. and Baker, C. (2006) *Bilingual Education*. Clevedon: Multilingual Matters.

García, O. and Kleifgen, J.A. (2010) *Educating Emergent Bilinguals: Policies, Programs, and Practices for English Language Learners*. New York: Teachers College Press, Columbia University.

Gelb, S. (1986) Henry H. Goddard and the immigrants, 1910–1917: The studies and their social context. *Journal of the History of the Behavioral Science* 22 (4), 324–332.

Gillborn, D. (2006) Rethinking white supremacy: Who counts in 'WhiteWorld'. *Ethnicities* 6 (3), 318–340.

Gilman, L. (1965) Hands across the border: Bienvenidos amigos. *I&N Reporter* (July), 61–63).
Glueck, B. (1913) The mentally defective immigrant. *New York Medical Journal* 98, 760–766.
Goddard, H. (1917) Mental tests and the immigrant. *Journal of Delinquency* 2, 243–277.
Goodenough, F.L. (1926) Racial differences in the intelligence of school children. *Journal of Experimental Psychology* 9 (5), 388–397.
Guidroz, K., and Berger, M.T. (2009) A conversation with founding scholars of intersectionality: Kimberlé Crenshaw, Nira Yuval-Davis, and Michelle Fine. In K. Guidroz and M.T. Berger (eds) *The Intersectional Approach: Transforming the Academy Through Race, Class, and Gender* (pp. 61–78). Durham, NC: University of North Carolina Press.
Haertel, E. and Herman, J.L. (2005) *A Historical Perspective on Validity Arguments for Accountability Testing.* Los Angeles, CA: National Center for Research on Evaluation, Standards, and Student Testing, Center for the Study of Evaluation, Graduate School of Education and Information.
Hage, J.T. (2012) *White Nation: Fantasies of White Supremacy in a Multicultural Society.* London: Routledge.
Hakuta, K. (1986) *The Mirror of Language: The Debate on Bilingualism.* New York: Basic Books.
Haney López, I. (2006) *White by Law 10th Anniversary Edition: The Legal Construction of Race.* New York: New York University Press.
Hanley, T.O. (1969) A western Democrat's quarrel with the language laws. *Nebraska History* 50, at. https://history.nebraska.gov/sites/history.nebraska.gov/files/doc/publications/NH1969LanguageLaws.pdf (accessed 13 May 2015).
Hansegård, N.E. (1968) *Tvåspråkighet eller halvspråkighet?* [Bilingualism or Semilingualism?] Stockholm: Alders/Banners.
Hansen, R. and King, D. (2001) Eugenic ideas, political interests, and policy variance: Immigration and sterilization policy in Britain and the US. *World Politics* 53 (2), 237–263.
Harney, A. and Stecklow, S. (2016) Exclusive: ACT Inc raises test prices abroad to fund cheating fight', Reuters, 8 December, at. https://www.reuters.com/article/us-college-cheating-act-price/exclusive-act-inc-raises-test-prices-abroad-to-fund-cheating-fight-idUSKBN13X1U8 (accessed 2 August 2017).
Harry, B. and Klingner, J. (2006) *Why Are so Many Minority Students in Special Education? Understanding Race and Disability in Schools.* New York: Teachers College Press, Columbia University.
Harry S. Truman Library and Museum (n.d.) The Truman public papers, at https://www.trumanlibrary.org/publicpapers/index.php?pid=2389 (accessed 12 July 2017).
Hemphill, F.C. and Vanneman, A. (2011) *Achievement Gaps: How Hispanic and White Students in Public Schools Perform in Mathematics and Reading on the National Assessment of Educational Progress* (Statistical Analysis Report NCES 2011-459). Washington, DC: National Center for Education Statistics.
Hernández, K.L. (2006) The crimes and consequences of illegal immigration: A cross-border examination of Operation Wetback, 1943 to 1954. *Western Historical Quarterly* 37 (4), 421–444.
Higgins, L. and Sun, C.H. (2002) The development of psychological testing in China. *International Journal of Psychology* 37 (4), 246–254.
Hing, B. (2004) *Defining America Through Immigration Policy.* Philadelphia, PA: Temple University Press.
Holt, G. (1915) *The Case for the Literacy Test.* New York: Immigration Restriction League.
Hornberger, N.H. (2005) Heritage/community language education: US and Australian perspectives. *International Journal of Bilingual Education and Bilingualism* 8 (2–3), 101–108.
Hornberger, N.H. (2006) Nichols to NCLB: Local and global perspectives on U.S. language

education policy. In O. García, T. Skutnabb-Kangas and M. Torres-Guzmán (eds) *Imagining Multilingual Schools: Languages in Education and Glocalization* (pp. 223–237). Clevedon: Multilingual Matters.

IBM (n.d.) IBM 805 (continued), at http://www-03.ibm.com/ibm/history/exhibits/specialprod1/specialprod1_10.html (accessed 12 June 2017).

ICF International (2011) *Records Study Comparison Report: U.S. Citizenship and Immigration Services' Records Study on Pass/Fail Rates for Naturalization Applicants* (RFQ/Project No. HSSCCG-09-Q-00228, DHS Professional and Program Management Support Services (PPMSS) BPA # GS-10F-06-LP-A-0007). Washington, DC: Department of Homeland Security, at https://www.uscis.gov/sites/default/files/USCIS/files/Records_Study_for_the_Naturalization_Test.pdf (accessed 29 October 2018).

IELTS (2017a) IELTS numbers rise to three million a year, at https://www.ielts.org/news/2017/ielts-numbers-rise-to-three-million-a-year (accessed 23 September 2017).

IELTS (2017b) IELTS for migration, at https://www.ielts.org/what-is-ielts/ielts-for-migration (accessed 23 September 2017).

ILTA (2000) International Language Testing Association Code of Ethics, at http://www.iltaonline.com/page/CodeofEthics (accessed 1 February 2017).

Jacobsen, E. (2017) A (mostly) brief history of the SAT and ACT tests, at http://erikthered.com/tutor/sat-act-history.html (accessed 2 January 2017).

Johnson, L.B. (1966) Public papers of the Presidents of the United States: Lyndon B. Johnson, 1966, at https://quod.lib.umich.edu/p/ppotpus?key=title;page=browse;value=1 https://quod.lib.umich.edu/p/ppotpus/4731549.1966.001?view=toc (accessed 2 June 2017).

Jørgensen, J.N. (2012) Ideologies and norms in language and education policies in Europe and their relationship with everyday language behaviours. *Language, Culture and Curriculum* 25 (1), 57–71.

Kachru, B.B. (2006) The English language in the outer circle. *World Englishes* 3, 241–255.

Kane, M.T. (2013) Validating the interpretations and uses of test scores. *Journal of Educational Measurement* 50 (1), 1–73.

Kang, O. (2012) Impact of rater characteristics and prosodic features of speaker accentedness on ratings of international teaching assistants' oral performance. *Language Assessment Quarterly* 9 (3), 249–269.

Kangas, S.E.N. (2014) When special education trumps ESL: An investigation of service delivery for Ells with disabilities. *Critical Inquiry in Language Studies* 11 (4), 273–306.

Kangas, S.E.N. (2017) 'That's where the rubber meets the road': The intersection of special education and bilingual education. *Teachers College Record* 119 (7), 1–36.

Kangas, S.E.N. (2018) Breaking one law to uphold another: Service provision for English learners with disabilities. *TESOL Quarterly*. Advanced online publication. doi:10.1002/tesq.431.

Kanno, Y. and Kangas, S.E.N. (2014) 'I'm not going to be, like, for the AP': English language learners' limited access to advanced college-preparatory courses in high school. *American Educational Research Journal* 51 (5), 848–878.

Kates, S. (2006) Literacy, voting rights, and the citizenship schools in the South, 1957–1970. *College Composition and Communication* 57 (3), 479–502.

Kelly, F.J. (1916) The Kansas Silent Reading Tests. *Journal of Educational Psychology* 7 (2), 63.

Kelly, W.F. (1954) The wetback issue. *I&N Reporter* 2 (3), 37–39.

Kennedy, E.M. (1981) The Refugee Act of 1980. *International Migration Review* 15 (1), 141–156.

Kevles, D.J. (1985) *In the Name of Eugenics: Genetics and the Uses of Human Heredity*. Cambridge, MA: Harvard University Press.

Kevles, D.J. (1995) *The Physicists: The History of a Scientific Community in Modern America*. Cambridge, MA: Harvard University Press.

Khan, K. (2017) Citizenship, securitization and 'suspicion' in UK ESOL policy. In K. Arnaut, M.S. Karrabaek and M. Spotti (eds) *Engaging with Superdiversity* (pp. 303–320). Bristol: Multilingual Matters.

Khan, K. and McNamara, T. (2017) Citizenship, immigration laws, and language. In S. Canagarajah (ed.) *The Routledge Handbook of Migration and Language* (pp. 451–467). London: Routledge.

Kieffer, M.J. and Parker, C.E. (2016) *Patterns of English Learner Student Reclassification in New York City Public Schools* (REL 2017-200). Washington, DC: US Department of Education, Institute of Education Sciences, National Center for Education Evaluation and Regional Assistance, Regional Educational Laboratory Northeast and Islands, at https://ies.ed.gov/pubsearch/pubsinfo.asp?pubid=REL2017200 (accessed 29 October 2018).

Kieffer, M.J. and Parker, C.E. (2017) *Graduation Outcomes of Students Who Entered New York City Public Schools in Grade 5 or 6 as English Learner Students* (REL 2017-237). Washington, DC: US Department of Education, Institute of Education Sciences, National Center for Education Evaluation and Regional Assistance, Regional Educational Laboratory Northeast and Islands, at http://ies.ed.gov/ ncee/edlabs (accessed 29 October 2018).

Kieffer, M.J., Lesaux, N.K., Rivera, M. and Francis, D.J. (2009) Accommodations for English language learners taking large-scale assessments: A meta-analysis on effectiveness and validity. *Review of Educational Research* 79 (3), 1168–1201.

Kieffer, M.J., Rivera, M. and Francis, D.J. (2012) *Practical Guidelines for the Education of English Language Learners: Research-Based Recommendations for the Use of Accommodations in Large-Scale Assessments*. Portsmouth, NH: RMC Research Corporation, Center on Instruction.

Kirkpatrick, C. (1926) *Intelligence and Immigration*. Philadelphia, PA: Williams & Wilkins.

Klein, C. A. (1996) Treaties of conquest: Property rights, Indian treaties, and the Treaty of Guadalupe Hidalgo. *NML Review* 26, 201.

Knowles, J. and Carlson, D. (2016) Reclassifying English language learners: What's the effect on Wisconsin high schoolers?, at https://www.brookings.edu/blog/brown-center-chalkboard/2016/03/09/reclassifying-english-language-learners-whats-the-effect-on-wisconsin-high-schoolers (accessed 21 December 2016).

Knox, H.A. (1913) The moron and the study of alien defectives. *Journal of the American Medical Association* 60 (2), 105–106.

Kobrin, J., Patterson, B., Shaw, E., Mattern, K. and Barbuti, S. (2008) *Validity of the SAT® for Predicting First-Year College Grade Point Average*. New York: College Board, at https://research.collegeboard.org/sites/default/files/publications/2012/7/researchreport-2008-5-validity-sat-predicting-first-year-college-grade-point-average.pdf (accessed 29 October 2018).

Kohler, M.J. (1912) *The Injustice of a Literacy Test for Immigrants*, at http://www.ajcarchives.org/AJC_DATA/Files/F-31.PDF (accessed 29 October 2018).

Kopriva, R. (2008) *Improving Testing for English Language Learners*. New York: Routledge.

Kraut, A.M. (1995) *Silent Travelers: Germs, Genes, and the Immigrant Menace*. Baltimore, MD: JHU Press.

Kuhl, S. (2002) *The Nazi Connection: Eugenics, American Racism, and German National Socialism*. Oxford: Oxford University Press.

Kulish, N., Dickerson, C. and Robbins, L. (2017) Reports of raids have immigrants bracing for enforcement surge, *New York Times*, 10 February, at https://www.nytimes.com/2017/02/10/us/immigration-raids-enforcement.html (accessed 3 March 2017).

Lado, R. (1961) *Language Testing: The Construction and Use of Foreign Language Tests. A Teacher's Book*. New York: McGraw-Hill.

Lambert, W.E., Hodgson, E.R., Gardner, R.C. and Fillenbaum, S. (1960) Evaluation reactions to spoken languages. *Journal of Abnormal and Social Psychology* 60, 44–51.

Lay, N.D.S., Carro, G., Tien, S., Niemann, T.C. and Leong, S. (1999) Connections: High school to college. In L. Harklau, K. Losey and M. Siegal (eds) *Language Minority Students, ESL, and College Composition* (pp. 175–190). Mahwah, NJ: Erlbaum.

Lee, E. and Yung, J. (2010) *Angel Island: Immigrant Gateway to America*. Oxford: Oxford University Press.

Lee, J. (2012) *U.S. Naturalizations: 2011*. Washington, DC: Office of Immigration Statistics, Department of Homeland Security, at http://www.dhs.gov/xlibrary/assets/statistics/publications/natz_fr_2011.pdf (accessed 3 March 2017).

Leibowitz, A.H. (1969) English literacy: Legal sanction for discrimination. *Notre Dame Lawyer* 45 (1), 7–67.

Leibowitz, A.H. (1984) The official character of language in the United States: Literacy requirements for immigration, citizenship, and entrance into American life. *Aztlan: A Journal of Chicano Studies* 15 (1), 25–70.

Leung, C., and Scarino, A. (2016) Reconceptualizing the nature of goals and outcomes in language/s education. *Modern Language Journal* 100 (suppl. 1), 81–95.

Levin, B. (1982) *The Making (and Unmaking) of a Civil Rights Regulation: Language Minority Children and Bilingual Education*. Stanford University, California Institute for Research on Educational Finance and Governance. Washington, DC: National Institute of Education.

Lewin, T. (2013) Testing, testing: More students are taking both the ACT and SAT, *New York Times*, 2 August, at http://www.nytimes.com/2013/08/04/education/edlife/more-students-are-taking-both-the-act-and-sat.html?mcubz=1 (accessed 1 March 2016).

Lind, D. (2017) Fewer immigrants are being deported under Trump than under Obama but it's not because Trump isn't trying, *Vox*, 10 August, at https://www.vox.com/policy-and-politics/2017/8/10/16119910/trump-deportations-obama (accessed 2 September 2017).

Lindquist, E.F. (1935) Cooperative achievement testing. *Journal of Educational Research* 28 (7), 511–552.

Linquanti, R. and Cook, H.G. (2015) *Re-examining Reclassification: Guidance from a National Working Session on Policies and Practices for Exiting Students from English Learner Status*. Washington, DC: Council of Chief State School Offices.

Linquanti, R. and Cook, H.G. (2017) *Innovative Solutions for Including Recently Arrived English Learners in State Accountability Systems: A Guide for States*. US Department of Education Report ED-ESE-12-C-0067, at https://statesupportnetwork.ed.gov/system/files/real-guidefinal.pdf (accessed 22 January 2018).

Lira, N. and Stern, A.M. (2014) Mexican Americans and eugenic sterilization. *Aztlan* 39 (2), 9–34.

Llosa, L., Kieffer, M.J. and Lee, O. (2016) *How Can Educational Systems Better Serve English Learners?* (Education Solutions Initiative). New York: NYU Steinhardt.

Losen, D.J. and Orfield, G. (eds) (2002) *Racial Inequity in Special Education*. Cambridge, MA: Harvard Education Press.

Lowenstein, E. (ed.) (1958) *The Alien and the Immigration Law: A Study of 1446 Cases Arising Under the Immigration and Naturalization Laws of the United States*. Dobbs Ferry, NY: Oceana Publications.

Ludmerer, K.M. (1972) Genetics, eugenics, and the Immigration Restriction Act of 1924. *Bulletin of the History of Medicine* 46 (1), 59.

Luebke, F. (1968) The German–American Alliance in Nebraska, 1910–1917. *Nebraska History* 49, at http://www.nebraskahistory.org/publish/publicat/history/full-text/NH1968GermanAlliance.pdf (accessed 15 October 2016).

Lynch, B.K. (2001) Rethinking assessment from a critical perspective. *Language Testing* 18 (4), 351–372.

MacSwan, J. (2000) The threshold hypothesis, semilingualism, and other contributions to a deficit view of linguistic minorities. *Hispanic Journal of Behavioral Sciences* 22 (1), 3–45.

Makoni, S. and Pennycook, A. (eds) (2007) *Disinventing and Reconstituting Languages*. Clevedon: Multilingual Matters.

Manohar, U. and Appiah, O. (2016) Perspective taking to improve attitudes towards international teaching assistants: The role of national identification and prior attitudes. *Communication Education* 65 (2), 149–163.

Martin-Jones, M. and Romaine, S. (1986) Semilingualism: A half-baked theory of communicative competence. *Applied Linguistics* 7, 26–38.

Matthews, D. (2013) Heritage study co-author opposed letting in immigrants with low IQs, article, at https://www.washingtonpost.com/news/wonk/wp/2013/05/08/heritage-study-co-author-opposed-letting-in-immigrants-with-low-iqs/?utm_term=.f00362e80b68 (accessed 15 April 2016).

May, V.M. (2015) *Pursuing Intersectionality, Unsettling Dominant Imaginaries*. London: Routledge.

McCammon, E. (2016) Can you get into graduate schools without GRE scores?, at https://www.prepscholar.com/gre/blog/no-gre-required-graduate-school (accessed 14 November 2018).

McNamara, T. (1998) Policy and social considerations in language assessment. *Annual Review of Applied Linguistics* 18, 304–319.

McNamara, T. (2005) 21st century shibboleth: Language tests, identity and intergroup conflict. *Language Policy* 4 (4), 351–370.

McNamara, T. (2008) The social-political and power dimensions of tests. In E. Shohamy and N.H. Hornberger (eds) *Encyclopedia of Language and Education, Vol. 7: Language Testing and Assessment* (2nd edn) (pp. 415–427). Dordrecht: Springer.

McNamara, T. (2009) Australia: The dictation test redux? *Language Assessment Quarterly* 6 (1), 106–111.

McNamara, T. and Ryan, K. (2011) Fairness versus justice in language testing: The place of English literacy in the Australian Citizenship Test. *Language Assessment Quarterly* 8 (2), 161–178.

Menken, K. (2008) *English Learners Left Behind: Standardized Testing as Language Policy*. Clevedon: Multilingual Matters.

Messick, S. (1980) Test validity and the ethics of assessment. *American Psychologist* 35 (11), 1012.

Messick, S. (1989) Validity. In R.L. Linn (ed.) *Educational Measurement* (3rd edn) (pp. 13–103). New York: Oryx Press.

Messick, S. (1990) Validity of test interpretation and use. *ETS Research Report Series* 1, 1487–1495.

Messick, S. (1993) Foundations of validity: Meaning and consequences in psychological assessments. *ETS Research Report Series* 2, 1–18.

Messick, S. (1994) The interplay of evidence and consequences in the validation of performance assessments. *Educational Researcher* 23 (2), 13–23.

Messick, S. (1996) Validity and washback in language testing. *Language Testing* 13 (4), 241–257.

Messick, S. (1998) Test validity: A matter of consequence. *Social Indicators Research* 45 (1–3), 35–44.

Meyer, K.R. and Mao, Y. (2014) Comparing student perceptions of the classroom climate created by U.S. American and international teaching assistants. *Higher Learning Research Communications* 4 (3), 12–22.

Migration Policy Institute (2013) Major U.S. immigration laws, at http://www.migrationpolicy.org/research/timeline-1790 (accessed 16 June 2017).

Miller, W.B. (1948) Foreign born in the United States army during World War II, with special reference to the alien. *Immigration and Naturalization Service Monthly Review* 6 (4), 48–54, at https://www.uscis.gov/sites/default/files/USCIS/History%20and%20Genealogy/Our%20History/INS%20History/WWII/INSMRev1948.10.pdf (accessed 16 June 2017).

Mills, C. W. (2003) White supremacy as sociopolitical system: A philosophical perspective. In *White Out: The Continuing Significance of Racism* (pp. 35–48). London: Taylor & Francis.

Mitchell, C. (2017) Is the new English-proficiency test too hard? Educators and experts debate, at http://www.edweek.org/ew/articles/2017/08/04/is-a-new-english-proficiency-test-too-hard.html (accessed 4 August 2017).

Moran, R. (1988) The politics of discretion: Federal intervention in bilingual education. *California Law Review* 76 (6), 1249.

Murray, C. (2013) In defense of Jason Richwine, at http://www.nationalreview.com/article/348323 (accessed 21 February 2016).

Nahm, R. (n.d.) From Japanese-occupied Korea to Angel Island: Immigration story of Lee Bum Young and Kim Hey Soo, at. http://www.aiisf.org/immigrant-voices/stories-by-author/from-japanese-occupied-korea-to-angel-island-immigration-story-of-lee-bum-young-and-kim-hey-soo (accessed 14 November 2016).

National Archives (2016) Documents related to *Brown v. Board of Education*, Background, at https://www.archives.gov/education/lessons/brown-v-board (accessed 16 September 2016).

National Center for Education Statistics (2016) *Public High School 4-Year Adjusted Cohort Graduation Rate (ACGR), by Selected Student Characteristics and State: 2010–11 Through 2013–14*, at http://nces.ed.gov/programs/digest/d15/tables/dt15_219.46.asp (accessed 13 April 2017).

National Center for Research on Evaluation, Standards, and Student Testing (2010) *When to Exit ELL Students: Monitoring Success and Failure in Mainstream Classrooms After ELLs' Reclassification* (CRESST Report 779). Los Angeles, CA: National Center for Research on Evaluation, Standards, and Student Testing, at http://files.eric.ed.gov/fulltext/ED520430.pdf (accessed 1 November 2018).

National Park Service (n.d.) History of Ellis Island 1892 to 1954, at https://www.nps.gov/elis/learn/historyculture/history-of-ellis-island-from-1892-to-1954.htm (accessed 16 September 2016).

National Research Council (2002) *Minority Students in Special and Gifted Education*. Committee on Minority Representation in Special Education, Division of Behavioral and Social Sciences and Education. Washington, DC: National Academy Press.

New York State Allies for Public Education (2016) 2016 NY refusal policy and counts, Google spreadsheet, at. https://docs.google.com/spreadsheets/d/1swri_N2ecebFJcY-1eiESLtGn1k6yAVW5XaGSi6mg9Pg/htmlview?pli=1#gid=0 (accessed 11 December 2016).

Ngai, M.M. (1999) The architecture of race in American immigration law: A reexamination of the Immigration Act of 1924. *Journal of American History* 86 (1), 67–92.

Ngai, M.M. (2005) Transnationalism and the transformation of the 'other': Response to the presidential address. *American Quarterly* 57 (1), 59–65.

NPR (2017) This simple puzzle test sealed the fate of immigrants at Ellis Island', at http://www.npr.org/2017/05/17/528813842/this-simple-puzzle-test-sealed-the-fate-of-immigrants-at-ellis-island (accessed 31 July 2017).

Núñez, A.M. (2014) Employing multilevel intersectionality in educational research: Latino identities, contexts, and college access. *Educational Researcher* 43 (2), 85–92.

Office of English Language Acquisition (2017) *Students with Disabilities Who Are English Learners*. Washington, DC: US Department of Education.

Office of Technology Assessment (1992) *Testing in American Schools: Asking the Right Questions*. Washington, DC: US Government Printing Office, at https://www.princeton.edu/~ota/disk1/1992/9236/9236.PDF accessed 29 October 2018.

Okeowo, A. (2016) Hate on the rise after Trump's election, *New Yorker*, at http://www.newyorker.com/news/news-desk/hate-on-the-rise-after-trumps-election (accessed 3 February 2017).

Omi, M. and Winant, H. (1993) On the theoretical status of the concept of race. In C. McCarthy and W. Critchlow (eds) *Race, Identity and Representation in Education* (pp. 3–10). New York: Routledge.

Otheguy, R., García, O. and Reid, W. (2015) Clarifying translanguaging and deconstructing named languages: A perspective from linguistics. *Applied Linguistics Review* 6 (3), 281–307.

Park, S., Magee, J., Martinez, M.I., Willner, L.S. and Paul, P. (2016) *English Language Learners with Disabilities: A Call for Additional Research and Policy Guidance.* Council of Chief State School Officers, at http://www.ccsso.org/Resources/Publications/English_Language_Learners_with_Disabilities_A_Call_for_Additional_Research_and_Policy_Guidelines.html (accessed 12 January 2017).

Pennock-Roman, M. and Rivera, C. (2007) *Test Validity and Mean Effects of Test Accommodations for ELLs and non-ELLs: A Meta-analysis.* Washington, DC: Center for Equity and Excellence in Education, George Washington University.

Pintner, R. (1927) Intelligence tests. *Psychological Bulletin* 24 (7), 391.

Pintner, R. and Keller, R. (1922) Intelligence tests of foreign children. *Journal of Educational Psychology* 13 (4), 214–222.

Pizmony-Levy, O. and Green Saraisky, N. (2016) *Who Opts Out and Why? Results from a National Survey on Opting Out of Standardized Tests.* New York: Columbia University.

Popham, W.J. (2001) Teaching to the test? *Educational Leadership* 58 (6), 16–21.

Prall, J. (1922) *With the Children on Ellis Island.* Albany, NY: Congregational Home Missionary Society.

Pressey, S.L. and Pressey, L.C. (1922) *Introduction to the Use of Standardized Tests.* Yonkers, NY: World Book Company.

Ragan, A. and Lesaux, N. (2006) Federal, state, and district level English language learner program entry and exit requirements: Effects on the education of language minority learners. *Education Policy Analysis Archives/Archivos Analíticos de Políticas Educativas* 14 (20).

Redden, E. and Jaschik, S. (2015) Indicted for cheating. *Inside Higher Ed*, 29 May, at https://www.insidehighered.com/news/2015/05/29/chinese-nationals-indicted-elaborate-cheating-scheme-standardized-admissions-tests (accessed 3 September 2016).

Reuters (n.d.) Inside the business of standardized testing and college admissions cheat sheet, at http://www.reuters.com/investigates/section/cheat-sheet (accessed 2 February 2016).

Richards, D. (2003) An overview of §504', at https://schoolcounselor.org/asca/media/asca/Resource%20Center/Disabilities-Special%20NeedsLearning%20Disorders/Sample%20Documents/504_Overview_Fall_2003.pdf (accessed 1 June 2016).

Richardson, J. (2003) Howard Andrew Knox and the origins of performance testing on Ellis Island, 1912–1916. *History of Psychology* 6 (2), 143–170.

Richardson, J. (2011) *Howard Andrew Knox: Pioneer of Intelligence Testing at Ellis Island.* New York: Columbia University Press.

Richwine, J. (2009) IQ and immigration policy. Doctoral dissertation, Harvard University.

Rigney, S.L., Wiley, D.E. and Kopriva, R. (2008) The past as preparation: Measurement, public policy and implications for access. In R. Kopriva (ed.) *Improving Testing for English Language Learners* (pp. 37–63). New York: Routledge.

Rivera, C. (2008) Defining and refining accommodations appropriate for English language learners, paper presented at the Addressing Achievement Gaps: Language Acquisition and Educational Achievement of ELLs conference hosted by the Educational Testing Service, 15–16 January.

Rivera, C. and Collum, E. (2006) *State Assessment Policy and Practice for English Language Learners: A National Perspective.* Mahwah, NJ: Lawrence Erlbaum Associates.

Roberts, D.E. (1998) Who may give birth to citizens? Reproduction, eugenics, and immigration, at http://scholarship.law.upenn.edu/faculty_scholarship/1372 (accessed 14 May 2013).

Robertson, K. and Lafond, S. (2008) Getting ready for college: What ELL students need to know, *Colorin Colarado*, at. http://www.colorincolorado.org/article/getting-ready-college-what-ell-students-need-know (accessed 1 September 2017).

Romaine, S. (1999) Early bilingual development: From elite to folk. In G. Extra and L. Verhoeven (eds) *Bilingualism and Migration* (pp. 61–73). Berlin: Walter de Gruyter GmbH.

Roorda, M. (2016) Enabling English learners to show what they know, at http://equityinlearning.act.org/press-releases/enabling-english-learners-show-know (accessed 24 March 2017).

Rosa, J.D. (2016) Standardization, racialization, languagelessness: Raciolinguistic ideologies across communicative contexts. *Journal of Linguistic Anthropology* 26 (2), 162–183.

Rosa, J.D. and Flores, N. (2017) Do you hear what I hear? Raciolinguistic ideologies and culturally sustaining pedagogies. In D. Paris and H.S. Alim (eds) *Culturally Sustaining Pedagogies: Teaching and Learning for Justice in a Changing World* (pp. 175–190). New York: Teachers College Press, Columbia University.

Safari, P. (2016) Reconsideration of language assessment is a MUST for democratic testing in the educational system of Iran. *Interchange* 47 (3), 267–296.

Sánchez, G.I. (1932) Group differences and Spanish-speaking children – a critical review. *Journal of Applied Psychology* 16 (5), 549–558.

Sánchez, G.I. (1940) *Forgotten People: A Study of New Mexicans*. Albuquerque, NM: University of New Mexico Press.

Schissel, J.L. (2009) Narrative self-constructions of Senator Ralph Yarborough in the 1967 Congressional hearings on the Bilingual Education Act. *Working Papers in Educational Linguistics* 24 (1), 79–99.

Schissel, J.L. (2010) Critical issues surrounding test accommodations: A language planning and policy perspective. *Working Papers in Educational Linguistics* 25 (1), 17–35.

Schissel, J.L. (2012) The pedagogical practice of test accommodations with emergent bilinguals: Policy-enforced washback in two urban schools. Doctoral dissertation, University of Pennsylvania.

Schissel, J.L. and Kangas, S.E.N. (2018) Reclassification of emergent bilingual with disabilities: The intersectionality of improbabilities. *Language Policy Journal* 17 (4), 567–589.

Schneider, J. (2010) Memory test: A history of US citizenship education and examination. *Teachers College Record* 112 (9), 2379–2404.

Shepard, L.A. (1997) The centrality of test use and consequences for test validity. *Educational Measurement: Issues and Practice* 16 (2), 5–24.

Shohamy, E. (1998) Critical language testing and beyond. *Studies in Educational Evaluation* 24 (4), 331–45.

Shohamy, E. (2001) *The Power of Tests: A Critical Perspective on the Uses of Language Tests*. Harlow: Longman.

Shohamy, E. (2006) *Language Policy: Hidden Agendas and New Approaches*. London: Routledge.

Shohamy, E. (2011) Assessing multilingual competencies: Adopting construct valid assessment policies. *Modern Language Journal* 95 (3), 417–429.

Shohamy, E. (2016) Critical language testing. In E. Shohamy, I.G. Or and S. May (eds) *Language Testing and Assessment* (pp. 1–15). New York: Springer International.

Sireci, S.G. (2009) Packing and unpacking sources of validity evidence. In S.G. Sireci (ed.) *The Concept of Validity: Revisions, New Directions and Applications* (pp. 19–37). Charlotte, NC: Information Age Publishing.

Sireci, S.G. (2016) On the validity of useless tests. *Assessment in Education: Principles, Policy and Practice* 23 (2), 226–235.

Skutnabb-Kangas, T. (1981) *Bilingualism or Not: The Education of Minorities*. Clevedon: Multilingual Matters.

Skutnabb-Kangas, T. and Toukomaa, P. (1976) *Teaching Migrant Children's Mother Tongue and Learning the Language of the Host Country in the Context of the Socio-cultural Situation of the Migrant Family*. Helsinki: National Commission for UNESCO.

Sledd, J. (1969) Bi-dialectalism: The linguistics of white supremacy. *English Journal* 58 (9), 1307–1329.

Smith, A. (2012) Indigeneity, settler colonialism, white supremacy. In D.M. HoSang, Oneka LaBennett and L. Pulido (eds) *Racial Formation in the Twenty-First Century* (pp. 66–90). Berkeley, CA: University of California Press.

Smith, A. (2016) Heteropatriarchy and the three pillars of white supremacy: Rethinking women of color organizing. In B.K. Scott, S.E. Cayleff, A. Donadey and I. Lara (eds) *Women in Culture: An Intersectional Anthology for Gender and Women's Studies* (p. 404). Oxford: Wiley-Blackwell.

Smith, J. (1995) A nation that welcomes immigrants? An historical examination of United States immigration policy. *U.C. Davis Journal of International Law and Policy* 227 (1), 229–230.

Smith, W. (1990) Policy regarding the treatment of national origin minority students who are limited English proficient, at http://www2.ed.gov/about/offices/list/ocr/docs/lau1990_and_1985.html (accessed 22 May 2015).

Sneeringer, S.G. (1974) Constitutional law – bilingual-bicultural education in Texas. *Urban Law Annual; Journal of Urban and Contemporary Law* 7, 400–407.

Snyderman, M. and Herrnstein, R.J. (1983) Intelligence tests and the Immigration Act of 1924. *American Psychologist* 38 (9), 986.

Sohoni, D. and Vafa, A. (2010) The fight to be American: Military naturalization and Asian citizenship. *Asian American Law Journal* 17, 119–151.

Solano-Flores, G. (2008) Who is given tests in what language by whom, when, and where? The need for probabilistic views of language in the testing of English language learners. *Educational Researcher* 37 (4), 189–199.

Solano-Flores, G. (2011) Assessing the cultural validity of assessment practices: An introduction. In M. del Rosario Basterra, E. Trumbull and G. Solano-Flores (eds) *Cultural Validity in Assessment: Addressing Linguistic and Cultural Diversity* (pp. 3–21). New York: Routledge.

Solano-Flores, G. and Nelson-Barber, S. (2001) On the cultural validity of science assessments. *Journal of Research in Science Teaching* 38 (5), 553–573.

Spolsky, B. (1995) *Measured Words: The Development of Objective Language Testing*. Oxford: Oxford University Press.

Stecklow, S. (2016) Exclusive: ACT cancels test scores in Asia after leak of essay question, Reuters, at. https://www.reuters.com/article/us-college-testing-act-exclusive/exclusive-act-cancels-test-scores-in-asia-after-leak-of-essay-question-idUSKBN12Y2NM (accessed 5 August 2017).

Stern, A.M. (2005) Sterilized in the name of public health: Race, immigration, and reproductive control in modern California. *American Journal of Public Health* 95 (7), 1128–1138.

Stern, A.M. (2015) *Eugenic Nation: Faults and Frontiers of Better Breeding in Modern America*. Berkeley, CA: University of California Press.

Stern, A.M. (2016) Eugenics, sterilization, and historical memory in the United States. *História, Ciências, Saúde-Manguinhos* 23 (suppl. 1), 195–212.

Stewart, D.M. and Johanek, M.C. (1996) The evolution of college entrance examinations. In J.B. Baron and D.P. Wolf (eds) *Performance-Based Student Assessment: Challenges and Possibilities* (pp. 261–286). Chicago, IL: University of Chicago Press.

Subtirelu, N.C. (2017) Students' orientations to communication across linguistic difference with international teaching assistants at an internationalizing university in the United States. *Multilingua* 36 (3), 247–280.

Supovitz, J. (2009) Can high stakes testing leverage educational improvement? Prospects from the last decade of testing and accountability reform. *Journal of Educational Change* 10 (2–3), 211–227.

Tamura, E. (1994) *Americanization, Acculturation, and Ethnic Identity: The Nisei Generation in Hawaii*. Champaign, IL: University of Illinois Press.

Taylor, G.A. (1926) The mental ability of foreign-born children. *Journal of Educational Psychology* 17 (8), 571–573.

Terman, L. (1916) *The Measurement of Intelligence*. Boston, MA: Houghton Mifflin.

Test Optional Survey (2016) 'Test optional colleges and universities for international students, August 2016', at https://drive.google.com/file/d/0BwoRNCiIYbSxUGxLbGZPU0QyVGVxRU9sQm5NWXo0aXh4YnFB/view (accessed 14 November 2018).

Thielman, S.B. (1985) Psychiatry and social values: The American Psychiatric Association and immigration restriction, 1880–1930. *Psychiatry* 48 (4), 299–310.

Thompson, K. D. (2017) English learners' time to reclassification: An analysis. *Educational Policy* 31 (3), 330–363.

Thurlow, M. L. and Bolt, S. (2001) *Empirical Support for Accommodations Most Often Allowed in State Policy* (Synthesis Report 41). Minneapolis, MN: National Center on Educational Outcomes, University of Minnesota.

Toukomaa, P. and Skutnabb-Kangas, T. (1977) *The Intensive Teaching of the Mother Tongue to Migrant Children at Pre-school Age*. Tampere: Department of Sociology, University of Tampere.

Truman, H.S. (1952) Veto of bill to revise the laws relating to immigration, naturalization, and nationality, at https://www.trumanlibrary.org/publicpapers/index.php?pid=2389 (accessed 14 November 2018).

Twine, F.W. (1998) *Racism in a Racial Democracy: The Maintenance of White Supremacy in Brazil*. New York: Rutgers University Press.

United Opt Out National (n.d.) At http://www.unitedoptoutnational.org (accessed 29 October 2018).

University of Milwaukee (n.d.) English for Academic Purposes (EAP) information for international teaching assistants, at https://uwm.edu/esl/programs/teaching-assistants (accessed on 8 October 2016).

University of Minnesota (2012) Language proficiency requirements for international teaching assistants, at https://policy.umn.edu/hr/language (accessed on 8 October 2016).

US Army Medical Department: Office of Medical History (2011) The Medical Department of the United States Army in the World War, Volume XIII, at http://history.amedd.army.mil/booksdocs/wwi/VolXIII/Default1.html (accessed 27 June 2016).

US Bureau of Immigration (1892–1924) *Annual Report of the Commissioner General of Immigration to the Secretary of Labor*. Washington, DC: US Government Printing Office.

US Census Bureau (2010) The Hispanic population: 2010, at http://www.census.gov/prod/cen2010/briefs/c2010br-04.pdf (accessed 29 October 2018).

US Census Bureau (2015) Census Bureau reports at least 350 languages spoken in U.S. homes (CB15-185), at https://www.census.gov/newsroom/press-releases/2015/cb15-185.html (accessed 29 October 2018).

US Citizenship and Immigration Services (2013) Origins of the naturalization civics test, at https://www.uscis.gov/history-and-genealogy/history-and-genealogy-news/origins-naturalization-civics-test (accessed 14 May 2016).

US Citizenship and Immigration Services (2014) INS records for 1930s Mexican repatriations, at https://www.uscis.gov/history-and-genealogy/our-history/historians-mailbox/ins-records-1930s-mexican-repatriations (accessed 16 October 2015).

US Citizenship and Immigration Services (2015) English and civics testing, at http://www.uscis.gov/policymanual/HTML/PolicyManual-Volume12-PartE-Chapter2.html#S-D (accessed 4 May 2017).

US Citizenship and Immigration Services (2016) Applicant performance on the naturalization test, at https://www.uscis.gov/us-citizenship/naturalization-test/applicant-performance-naturalization-test (accessed 2 March 2017).

US Citizenship and Immigration Services (2018) Applicant performance on the naturalization test, at https://www.uscis.gov/us-citizenship/naturalization-test/applicant-performance-naturalization-test (accessed 14 November 2018).

US Department of Commerce (1975) Historical statistics of the United States, at https://www2.census.gov/prod2/statcomp/documents/HistoricalStatisticsoftheUnitedStates1789-1945.pdf (accessed 12 April 2017).

US Department of Education (1999) *Peer Reviewer Guidance for Evaluating Evidence of Final Assessments Under Title I of the Elementary and Secondary Education Act*. Washington, DC: US Department of Education.

US Department of Education (2003) National Symposium on Learning Disabilities in English Language Learners October 14–15, 2003, symposium summary, at https://www2.ed.gov/about/offices/list/osers/products/ld-ell/ld-ell.pdf (accessed 12 March 2015).

US Department of Education (2015) Office of English Language Acquisition, Fast facts: English learners (ELs) and college and career readiness, at. https://www.ncela.us/files/fast_facts/OELA_FastFacts_ELsandCRDC_CollegeReadiness.pdf (accessed 2 April 2017).

US Government Accountability Office (GAO) (2016) *Better Use of Information Could Help Agencies Identify Disparities and Address Racial Discrimination* (GOA-16-345). Washington, DC: GAO.

US Holocaust Memorial Museum (n.d.) Refugees: Key facts. In *Holocaust Encyclopedia*, at https://www.ushmm.org/wlc/en/article.php?ModuleId=10005139 (accessed 1 July 2016).

Vakili, B., Pasquarella, J. and Marcano, T. (2016) *Discharged, Then Discarded: How U.S. Veterans are Banished by the Country They Swore to Protect*. ACLU of California, at https://www.aclusandiego.org/wp-content/uploads/2017/06/DischargedThenDiscarded-ACLUofCA.pdf (accessed 2 March 2017).

Valdés, G. (2004) Between support and marginalisation: The development of academic language in linguistic minority children. *International Journal of Bilingual Education and Bilingualism* 7 (2–3), 102–132.

Valdés, G. and Figueroa, R.A. (1994) *Bilingualism and Testing: A Special Case of Bias*. New York: Ablex Publishing.

Villazor, R. (2015) Chae Chan Ping v. United States: Immigration as property. *Oklahoma Law Review* 68 (1), 137–164.

Wagner, E. (2016) A study of the use of the 'TOEFL iBT'® test speaking and listening scores for international teaching assistant screening (RR-16-18). *ETS Research Report Series* 1, 1–48.

Wall, D. (1997) *Impact and Washback in Language Testing*. Dordrecht: Kluwer Academic.

Wang, S.L. (1926) A demonstration of the language difficulty involved in comparing racial groups by means of verbal intelligence tests. *Journal of Applied Psychology* 10 (1), 102–106.

Wasem, R.E. (2011) *Diversity Immigrant Visa Lottery Issues*. Washington, DC: Congressional Research Service.

Wasem, R.E. (2016) *Cuban Migration to the United States: Policy and Trends*. Washington, DC: Congressional Research Service.

Werner, E.E. (2009) *Passages to America: Oral Histories of Child Immigrants from Ellis Island and Angel Island*. Lincoln, NE: Potomac Books.

Wiener, J. (2013) Why did Harvard give a PhD for a discredited approach to race and IQ?, at https://www.thenation.com/article/why-did-harvard-give-phd-discredited-approach-race-and-iq (accessed 1 March 2017).

Wiley, T.G. (1998) *Literacy and Language Diversity in the United States*. Washington, DC: Center for Applied Linguistics.

Wiliam, D. (2010) Standardized testing and school accountability. *Educational Psychologist* 45 (2), 107–122.

Winke, P. (2011) Investigating the reliability of the civics component of the U.S. naturalization test. *Language Assessment Quarterly* 8 (4), 317–341.
Wixom, M.A. (2015) *ECS and National Experts Examine: State-Level English Language Learner Policies*. Denver, CO: Education Commission of the States.
Wright, W. (2005) *Evolution of Federal Policy and Implications of No Child Left Behind for Language Minority Students*. Tempe, AZ: Educational Policy Studies Laboratory.
Wright, W. (2016) The Every Student Succeeds Act and English language learners, at https://www.youtube.com/watch?v=p05nPGSBsSY (accessed 4 October 2017).
Xavier University: Center for the Study of the American Dream (2012) Civic illiteracy: A threat to the American dream, blog, at http://xuamericandream.blogspot.com (accessed 14 January 2017).
Yerkes, R.M. (ed.) (1921) Psychological examining in the United States Army. *Memoirs of the National Academy of Science* 15, 7–10.
Yoshioka, J.G. (1929) A study of bilingualism. *Journal of Genetic Psychology* 36 (3), 473–479.
Yung, J. and Lee, E. (2015) Angel Island Immigration Station, in *Oxford Research Encyclopedia of American History*, at http://americanhistory.oxfordre.com/view/10.1093/acrefore/9780199329175.001.0001/acrefore-9780199329175-e-36 (accessed 2 May 2016).
Zehr, M.A. (2011) 'Ed. Department backs English-proficiency tests for common standards, at http://www.edweek.org/ew/articles/2011/01/10/17ellassess.h30.html?r=1503872482 (accessed 7 October 2013).
Zenderland, L. (1998) *Measuring Minds*. Cambridge: Cambridge University Press.
Zhang, H.C. (1988) Psychological measurement in China. *International Journal of Psychology* 23, 101–117.
Zheng, X. (2017) Translingual identity as pedagogy: International teaching assistants of English in college composition classrooms. *Modern Language Journal* 101, 29–44.
Zuckerbrod, N. (2007) Changes to No Child Left Behind expected, at http://abcnews.go.com/Politics/WireStory?id=2865819&page=1 (accessed 4 May 2014).

Index

14th Amendment to the US Constitution, 38, 52, 53, 99
15th Amendment to the US Constitution, 51
1790 Naturalization Act, 37
1913 Mocklett law, 99
1917 Immigration Act, 38
1921 Emergency Quota Act, 39
1982 Amerasian Act, 42

accountability, 10, 19, 107, 149, 152, 161, 163
ACT, 10, 124, 129, 133–135, 142, 148, 152–156, 161
AFQT, 62
Alien and Sedition Acts, 37
Amerasian Homecoming Act of 1987, 42
amnesty, 43, 59
Angel Island, 5, 6, 12, 37, 38, 77, 78, 81, 91–97, 149, 151, 156, 163, 164
Army Alpha, 8, 21, 23, 62, 64, 109
Army Beta, 8, 20, 64
ASVAB, 62, 63, 68, 69, 148

BEA, 101, 102, 104–106, 150
Border Patrol, 40
Bracero Program, 39, 40
Brown v. Board of Education, 104, 105, 158

Chinese Exclusion Act of 1882, 38, 91
citizenship, 12, 37, 38, 40, 41, 45, 53–63, 67–76, 82, 91, 93, 126, 131–135, 137, 144, 152, 154, 156, 160–163
civic participation, 6, 12, 37, 58, 75, 144
civics test, 58–61, 162

Cold War, 5, 39
College Board, 7, 130–132, 136
Common Core State Standards, 11, 106, 125, 150
consequential validity, 26, 28, 29, 33, 34, 143, 145
Cuban Adjustment Act of 1966, 42

Deported Veterans' Support House, 73

Ellis Island, 5, 12, 37, 38, 77–92, 96, 97, 109, 148–152, 158, 159, 163
ELPA21, 125
English language learner, 1–4, 58, 144, 152, 159
English proficiency, 2, 3, 11, 13, 18, 26, 45, 53–58, 60, 62, 103, 105–108, 118, 119, 122, 123, 125, 126, 129, 130, 135–142, 145, 149
Enhanced Border Security and Visa Entry Reform Act, 44
entry into the United States, 6, 34, 38, 39, 79, 84, 144
ESSA, 6, 104, 105, 106, 107, 110, 123
eugenics, 8, 20, 22, 62, 78, 79, 81, 86–91, 115, 116, 156, 159

fairness, 28, 31–33, 85, 102, 122
Farrington v. Tokushige, 100

GRE, 10, 11, 129, 134, 135, 137, 142, 151, 157
Great Depression, 26, 39, 50
Guey Heung Lee v. Johnson, 104

higher education opportunities, 6, 99
Homeland Security Act, 44

IASA, 105, 106, 120

165

IELTS, 130, 136, 138, 139, 141, 142, 148, 154
Immigration Act of 1924, 24, 91, 96, 115, 136, 158
Immigration and Naturalization Act of 1965, 41
Immigration and Naturalization Act of 1952, 39, 56 (*see also* McCarran–Walter Act)
Immigration and Naturalization Act of 1990, 43
Immigration Reform and Control Act, 43
Immigration Restriction League, 58, 153
immigration restrictions, 77, 110, 115
Independent School District v. Salvatierra, 104
Indochina Migration and Refugee Assistance Act, 42
institutionalization, 8, 79, 86, 88
intelligence tests, 8, 21, 22, 24–27, 45, 48, 62, 67, 76, 79, 84–86, 88, 90, 97, 108, 109, 110–112, 117, 118, 127, 144, 163
Internal Security Act, 56
intersectionality, 12, 15–17, 144, 148, 150, 158, 160
ITAs, 139–142

justice, 7, 32, 33, 157

Katzenbach v. Morgan, 52
Keyes v. School District Number One, 105

language-minoritized bilinguals, 1–4, 6, 12–27, 30–37, 41, 44, 45, 48–53, 56, 58–64, 66–69, 74–82, 86, 89, 90, 91, 96, 97, 99, 100, 104–117, 119–135, 139, 141–147
language-minoritized bilinguals with disabilities, 111
language-minoritized bilingual test-takers, 1, 2, 4, 14, 15, 26, 32, 48, 56, 66, 70, 75, 76, 101–105, 108–115, 118–124, 127, 144
Lau v. Nichols, 102, 123
literacy test, 38, 45–52, 55, 58–60, 150

Madrigal v. Quilligan, 117
McCarran–Walter Act, 39, 40, 41, 59
Meyer v. Nebraska, 99
Migration and Refugee Assistant Act of 1962, 42
military testing, 22, 62, 79, 81, 148
Mo Hock Ke Lok Po v. Stainback, 100
multiple-choice, 7, 8, 10, 109

NAEP, 10, 120
naturalization, 12, 18, 40, 45, 50–62, 69, 74, 75, 78, 161–163
Naturalization Act of 1906, 38, 54
NCLB, 6, 10, 104–106, 110, 119, 120, 123, 153
negative consequences, 14, 22, 30, 31, 34, 35, 56, 61–63, 142, 146, 147
not yet proficient in English, 2, 19, 32, 144, 145
NPRM, 123

objectivity, 5, 7, 8
Operation Wetback, 39, 40, 153

paper sons, 93, 96
PiCAT, 63, 68, 149

racial prerequisite trials, 8, 53–58, 62, 75, 144
raciolinguistic ideologies, 16
Refugee Act of 1980, 42, 154

SAT, 8, 10, 26, 129–135, 142, 149, 152, 154–156
scientific racism, 78, 116
segregation, 104, 105
social consequences of testing, 14, 15, 17, 19, 26, 27, 33, 34, 37, 68, 90, 91, 99, 108, 128, 143, 145–147
social isolation, 8, 79
sterilization, 8, 22, 79, 81, 87, 88, 108, 110, 115–118, 127, 153, 156, 161

test accommodations, 27, 119–122, 133, 135, 142, 160
TOEFL, 11, 26, 62, 126, 130, 136–142, 152, 163
Treaty of Guadalupe Hidalgo, 37

United Opt Out National, 11, 162
United States v. Texas, 104
US Civil Rights Movement, 5, 41, 117
US Civil War, 5, 7, 37, 38, 51, 53, 68
use-oriented testing, 1, 4, 5, 15, 31, 34, 75, 143, 146

validity, 12, 13, 15, 19–34, 88, 109, 122, 143–145, 155, 157, 160, 161
Vietnam War, 41, 42, 68
visa diversification program, 43

Voting Rights Act of 1965, 51, 59

'War on Terror', 5, 44
white supremacy, 12, 15, 17–19, 37, 53, 56, 62, 67, 114, 143, 145, 148, 152, 161
WIDA consortium, 125
World War I, 5, 21, 38, 53, 62, 63, 67, 69, 76, 79, 91, 99, 136
World War II, 5, 26, 39, 59, 62, 63, 69, 70, 76, 130, 131, 134, 157

For Product Safety Concerns and Information please contact our EU Authorised Representative:

Easy Access System Europe

Mustamäe tee 50

10621 Tallinn

Estonia

gpsr.requests@easproject.com

www.ingramcontent.com/pod-product-compliance
Lightning Source LLC
Chambersburg PA
CBHW070617300426
44113CB00010B/1565